# GAMBLING
## *Don't Bet on It*

# GAMBLING
## *Don't Bet on It*

REX M. ROGERS

**Kregel**
*Publications*

*Gambling: Don't Bet on It*
© 2005 by Rex M. Rogers

Published by Kregel Publications, a division of Kregel Inc., P. O. Box 2607, Grand Rapids, MI 49501.

A revised edition of *Seducing America: Is Gambling a Good Bet?* © 1997 by Rex M. Rogers.

ISBN 0-8254-3646-x

05 06 07 08 09 / 5 4 3 2 1

*Printed in the United States of America*

*To my parents,*
*Ernest and Yvonne Rogers,*
*who taught me right from wrong.*

# CONTENTS

# ACKNOWLEDGMENTS

Dr. Warren W. Wiersbe offered helpful comments on the first manuscript and still more encouragement. I count it a privilege to have learned from him.

First Maxine Nelson and later Marsha Sweet, my executive assistants at Cornerstone University, organized the office and kept my administrative duties on track as I juggled multiple responsibilities. With the first publication of this book, Ray Doerksen, a librarian at the university, and then with the revision, Dr. Fred Sweet, director of the Cornerstone University Miller Library, provided me with professional assistance in online searches and in locating difficult-to-find materials. Ray also provided me with intellectual interchange on the subject of gambling. For all of these friends I am grateful.

I published an article titled "Is Gambling a Good Gamble?" in *The Baptist Bulletin,* April 1995. Vernon Miller, the editor, graciously gave me permission to use some of that material in this book.

Since writing and publishing the first edition of this book as *Seducing America: Is Gambling a Good Bet?* (Baker, 1997), I've been involved as a speaker, consultant, or supporter in a variety of state or local opposition efforts attempting to thwart the expansion of legalized commercial gambling. In those experiences with democracy in action, I've learned to esteem highly the American citizens who hold to eternal values, who live by principle, and who are willing to put their time, money, and sometimes their reputations on the line for what they consider to be a good cause in the name of family and community well-being. To all those men and women from whom I have learned and with whom I have been privileged to work I say, "Thank you," for your example in fighting the good fight. Your resolve encouraged me.

Finally, I am especially thankful for the support of a loving wife, Sarah, four adult children, a son-in-law, and now two grandchildren, who granted me the time to focus on the project. It is my hope and prayer that this book has a positive impact on families everywhere.

# Introduction

# PITCHING PENNIES

Chet Forte's name is not known to many, but his work is. For twenty-four years he was on staff at ABC television. He won eleven Emmy awards as director of Monday Night Football, seven Olympic Games, Super Bowls, major-league baseball, the Indianapolis 500, Kentucky Derbies, and the NBA play-offs. A close friend of Howard Cosell, Forte was fired from ABC in 1987, admitting to a gambling problem that at times cost him $10,000 per day.

"I lost all my money. I lost all my respect," Forte said in 1992. "I hurt my family, and I hurt my friends." He gambled away nearly $4 million and lost his million-dollar home in Saddle River, New Jersey. Forte's mother declared bankruptcy after helping him financially. He defrauded a New Jersey businessman of $100,000 to get gambling money, and he got into trouble with the IRS, pleading guilty to mail and wire fraud as well as income tax evasion. Forte bet at casino tables and even bet on games he was directing. He died at sixty years of age in early 1996, still plagued by a gambling problem that began in the early 1960s.

Chet Forte is not unique. He's not even rare. He's just a real-life, unfortunate example of a growing statistic.

Forte was a human being seduced by gambling. Yet he never really intended it to be that way. He started out small, just having a little fun, but what started as a game turned into pain. His story is repeated every day in every state in the country.

So what's wrong with pitching pennies? It's not much. It's just a little fun, isn't it? Those were the questions I asked my mother forty years ago. I've wondered about gambling ever since.

I grew up in what I've come to understand was a typical conservative Christian home. My parents considered gambling wrong in all its forms. As a youth I had a difficult time understanding why gambling was considered such a dubious activity. I struggled with the idea that, "Hey, it's my money. I can do with it what I want." Or, "What's the difference in my losing 10 dollars in gambling or spending 10 bucks on a few games of putt-putt golf? It's just harmless entertainment, isn't it?"

My non-Christian friends weren't into gambling either. In fact, most of their parents warned them away from it too. And as far as I could tell, those parents avoided gambling as well. My town had a lot of problems, but gambling to excess was not one of them.

Now I don't think my growing-up experience was unique. Our outlook on gambling reflected the spiritual and cultural understanding of the day. Gambling was a socially suspect activity. It was typically part of the *don't* list.

I'm not saying that gambling didn't take place. Of course it did. In fact, illegal gambling along with legal gambling in Nevada and a few racetracks were major financial enterprises even when I was young. But gambling was still an activity that was held at arm's length, something tolerated by society, not promoted.

Forty years ago the availability of gambling was really quite limited. You had one of three choices: Either you got involved in some kind of illegal gambling, you traveled to Las Vegas or scattered racetracks, or you participated in some social or friendly gambling in a variety of competitive games. Today that's not the case.

Beginning with lotteries in the sixties and followed by casinos in the nineties, Americans have plunged headlong into legalized gambling in virtually every form. Gambling that was once a social taboo, or at least limited to certain leisure expressions in restricted areas, is now an accepted part of everyday life. It's as easy as buying milk. Just pick up a lottery ticket at the convenience store.

Gambling has gone from "Don't you dare" to "Who cares?" It's a virtual nonissue. Most Christian groups and churches don't pay much attention to it. Gambling is so much a part of the social landscape that we don't see it anymore.

What happened? What kind of moral seismic shift took place to bring gambling out of the darkness into the light? How is it that a human behavior that virtually every civilized society for the past five hundred years has tried to limit is now embraced with such abandon? And where is the Christian conscience?

Should Christians resist America's renewed desire to legalize and legitimize gambling? The Catholic Church has never been that bothered by gambling, but Protestant denominations have historically considered gambling the devil's game. That's what makes the past fifteen years so strange. In the face of America's rush to build "temples of chance," Christians have been oddly silent—or at least very quiet.

If the Christian community has concluded that there is really nothing wrong with shooting craps, I haven't heard any discussion about it. Walk through any public bookstore in the country and you'll discover dozens of books on how to win at keno, blackjack, or poker. Check your local Christian bookstore, and you'll find very little on the subject of gambling.

That's where I hope this book fits. This is not the last word on gambling. I don't have all the answers. However, I would like to say to the Christian community, "Hey, there's something out there that we need to be thinking about. It entails enormous social, cultural, economic, and even political implications. It's affecting the church, and its abuse involves dangerous, even deadly, consequences for certain individuals."

This book provides a brief overview of the gambling paradigm shift that has taken place in our culture both in attitudes and activities. The book attempts to develop a Christian view of gambling, examines some moral and economic arguments for and against gambling, considers charity gambling, reviews growing concerns with problem gambling, and describes the emergence of online or Internet gambling. Finally, I consider the future of legalized gambling and offer a few recommendations for what we should be thinking, saying, and doing about it.

For now, let me say that the history of gambling is a record of broken promises, broken dreams, and broken lives. Without fail, gambling produces detrimental personal and social consequences that are a lot more serious than losing a few pitched pennies.

# 1

# Taking a Chance
## *Rediscovering an Old Vice*

Dan is a gambler.[1] He's not a professional, but he's a gambler nonetheless. Dan is employed by the state in a local office, works hard five days a week, drinks a little on the weekend but not a lot, tries to take care of his family, and in general is a pretty nice guy. He loves his wife, and he doesn't kick his dog.

Dan started gambling about five years ago. At first it was just a few games of poker with the boys. Then a casino opened on a nearby Native American reservation. Dan experimented with blackjack and keno. He enjoyed roulette, but most of all he liked the slot machines. There was something exciting about the anticipation of winning or losing.

He didn't lose much—at least not at first. It was just nickels and quarters anyway. After a while, though, things got a little tougher. These last few months have not been pleasant. Joan, his wife of twenty-three years, doesn't appreciate Dan losing their "walking around money," and she worries even more about the time he spends in the casino. The more Dan gambles, the more his problems seem to grow. The more his problems grow, the more he gambles. Dan is depressed. Joan is desperate.

Joan says, "Dan is a good man. He doesn't think he has a problem. He spends all his free time at the casino. We're growing apart. The neighbors aren't much help. They gamble too."

**Gambling to Gaming**
The words *game, gamble, gambler,* and *gambling* derive from the Old English *gamen* (game) and *gam(e)man* (to sport or to play or to game). "Not all games are gambling, but all gambling is fundamentally a game."[2]

"Gambling may be defined as an activity in which a person subjects something of value—usually money—to a risk involving a large element of chance in the hopes of winning something of greater value, which is usually more money."[3] A game must contain three elements to be gambling:

1. a consideration or a pay-to-play arrangement (the stakes)
2. a prize or an opportunity to win something
3. chance, a disposition of results in which knowledge and skill are either not involved or play a very limited role dominated by chance

In Dr. Samuel Johnson's *Dictionary of the English Language* (1755), he gives no noun for *gamble,* but *gambler* is defined as "a knave whose practice it is to invite the unwary to game and cheat them." *To game* was defined by Johnson as "to play wantonly and extravagantly for money."[4]

Today the term *gaming* is usually applied to casinos, while the term *gambling* is used inclusively of all forms of gambling activity. However, in recent years the *gambling industry* has preferred the historically less pejorative *gaming industry* and uses the latter term in publications and promotions.

Sports betting and race betting are typically called *wagering.* In conversational use, the terms *betting* and *wagering* are employed interchangeably.

The owners and operators of commercial gambling establishments always have a guaranteed advantage or edge; they always get their cut. The edge varies by game. The house edge in craps may range from 1.4 percent to 16.7 percent. Blackjack's house edge ranges from a negative or player's advantage to above 6 percent. For casino table games, the edge may be 2.6 percent up to 11.6 percent for slot machines.[5]

Gambling can be understood by type of play as well as by form of game:

1. *Casual gambling,* sometimes called social gambling, is conducted on impulse or happenstance.
2. *Occasional gambling* is a determined act for escape or special occasion, or just a matter of hope. A payoff is sometimes the motivation.
3. *Risky gambling* seeks risk rather than a game.

4. *Professional gambling* is work, not leisure or entertainment, and seeks productive economic gain.
5. *Habitual gambling* is generally integrated with the rest of life and is incidental to other behaviors.
6. *Serious gambling* is the pursuit of gambling as a hobby.
7. *Obsessive gambling* seeks escape into a different order, but with the gambler still in control.
8. *Compulsive gambling* steps beyond obsession into personality disorder with no control.

The first six types of gambling may be called *conventional gambling,* in which the losses are discretionary consumer spending for the value of leisure and entertainment received. These types of gambling are considered voluntary and meet a variety of needs sometimes called play.

*Obsessive* and *compulsive gambling* are qualitatively different from the others and can absorb large portions or all of the gambler's income.[6] Both of the latter types of gambling are sometimes referred to as "pathological gambling."

*Problem gambling* is a term frequently used to refer to any form of habitual gambling, whether avocational or obsessive, compulsive or pathological. *Problem gambling* is perhaps the most inclusive term currently employed and may be used any time gambling seems to cause negative personal and social effects.

Another name for casual gambling is *social gambling.* This is the kind with which most people are familiar. Social gambling is "that form of gambling which is not conducted for the profit of any person, cause, or organization; is not public and makes no appeal to the public or any segment thereof; is not connected in any way with gambling machines, gambling devices, or professional gambling; is participated in only by natural persons, none of whom are professional gamblers or promoters of professional gambling; does not breach the peace and is engaged in solely for pastime and recreation based on a bona fide social relationship."[7]

The primary characteristic of social gambling, even though stakes may rise to considerable dollar amounts, is that gamblers participate on equal terms. In addition, in social gambling no agency or professional organization takes a piece of the action.

In everyday conversation, the terms *casual* or *social gambling* and *compulsive* or *pathological gambling* are the most often used. *Excessive gambling* is a term more often used in Australia and Great Britain than the United States and means about the same thing as problem gambling, compulsive gambling, or pathological gambling.[8]

*Commercial gambling* is legalized or decriminalized gambling arranged for the profit or gain of gaming owners or agencies, along with a very limited number of individual gambling winners. Unlike most casual or social gambling, commercial gambling is marketed to the public and always provides for a guaranteed profit to the gaming owners. Commercial gambling creates a gambling environment in which all forms of gambling can take place.

## A Dollar and a Dream

Gambling is this country's newest Great American Pastime. Winning the lottery is now the number one American fantasy.

High schools are scheduling mock casino nights. Slot machines are available in restaurants. Charities are graduating from bingo to Las Vegas Nights and Millionaire Parties. Grandparents are giving children lottery tickets for birthdays and Christmas. Retail outlets are selling toys that look like slot machines, as well as a variety of playable card games used in gambling houses.

Beginning in 1964 with New Hampshire, lotteries now exist as state-sponsored revenue enhancers in thirty-nine states and the District of Columbia.[9] State lottery commissions lure participants with patriotism, "The American Way to Play," or a desire for wealth, "Now Money Grows on Trees—Play Money Tree Instant Lotto," or just fantasy, "All You Need Is a Dollar and a Dream."

Mayors in several cities, including Chicago, Philadelphia, and Pittsburgh, have become supporters of city-sponsored gambling operations. Virtually every major city (and many smaller ones) in the country has proposals percolating. Once-quiet towns like Deadwood, South Dakota, and Biloxi, Mississippi, are now centers of gambling action, with the twenty-six miles of floating casinos on the Gulf shoreline near Biloxi marketed as Mississippi Beach. Old mining towns like Black Hawk and Cripple Creek, Colorado, have added casinos and bill themselves as "the new gold rush."[10]

Ed McMahon's Publishers Clearing House "You May Have Already Won" has given way to "Eat, Drink, and Make Money!" Or, "You're just one pull away from a multimillion-dollar jackpot. Hit it and buy your dream house. Or your dream car. Or your dream vacation, year after year after year." For the Massachusetts lottery, it's "No Matter What You Do for a Living, There's an Easier Way to Make Money." In Michigan, you can play "Win to Live: You Keep Living, We Keep Giving."

## Upping the Ante

In 1974, according to a Gallup poll, 61 percent of Americans gambled, wagering $17.4 billion legally. In 1989, 71 percent of Americans gambled, wagering $246 billion, a 1400 percent increase in fifteen years.[11] In 1974, less than 1 percent of the population gambled compulsively. Today the figure is estimated to be closer to 3 to 4 percent who gamble compulsively with as high as 6 to 7 percent considered problem gamblers.[12]

Gambling fever has swept the country. Gambling is a new national phenomenon. According to *International Gaming and Wagering Business Magazine*, an estimated $330 billion was wagered *legally* in the United States in 1992, an increase of 162 percent in a decade. Gambling expenditures each year exceed the amount of money spent on films, books, amusements, and music entertainment combined. Americans gamble about five times as much each year as they spend on toys.[13]

*Gambling expenditures each year exceed the amount of money spent on films, books, amusements, and music entertainment combined.*

In 1993, approximately $400 billion was wagered in the United States. In 1994, the total dollars legally gambled in the United States jumped to $482 billion, a 22.3 percent increase over the year before. Since 1982, the total amount gambled in the United States has nearly quadrupled. In a short time, legal gambling has surpassed all other forms of entertainment in total revenues.[14]

From 1975 to 1999, revenues from legal wagering grew nearly 1900 percent from $3 billion to $58 billion, meaning that throughout the 1980s and 1990s, double digit growth characterized the gambling industry in the United States.[15] By 2002, even in major markets, annual gaming revenues were in the billions of dollars with Las Vegas leading the way at $4.7 billion, Atlantic City second at $4.4 billion, followed by Chicagoland at $2.3 billion and Detroit at $1.1 billion.[16] Total gross gaming revenue (the amount wagered minus the winnings returned and overhead costs, i.e., taxes, salaries, and other expenses) moved from $34.7 billion in 1993 to $72.87 billion in 2003, an amount that does not include deepwater cruise ships, cruise-to-nowhere, or casino devices.[17] Of this $72.87 billion, commercial casinos accounted for $28.69 billion, lotteries kept $19.93 billion, Indian casinos $16.82 billion, pari-mutuel wagering $3.786 billion, charitable games and bingo $2.67 billion, card rooms $851.3 million, and legal book making $128.6 million.[18]

What began as a trickle with state lotteries became a hyperspeed flood in 1988 when Native American tribes began taking advantage of a federal law permitting them to operate casinos. Before this date, legal casinos existed in only two municipalities: Las Vegas, Nevada, and Atlantic City, New Jersey.

Some kind of Vegas-style gambling is now legal in a majority of states due to more than 150 gaming compacts, with more than 140 Native American tribes participating by the mid-nineties.[19] Additional tribes are vying for a stake in what some have called "the new buffalo." Michigan, for example, has 23 casinos (20 Native American and 3 non-Native American owned).

By 1995, 28 states had legalized casinos, and more are coming.[20] "Rug Joints," as casinos are called, were once isolated in remote areas or foreign resort playgrounds of the rich. Now they're within a day's drive of most Americans. By 2004, the number of states with casino gambling had increased to 34.

Between 1990 and 1993, the number of American households visiting casinos doubled from 46 million to 92 million, with more than 35 million of the increase at casinos outside New Jersey and Nevada. In 1993, more people visited casinos for the first time than purchased tickets to major-league baseball parks. More than 100 million people patronized casinos, video gaming, and sports betting enterprises.[21] According to a 2001 Harrah's Entertainment study, Americans averaged a trip to a casino once every two months, or 5.7 times per year.[22]

## Better Bettors

The amount Americans are betting is also increasing. In 1994, the amount wagered was $482 billion, which is 8.45 percent of U.S. personal income. Between 1993 and 1994, personal income went up 6 percent in the United States while the amount gambled increased 22 percent. In the past decade, legal wagers grew at two times the rate of personal income.[23] This rate did not slow until 2000 when gambling increased 5.4 percent and personal income rose 7.3 percent.[24]

We are gambling at a much faster rate than the economy is growing. Our gambling is increasing faster than our discretionary income. In other words, we're becoming better bettors, depending on how you define *better*.

Of the $482 billion wagered in 1994, more than $40 billion went to the "house." The total amount gambled is called the "handle," and the total the house wins is called the "hold." Of course the hold is the sum total of the money lost by patrons. The gambling industry earns about 15 percent in yearly profits, compared to an average of 5 to 8 percent for all other American businesses.[25]

Gambling is increasing in every form. Riverboat, dockside, and other offshore gambling enterprises, including cruise ships, are being proposed in several states as limited gambling. The idea is that if gambling is taking place on floating casinos, it is somehow more palatable to the public. Colorado citizens have tolerated a reintroduction of commercial gaming with limited stakes gambling, which establishes a cap on the amount that may be wagered at any time.

Offtrack, pari-mutuel, jai alai, keno, and video betting are also increasing. So are raffles and bingo. *Business Week* observed that gambling outlets are becoming "almost ubiquitous" as "mob-affiliated bookies and numbers runners are being supplanted by state governments, charitable and religious groups, and blue-chip entertainment-leisure conglomerates that say they're in the 'gaming' business."[26]

While the barrage of new casinos and card houses have hurt some tracks, people continue to wager on dog and horse racing. Offtrack betting is expanding, and the use of advanced technology to simulcast races is increasing.

No one really knows how much money goes through illegal bookmaking and the numbers racket each year. Estimates of illegal gambling place the figure at an amount at least equal to the amount gambled legally.

Casinos are making millions of dollars per day, and state lotteries are transforming from monthly and weekly drawings to aggressively promoted dailies and instant games. Now state lottery commissions are offering multiple drawings daily, something that is irresistible to problem gamblers.

During the past three decades, the gambling industry has grown more rapidly and more explosively than any business in American history. Americans spend more than six and one-half times as much money on gambling as they do on spectator sports or trips to theme parks. Legalized commercial gambling is now one of the largest industries in the U.S. leisure economy.[27]

Clearly, what was once a social taboo and a restricted form of dubious entertainment is now vogue behavior. "Everyone" does it.

## The Vice of Choice

Gambling is the "vice of choice" for the masses.

> The phenomenon of gambling is ubiquitous, recognizing no geographic, social or intellectual boundaries. Its mystery and appeal are a sometimes random mixture of superstition, excitement, hope, escapism, greed, snobbery, and mathematical fascination. Gambling is a vital part of some lives and an important sidelight for many others. It is in some cases destructive and potentially addictive, and in others a delight and a diversion.[28]

Studies show the following statistics for U.S. citizens:

> 95 percent have gambled at some time in their lives.
> 82 percent have played the lottery.
> 75 percent have played slot machines.
> 50 percent have bet on horse or dog races.
> 44 percent play cards.
> 34 percent play bingo.
> 26 percent have bet on sports events.
> 74 percent have frequented casinos.
> 89 percent approve of casino gambling.[29]

The acceptance of gambling into everyday life is a historic shift in cultural philosophy. University of Nevada, Las Vegas, professor William N. Thompson observed that

> the era of expanded legalized gambling has coincided with a trend toward increased permissiveness in society. There certainly is a connection between attitudes about lifestyle, sex, pornography—even abortion and occasional drug use—and attitudes toward gambling. The notion that government has no business in our bedrooms relates to the notion that government has no business telling us how to spend our leisure time and our own money as long as we are doing so without coercion or harm to others.[30]

The ethic of saving, self-denial, and capital accumulation is being replaced with a hedonistic consumerism, what Christopher Lasch called the "culture of narcissism."[31] Deferred gratification is shelved in favor of instant demand. We want more, and we want it now.

Legalization is followed by legitimation. Gambling by virtue of its governmental sanction is becoming legitimized. One author saw it clearly: "A devil is being exorcised from gambling games, and Americans are granting themselves absolution from a traditional sin."[32]

Gambling is no longer an entertainment pariah played in secret, smoke-filled rooms, back alley speakeasies, or Vegas. It's now relativized, no more harmful than Monopoly or bridge.

### It's Not in the Cards

Perhaps the most amazing thing about the story of legalized gambling's resurrected social acceptance is the nonchalance with which this trend has been greeted in the Christian community. There have been scattered battles of resistance in local areas, but only very limited attention has been given to the phenomenon on a national scale.

This Christian apathy is startling, even perplexing. Historically, many Protestant Christians vigorously opposed gambling and the "Sin City" activities usually associated with it. Christians condemned gambling as "the moral economy of vice." Yet a review of Christian periodical indexes for the past three decades yields only a few articles in popular magazines, even fewer well-researched articles in journals, and only a handful of books on the topic.

Christian bookstores offer few titles, if any. Yet secular bookstores feature entire sections devoted to gambling, books with titles like *Winner Take All*, *Video Poker Mania*, *The Winner's Guide to Gambling*, *Blackjack Made Simple*, and *Beat the Dealer: The Bible for Blackjack Players*.

Our forebears considered gambling a moral threat, and they acted against it accordingly. Not just the theological conservatives either; theologically liberal churches also resisted gambling. But now, people on both ends of the theological spectrum seem to have lost interest in the subject.[33] What has happened to us?

Several reasons may explain why Christians have been rather slow to respond to the spread of legalized commercial gambling:

1. Since the political coming of age of conservative Christians in the 1970s, many Christian groups from the Moral Majority

to the Christian Coalition have focused on issues like abortion, pornography, crime, gun control, sex education, creationism, family values, and prayer in public schools. Gambling was not on the list.

2.  Conservative Christians, particularly those who call themselves fundamentalists, have been historically reticent to get involved in politics or social concerns. While theologically conservative pastors may preach on gambling as part of the stewardship of one's finances, they are less likely to mount local campaigns to thwart the development of gambling enterprises in the community.

3.  The abstract nature of the gambling issue makes it difficult to confront. There are no direct biblical commands declaring gambling off limits. And unlike narcotics, which exercise an immediate negative impact on the user, abuses of gambling take longer to reveal themselves. Moral arguments against gambling are, therefore, more difficult to develop and do not come in neat sound-bite packages.

4.  This generation of Christians is uninformed about the rapid growth of commercial gambling, unaware of its financial and moral dangers, and, consequently, unconcerned about gambling as a social question.

5.  Ambivalence toward the morality of gambling stems from lack of awareness of the history of gambling, the abstract nature of the issue, and ignorance of biblical principles. Few Christians seem to be able to say forthrightly whether gambling is a virtue or a vice and why.

6.  Christians have been lulled to sleep by "gambling creep"—the gradual but steady introduction of gambling into mainstream American life. Lotteries are both everywhere and invisible. Lotteries, and now slot machines and video poker, are available right in your neighborhood.

7.  Christians are just as materialistic as anyone else. We're victims of what Bill Hybels labeled "the Monster called 'More.'" We're susceptible to the lure of quick riches, the easy dollar, and the free lunch. So Christians gamble too.[34]

8.  Gambling is not yet a national issue. Resistance battles so far have been fought on local and state fronts. It's easy to miss or selectively ignore social questions that are someone else's problem.

For these reasons and perhaps others, theological disapproval does not always translate into social or political opposition. Saying most Christians are against gambling is one thing. Demonstrating Christian anti-gambling activity is another.

In 1976, the Commission on the Review of the National Policy Toward Gambling noted that traditional Protestant opposition to gambling that argued from moral principles and socioeconomic consequences was as strong as ever.[35] This is not the case thirty years later.

A writer for *Christianity Today* crystalized the problem. While there is broad agreement across denominational lines against gambling, very little is done about it.[36] Part of the problem is apathy, part lack of awareness, part legal ambiguity and complexity, and part funding. Anti-gambling movements have always been hampered by these four barriers, religious or specifically Christian resistance even more so.

Churches have an advantage in that they can fight gambling locally. Despite the fact that some commentators have referred to conservative religious values as "traditional repressive cultural norms," churches can exercise an impact. Until the 1996 passage of Proposal E, the religious community of Detroit had been largely responsible for stopping repeated referendums calling for legalized gambling in that city.

Whatever their resource limitations, Christian groups and churches must do more than give up without a fight. The question is whether religious and specifically Christian groups are going to rise to the challenge of this moral moment.

At the national meeting of the Christian Coalition in 1995, Senator Richard Lugar (a candidate for the Republican Party presidential nomination in 1996) said,

> The spread of gambling is a measure of the moral erosion taking place in our country. . . . It says that if you play enough, you can hit the jackpot and be freed from the discipline of self-support through a job or the long commitment of ongoing education. . . . We cannot tolerate the "get rich quick" symbolism of gambling, while pleading with our children to avoid other "tosses of the dice" that lead to unhealthy living and destructive behavior.[37]

Lugar's point, according to journalist William Safire, was that the government may not be able to legislate morality, but the Christian Coalition should be involved in encouraging the government to stop legislating immorality. It was a point well-taken.

Ralph Reed, former executive director of the Christian Coalition, said, "Gambling is a cancer on the body politic, destroying families, stealing food from the mouths of children, turning wives into widows."[38]

Gary L. Bauer, former president of the Family Research Council and the current president of American Values, believes America's embrace of gambling is evidence that "a crass materialism has overtaken good sense." He contends that gambling spawns further growth in government, because government response is necessary to care for the negative spin-offs of gambling, and he argues for a national commission on gambling.[39]

> *"Gambling is a cancer on the body politic, destroying families, stealing food from the mouths of children, turning wives into widows."*

The Christian Coalition has been fighting legalized gambling at the state level since 1989. In 1996, the Christian Coalition joined with several Protestant denominations to call for a federal study of legalized gambling and to assist the National Coalition Against Legalized Gambling in opening its anti-gambling lobbying office in Washington, D.C.[40]

It remains to be seen, however, whether the Coalition or any other Christian group takes up Senator Lugar's challenge and acts on Ralph Reed's and Gary Bauer's perceptions of gambling in a more aggressive national campaign. Even if they do, the Coalition and other Christian social and political organizations may be a decade late and more than a dollar short. While the Christian community has focused on other important issues, the gaming industry has gained considerable financial, legal, and political clout.

### CasiNO!

To date, no denomination has done more to combat gambling than the United Methodist Church.[41] Methodist parishioners have won anti-gambling battles in several states. They are most prominently represented by Rev. Tom Grey, a United Methodist minister from Galena, Illinois, who has organized a number of successful anti-gambling efforts. Grey is considered by many in the media to be the national spokesman for anti-gambling Christian concern.

Rev. Grey is the "Riverboat Rambo" behind the formation of the

National Coalition Against Legalized Gambling. The National Coalition was formed in May 1995 in Galena, Illinois, and is comprised of more than thirty state organizations. A Washington, D.C., office was opened in 1996. Methodists and other Protestants, Mormons, and Catholics joining the group have faithfully and often successfully resisted what one Methodist minister called the "wizard of odds."[42]

"We're fighting a battle for the soul of America," Tom Grey says. His efforts and his organization count 21 victories in 23 attempts thus far—local efforts that stopped the expansion of legalized commercial gambling, at least for a time.[43]

Virginians Deserve Better joined with minority pastors to fight riverboat casinos in that state. Pennsylvanians Against Gambling Expansion and Michigan Citizens Against Casino Gambling are working with key legislators from both major parties to stall gambling bills in committees.

These organizations, along with Pennsylvania's Bucks County People Serving a Larger Mission, Missouri's Citizens for Life and Liberty, Wyomingites for a Better Economy Today and Tomorrow (WyBETT), Stand Up for Kansas, and many others, are all being networked by Grey's National Coalition. They're attempting to draw a line in the sand against the advance of commercial gambling.

In 2005, we still must observe that a national anti-gambling fight hasn't been a priority for the Christian community. The jury is still out on whether more Christians, particularly conservative ones, will respond to the juggernaut of legalized commercial gambling.

Why gambling might be morally wrong or personally threatening is not immediately clear to many people. It's gaming; it's entertainment. And if taxed properly, it's entertainment that produces a bundle of money for state governments. Why shouldn't this old-time vice be "virtue-ized"?

### Vice or Virtue?

Durand Jacobs noted that "public understanding of gambling is where our understanding of alcoholism was some 40 or 50 years ago. Unless we wake up soon to gambling's darker side, we're going to have a whole new generation lost to this addiction."[44] Jacobs believes gambling is a vice—one that impoverishes some victims in a moment of time and that grips others for a lifetime.

Others consider gambling at best a virtue, at worst a harmless entertainment. It's excitement; it's play; it's a way of raising dollars for good causes.

Whether vice or virtue, gambling has once again captured the fantasy and imagination of the American people. It is one of the leading political and cultural issues of the early twenty-first century. Not to understand legalized commercial gambling and not to respond to it is itself a gamble with our future.

# 2

# Seven Come Eleven
## *America's Gambling Past*

P. T. Barnum got his start selling lottery tickets. He's also the man who said, "There's a sucker born every minute."[1] History bears him out, especially when it comes to gambling.

Gambling has been around longer than money. It's been called the "world's second oldest diversion." It's been a pervasive activity in virtually every human society, and it is "no respecter of time, class, country, race, or civilization."[2]

### A Sucker Born Every Minute

The first records of gambling are Chinese, circa 2300 B.C., but it existed long before that. Gambling was practiced in ancient India, Persia, Egypt, Greece, and Japan. When Aristotle thought about gamblers, he also thought of robbers and thieves—there was no difference.[3]

Knucklebones, the six-sided bones from the legs of sheep or deer, were used as dice in India before 1000 B.C. Shaved or crooked dice have been found buried with the pharaohs. Greek soldiers shot craps. Loaded dice were found in the lava-drenched city of Pompeii. Among the artifacts discovered in the Roman Colosseum were a variety of gambling devices.

Lotteries were used as entertainment in Rome, in medieval festivals, and later by feudal princes as a source of revenue. Cards first appeared in Asia not long after the Chinese invented paper in the late first or early second century A.D. The first known European card decks were used in the fourteenth century in Italy and France.[4]

Anglo-Saxon and later English law evidenced both a tolerance of and an ambiguous attitude toward gambling. At first, neither gambling nor promotion of gambling was considered a crime. Shakespeare, for example, mentioned gambling thirteen times in seven plays.

The bewitching nature of gambling eventually caught up with English society, however, for England enacted a law against gambling in games in 1542, a law against all gambling in 1665, and a law making lotteries illegal in 1698. In one of the more prescient phrases of the English language, Lord Beaconsfield called gambling "a vast engine of national demoralization."[5]

Horse racing began as a gentleman's sport designed for the pleasure of competition or the measure of quality in breeding stock. It was not long, though, before horse racing became the focus of gambling, cheating, and other forms of fraud.

## America's Big Gamble

When the colonists arrived in America, gambling was already a widely practiced pastime of Native Americans. But colonial leaders were not interested in encouraging the activity. The New World's first law against gambling was enacted by the Puritans in 1638. Both the Puritans and the Pilgrims believed gambling undermined a sound work ethic, yielding idleness and debauchery. In 1670, the Massachusetts legislature banned cards and dice as a "great dishonor of God," and cards were considered the devil's playthings. In 1682, the Quakers decided to outlaw gambling, considering dice, cards, and so on, to be "enticing, vain, and evil sports and games."[6]

Yet "gambling in one form or another was as traditional in early America as the spelling-bee or barn-raising."[7] At one time or another all thirteen colonies operated lotteries, which were used extensively throughout the colonies to raise funds for public works. The armed forces got into the act during the Revolutionary War when troop supplies were purchased with funds from colonial lotteries. In 1775, the First Baptist Church of Providence, Rhode Island, was built using proceeds from a lottery.[8]

In 1832, there were more than 400 lotteries in 8 states, with a total ticket purchase of $66 million—5 times the federal budget of that year.[9] This continued in the new nation in which 24 of 33 states between 1790 and 1850 used lottery revenues to finance roads, buildings, canals, and bridges. In that same period, lotteries were employed by more than 50 colleges, 300 lower schools, and 200 churches, along with individuals and private charities. Even the religious leaders at Harvard used lotteries to help finance capital projects until 1793, as did university officials at Columbia and Brown.

During the period of June 10 to July 2, 1776, Thomas Jefferson kept notes of his backgammon, cards, and lotto winnings and losses even while he was writing the Declaration of Independence. Later, the Virginia legislature authorized Jefferson to conduct a lottery for private gain after his years in the presidency left him in dire financial need. The lottery never happened, for he died before it could be implemented.[10]

## Defying the Odds

Part of the enigmatic character of the history of gambling in America is that gambling has always lacked both sustained opposition and sustained support. It has never been so thoroughly opposed that it has been squelched forever, nor has it ever been so vigorously supported as to escape public disdain—until the 1990s.

Despite the absence of rousing opposition, most colonials still associated gambling with suicides, duels, and destruction of homes. Gambling was also blamed for the practice of marrying women for their money, then discarding them to impoverishment. Besides this, colonials believed gambling encouraged crimes, the gambling away of merchants' funds by their employees, and drunkenness.[11]

Betraying the attitude of many in his day, Dr. Samuel Johnson said that gambling was "the mode of transferring property without any intermediate good."[12]

## Pot of Gold

Slot machines were perfected by Charles Frey in San Francisco in 1895, and the face and pace of gambling haven't been the same since. Frey was a German immigrant whose machine, the Liberty Bell, was easy to use and relatively reliable.[13] Slots now make up almost 80 percent of some casino gambling profits.[14] More than 900,000 slot machines were placed by 2004, garnering $30 billion per year.[15]

*Approximately 50 million people played*
*slots at least once in 1995.*

The small bettors—low rollers—are what make casinos profitable, and low rollers like slot machines. In the 1970s, for example, about 40 percent of Nevada gambling came from 60,000 slot machines. By 1984, this figure increased to 53 percent. In the decade that followed, the number of slot machines in Nevada rose from 90,612 in 1985 to about 180,000. In 1991, Harrah's Mariner won more than $103,000 from each of its 1,739 slot machines. In virtually any other business, this kind of profit is un-imaginable. Average machine winnings per day in 1994 from Nevada slot machines was $27,460. In Atlantic City, there were 27,041 slots in 1994, producing an average house winnings per day of $84,950.[16] In 1995, $3.3 billion went to the house from casino slots in Las Vegas. Of the $7.5 billion in total Nevada gaming revenue that year, $4.5 billion came from slot machines.[17] In Las Vegas, there is one operating slot machine for every eight residents.[18]

Approximately 50 million people played slots at least once in 1995. That's twice the number who played golf and about the same number who have a vegetable garden.[19] In 2003, Harrah's Entertainment's annual survey found that every day the average slot machine take was $1 billion, providing casinos after overhead with a "hold" or profit of $30 billion annually and leading some to call slot machines "beautiful vaults." That is a greater gross than McDonald's, Wendy's, Burger King, and Starbucks combined. It dwarfs the 2003 movie gross of $9 billion and the $10 bil-lion gross in pornography.[20] Part of the reason for their popularity is that slot machines combine random rewards with seeming control—a seduc-tive mix. Slot machines are also glittery, emotionless, and individualistic. Players can stare at the machines for hours, make their own plays, and answer to no one. Some have suggested that this is one reason women are attracted to slots. If women make the wrong call at the roulette wheel or the wrong play at the blackjack table, they often must endure the ridicule of men. At slots, they can do their own thing without fear of embarrassment.

"Progressive slots," which link with other slot machines from several casinos and offer mega or super jackpots, also lure players. The jackpot grows with each pull of the handle. Megabucks is a $1.00 slot with one of the highest payoffs. Jackpots of $10,000 or even $1 million are possible.

Yet winning the big jackpot is not very probable. In fact, slot machines are money in the bank for slot machine owners. The basic machine has 3 reels with 20 symbols each, translating to a possibility of 8,000 different combinations.[21] Mathematically, it's not too difficult to understand why people can pour money in and not get much back.

"Without slot machines, there would be no Las Vegas as we know it to-day. These low rollers are perhaps even more important to the Las Vegas economy than are the high rollers. But both are essential."[22] Las Vegas slot machines work with 95 percent payouts to players, while many slots in other states pay less than 80 percent.[23]

## Electronic Jackpots

New technologies are making gambling faster, simpler, more attractive, more accessible, and more profitable for states, casino owners, and gamblers. Electronic gambling has changed casinos from formerly upper-class establishments to theme-decorated warehouses—"McGambling." Casinos are now patronized by "grind players" who sit for hours holding plastic cups full of coins and staring at blinking machines.[24]

> *Electronic gambling has changed casinos from formerly upper-class establishments to theme-decorated warehouses—"McGambling."*

Formerly nongambling establishments from interstate oases to restaurants to convenience stores are offering new video versions of slot machines and card games. Credit and debit cards are replacing cash; automated ticket machines dispense lottery tickets.

Gambling industry planning discussions feature video terminals in grocery stores and interactive television wagering at home.[25] In some cases the future has already arrived, with home lottery games being used in Europe and Asia.

International Game Technology (IGT) of Reno makes video poker games and envisions video slots in every neighborhood bar. Because the machines pay winners in paper script to be redeemed at cashiers, IGT calls the machines Video Lottery Terminals, "the one-armed bandits of the cashless society."[26]

IGT vice president for marketing, Bob Bittman, believes that computer technology "just opened up unbelievable numbers of models and variations and flexibility for casinos to offer a broader range of product that appeal to different kinds of people." IGT is experimenting with slot machines with touch pads that would enable gamblers to use PIN numbers, accessing bank accounts directly in ATM fashion. Some casinos already use slot machines that accept debit and credit cards.[27]

Technological changes make it easier for gamblers to lose their money without ever handling the hard currency. IGT product design vice president, Dick Sadler, indicated that gambling without money is the way to go: "The money handling is a nuisance for the casino and the player. The casinos spend a lot of time handling money, counting it, processing it. It's just a real big expense. Wrapping coins alone costs big bucks."[28]

Casino Data Systems of Las Vegas and IGT are developing new player tracking systems that will enable casino managers to monitor slot machine players in "real time." Most of these new tracking systems work via membership cards issued by casino slot clubs. Slot machine scanners read the cards, thus allowing players to become eligible for prizes, and casinos develop a database on each player using the cards.[29]

Slot cards together with cardless tracking systems provide managers with critical data on gambler behavior, thereby enhancing a casino's ability to tailor marketing directly to consumer behavior. This, of course, translates to higher-volume gambling and greater house profits.

Electronic gambling is not limited to slot machines. Other technological developments include:

- Gambling video games. New games are already hitting the market. Tiger Electronics, Inc., produces handheld Caesars Palace talking electronic games. Poker, blackjack, and roulette slots are also available in toylike form with advertisements claiming they are intended only for entertainment, not wagering. This is gambling preschool. International Gaming Technology recently offered "Winner's Choice," giving gamblers one hundred different gaming options.[30]
- Television gambling. In 1995, a new Lottery Channel was started in Providence, Rhode Island, by Cincinnati investment banker Roger Ach. The idea is to become the "CNN for gamblers." Ach envisions a nationwide cable channel with round-the-clock, play-at-home lottery games, drawings from different states, jackpots, gambling news, and entertainment.[31]

  Gaming Entertainment Television is based in Pittsburgh and offers a variety of gambling opportunities. This subscriber-supported station joins innumerable cousins on the cable channels in an endless pursuit of targeted markets. David Hawk, co-founder of a new network called Casino and Gaming Television, says, "The number of Americans who bet represents a vast potential audience." He notes that more than 50 million Americans travel to casinos annually, while only 25 million visit a golf course, so if the Golf Channel has succeeded while drawing from a smaller pool of potentially interested customers, why not gambling? From its first year of operation in 2004, the new gambling network hopes to reach 20 million homes in four years.[32]

  Since the World Poker Tour debuted on The Travel Channel in

2003, things haven't been the same. People are watching poker, and people are once again playing poker in ways reminiscent of the Old West.[33] Several television cable channels are now featuring an endless stream of "Inside Las Vegas" specials, movies like *The Godfather* and *Casino,* and, of course, World Poker Tour copy cats like The Bravo Channel's "Celebrity Poker Showdown" and ESPN's coverage of the World Series of Poker.[34] These programs and continuing mainstream acceptance of gambling have spawned a resurgence of poker interest nationwide, particularly among junior high, high school, and college students.[35] Whether this is a pop culture fad like Trivial Pursuit that eventually goes the way of the pet rock or whether poker is here to stay remains to be seen. For now, few people seem to be concerned about the possible downside of giving an entire generation a thirst for and knowledge of one of gambling's most infamous games.[36]

- Telephone gambling. In March 1995, a National Indian Lottery was proposed in Idaho by the Coeur d'Alene tribe. Sold via 1-800 telephone numbers, it is conceived as an "unrestricted lottery," offering both inter- and intrastate gambling.[37]
- Gambling on the Internet. Gambling updates have made their debut on the Internet. More than 31,000 gambling-related sites can be found on the World Wide Web, many of which offer real money wagering opportunities. Most of the actual gambling sites are operated overseas to avoid American gambling laws.

    Among other Web sites, one can visit Virtual Vegas (a commercial site of gaming software), Las Vegas Online (tourist information), Vegas COM (gaming information, casino listings, and so on). Online gambling discussion groups, interactive casino maps, and Atlantic City-related sites are also available.

New gambling is *de-skilled,* that is to say that games like lotteries, bingo, and slot machines are built strictly on chance. The less skill required, the greater the market of people who can play.

## Neon Nights

Two American cities are virtually synonymous with gambling—Las Vegas and Atlantic City. To understand these cities is to understand much about the history of gambling in America. To understand the gambling experience in these cities is to understand much about the negative impact of gambling on a community. No urban experience tells us more about dice and vice. Las Vegas and Atlantic City are case studies in how to make game owners rich, while others go wanting.

Las Vegas was founded in 1905 with the previously established Spanish name meaning "the meadows." It was an oasis in the Mojave Desert. Then Nevada legalized gambling in 1931. Today Vegas is the fastest-growing city in America with its population doubling in the 1980s and doubling again in the 1990s.[38]

Las Vegas as we know it today began as mobster Bugsy Siegel's dream at the end of World War II. He built the Flamingo Hotel and Casino. He was murdered in Beverly Hills in 1946. From its inception, casino gambling in Las Vegas was associated with organized crime, false promises, and broken lives. Siegel was the first and most famous example of gambling's tendency to create victims.

Today Las Vegas is a city of neon and computerized glitz. Thousands of miles of lighted neon tubing shines on downtown Las Vegas and along Las Vegas Boulevard—the Strip.

While the world's largest jackpot winner was a Las Vegas woman who took $27.58 million in November 1998, Las Vegas is much more about *excess* than it is *success*. Las Vegas is the "city of the eternal now," and unlike major commercial or manufacturing centers, it produces nothing tangible. Las Vegas built "the biggest casino in the world, then the biggest hotel in the world, the biggest man-made lake in the world, the hotel with the biggest rooms in the world, and so on and so on."[39] But "the casino industry has always had a lovers' quarrel with its image. Comfortable with big money action, sex, smoke and booze that permeates sports books, slot floors and table game pits, casino company executives are nonetheless touchy when gambling addiction and the somewhat sinful indulgences associated with the business are mentioned in the halls of Congress or splashed across the pages of *The New York Times* and *The Wall Street Journal.*"[40]

Beneath the glitz is another Las Vegas. A record number of people killed themselves in Clark County in 2001; 292 people committed suicide that year compared to 282 the previous year. Nevada records some 22.3 suicides per 100,000 people, while the national average is 10.7 suicides per 100,000. Even when the average population growth of 5,000 people per month is accounted for, mental health officials consider the suicide rate in Nevada, and in Clark County specifically, intolerable.[41]

Prostitution is no longer legal in Clark County and Las Vegas, but it is still legal in parts of Nevada and can be found nearby. Along the Strip, pimps aggressively pass out literature to visitors (it's a bit like running a pornography gauntlet), advertising exotic entertainers for private shows in one's room. Anything can be had in Las Vegas twenty-four hours a day—for a price.[42]

Las Vegas claims one of the nation's highest crime rates. Nevada lists the highest incarceration rate in the nation, and 40 percent of the felons jailed in Nevada are from out of state. In 1994, the FBI found that criminals in Las Vegas committed five times as many violent crimes as police were able to solve. This is the worst ratio of any large city in the United States.[43]

Nevada also has the highest per capita consumption of alcohol in the nation (much of it given away free in casinos). Eight times every day in Las Vegas there is a meeting of a Gamblers Anonymous group.[44]

Personal economics are taking a hit in Las Vegas too. Gambling thrives on destroyed lives, and the destruction always begins in the pocketbook. Annually, one in every sixty-six households files for bankruptcy in Nevada—the highest rate in the nation.[45]

Las Vegas is pulling in the dollars—big dollars. The only thing more blinding in Las Vegas than the lights is the speed with which money changes hands. The gambling industry in Las Vegas makes about $171 in profit per second.[46] But the glitzy glamour becomes an economic elixir, which in turn becomes a poison for those who imbibe.

Atlantic City's experience with gambling is no more encouraging than that of Las Vegas. A few casino owners have reaped enormous profits while the city and most gamblers have suffered financial loss.

Atlantic City approved gambling in 1976 as a "unique tool of urban development," and the first casino began operating two years later. During that first year, gambling revenues reached $134 million. Resorts International opened Memorial Day 1978, with a $1 million take. In nine months, Resorts International paid for its entire $77 million capital investment.[47]

In 1993, Atlantic City gambling revenue topped $34 billion. Atlantic City now attracts more than thirty million visitors a year. Nearly 46 percent of Atlantic City's casino gambling revenues comes from slot machines, the kind accessible to low rollers betting a nickel or quarter at a time.[48]

But not everything is coming up roses in Atlantic City:[49]

- New Jersey gave a license to the first Atlantic City casino, Resorts International, despite evidence of organized crime involved in the company's Bahamas operation.
- In 1979, ABSCAM, or "Abdul Scam," produced convictions for bribery of a U.S. senator, city mayor, and more.
- Illegal sports betting increased after casinos opened in Atlantic City.[50]
- Since casinos were introduced in Atlantic City, about 100 of 250 restaurants closed.[51] Gamblers eat in casinos and don't bother to patronize neighborhood businesses.
- From 1973 to 1976, Atlantic City averaged 4,700 major crimes per year. In 1990, total major crimes stood at 14,416. Two-thirds of these crimes occurred in the casinos.[52]
- In the first four years of casinos, pickpocket arrests went from 15 to 1,247. During the same period, purse snatchings increased 48 percent, shoplifting 342 percent, larceny from parked cars 347 percent, and larceny from buildings 430 percent. From 1978 to 1984, crimes in all categories increased dramatically: violent crimes 59 percent, crimes against property 76 percent, rape 54 percent, aggravated assault 76 percent, and robbery 49 percent.[53]
- The average population in Atlantic City dropped more than 25 percent since casinos arrived.
- The city has ten times the number of homeless people on the streets compared to other similar sized cities.[54]

As one might expect, anti-gambling experts are not impressed with the gambling industry's impact on Atlantic City. Arnie Wexler, executive director of the Council on Compulsive Gambling of New Jersey, says, "Fifteen years ago, Atlantic City was a hellhole. Today, it's a hellhole with 12 casinos sucking away the money."[55] I. Nelson Rose, a Whittier Law School professor and gaming industry authority, describes the city this way: "Atlantic City used to be a slum by the sea. Now it is a slum by the sea with casinos."[56]

## Happy Days Are Here Again?

Gambling is not new to the American experience. It has been an American entertainment option for at least four hundred years. What is new, however, is the current attitude of acceptance toward gambling. While Americans once attempted to contain gambling in certain places, gambling is now being welcomed into every community willing to gamble with its future.

The history of gambling in America is the history of lessons unlearned. No matter what the technology—knucklebone dice to lotteries to computerized slot machines—gambling creates its own morality and gradually debilitates the people it touches. That's the lesson of Las Vegas and Atlantic City, and that will be the lesson of the nation as gambling goes mainstream.

# 3

# GAMBLING GOES MAINSTREAM
## America's New Gambling Craze

Jimmy "the Greek" Snyder went to his reward April 21, 1996. He was a small-town kid from Steubenville, Ohio, who made it big as an odds-maker, first in Las Vegas, then on national television. Jimmy spent twelve years on CBS's *The NFL Today* pregame show, only to fall from fame for a few unwise and ill-chosen comments about African Americans.[1]

Jimmy the Greek was the first gambler to enjoy national acceptance. CBS gave him prominence at a time when commercial gambling was limited to Las Vegas, emerging state lotteries, and a few racetracks. Jimmy's celebrity came from the fact that his oddsmaking represented another world, a gambling arena not typically embraced or even understood by the average American.

It seems like such a long time ago. Jimmy's passing signaled the close of an era. We don't need "the Greek" anymore. Gambling has come of age.

Pick up any metropolitan newspaper in the country and you'll find odds on baseball games. One Great American Pastime is replacing another. There are odds on everything—basketball, racing, football, boxing, hockey. There are even odds on who'll win the Miss America Pageant or the presidency of the United States. Gambling is becoming a way of life.

### Prohibition to Promotion
Gambling expert I. Nelson Rose believes we're entering a *third wave* of legalized gambling in the United States.[2] The *first wave* began in colonial America when lottery management companies took their place among the largest early-nineteenth-century businesses.[3] A healthy economy together with lottery corruption contributed to the decline of legal lotteries by the 1820s.

The *second wave* of legal gambling began when Southern states looked for revenue after the Civil War. Gambling for profit was a thriving and open business in most American cities. Gambling was also a major diversion in late nineteenth-century Western gold and silver mining camps.

Legalized gambling's second wave of popularity ended in the 1880s with the Louisiana state lottery scandal. This fiasco attracted so much national attention that even today it is an oft-cited standard of greed and corruption. What began as a post–Civil War effort to refurbish the South ended with an ongoing moneymaking scam featuring corrupt government officials, intrigue, and even murder. Louisiana's lottery minions changed lotteries from local fund-raisers for specific projects into mail fraud and criminal interstate commerce.

By 1894, state lotteries were condemned by law, and thirty-six states adopted anti-lottery text in their state constitutions. Sporadic anti-gambling campaigns were conducted in most cities in the nineteenth century. But after 1900, open gambling faced more sustained and powerful attacks from public law enforcement bolstered by various reform groups.[4]

## Twentieth-Century Gamblers

Gambling declined until World War I but then experienced a comeback in the 1920s and 1930s. During these decades, states intermittently legalized various forms of gambling, but not enough to constitute a third wave of legalized gambling. A major development did occur in 1931, however, when Nevada authorized virtually all forms of gambling.

Two historical developments in the 1930s gave gambling a boost: the Great Depression, which encouraged some politicians to look for fiscal relief through legalized gambling, and the end of Prohibition, which made illegal gambling the new economic backbone of organized crime.

Illegal gambling would flourish in a city until the public eventually reacted by electing a reform administration. Then the gambling racketeers would move their games a short distance away, outside of their former political jurisdiction. The Al Capone gang, for example, moved their operation from Chicago to Cicero, Illinois, when it became too hot downtown.

During the 1940s, gambling was widespread in the military and among racketeers at home. Americans spent approximately $6 billion per year on illegal gambling, more than the combined profits of U.S. Steel, General

Motors, General Electric, and one hundred of the other largest American manufacturing companies.

While official anti-gambling attention waned from the 1920s to 1940s, illegal gambling attracted increasingly more wagerers. A 1945 Gallup poll indicated that 45 percent of the population gambled. By 1950, the figure was 57 percent. Gambling was becoming an increasingly popular pastime, but it was confined to Nevada or private and illegal venues.

Meanwhile organized crime continued to build its strength by using gambling money to pay off public officials or by laundering funds through legitimate businesses. In 1950, a select committee of the United States Senate, chaired by Estes Kefauver, finally turned federal attention toward criminal gambling and its influence on organized crime and interstate commerce. But government opposition to the underground gambling industry was at best inconsequential.

In the 1960s, Americans spent twice as much money on gambling as they did on medical care. The amount Americans spent on gambling was also twice the amount spent on religious and welfare activities, twice the amount expended for private research and education, and, once again, 20 percent more than combined net profits of the one hundred largest manufacturing companies in the country.[5]

## The Third Wave

In I. Nelson Rose's terms, the *third wave* of legalized gambling in the United States began in 1964 with the inception of the New Hampshire state lottery. By 1984, a majority of states had legalized lotteries.[6]

Bingo was legalized in 1937 in Rhode Island, 1949 in New Hampshire, and 1954 in New Jersey. Forty-seven states, the District of Columbia, and all the Canadian provinces have now legalized either charitable or Indian bingo.[7]

Horse-race betting is legal in 44 states and all Canadian provinces, dog-race betting in 19 states, and jai alai games in 4 states. All 10 Canadian provinces and 48 states now permit some form of legal gambling. By the year 2000, 40 percent of U.S. households participated in some form of gambling.[8]

The year 1994 was the first year that Americans spent more on gambling than on their children's toys. By 2000, total dollars wagered stood at $638.6 billion and total gambling revenues at $50.9 billion. Now Americans were spending more per year on gambling than on recorded music, concerts and plays, the cinema, and spectator sports combined.[9]

Canadians are also upping the ante, where net revenue from government-run lotteries, VLTs (video lottery terminals), and casinos rose from $2.7 billion in 1992 to $11.3 billion in 2002.[10] In both countries, "racinos" are now in fashion—horse racetracks where casino-style slot machines and other gambling devices have been added.[11]

Legalized commercial gambling is now growing at breakneck speed, spurred by cash-hungry governments, gambling industry promotion of gaming as entertainment, and the appeal of new, high-tech video gambling. "Decades of church-sponsored gambling has also tended to lend approval to games of chance."[12]

Only two states still refuse to legalize gambling—Hawaii and Utah. Hawaii debates the matter periodically. While 60 percent of Hawaiians polled favor a lottery, enough citizens are concerned about damaging the state's image as an island paradise that lotteries and other commercial gambling are consistently rejected.[13] If Hawaii's experience is similar to other states', gambling proponents will be successful in making economic arguments, and Hawaii will eventually pass a gambling bill.

In Utah, conservative Mormon values keep commercial gambling at bay. "There are long odds and there are Utah odds, and Utah odds are longer."[14] Mormon people in Utah are a good example of the impact a united religious people can exercise in a democratic polity.

Values play a role, and a significant role at that. Changing cultural values, what some may call "liberalizing," opened the way for increased legalized gambling in the United States. In the early 1970s, no form of gambling was approved by women. Men approved of legalizing bingo at only 53.6 percent and horse-race betting at 50.8 percent. No form of gambling received approval from a majority of black citizens, while a greater percentage of blacks than whites favored legalizing sports betting, slot machines, and street-level numbers gambling.

In other words, most black and white Americans disapproved of gambling. Values were changing, however. By 1982, a Gallup poll found that 80 percent of Americans favored some form of legalized gambling.[15] That is a significant swing in viewpoint in a relatively short time.

Unfortunately, many evangelical Christians have also set aside their forebears' condemnation of all forms of gambling. A nationwide survey conducted by the Barna Research Group in 2002 found that 27 percent of evangelicals, to varying degrees, consider gambling morally acceptable.[16] In related questioning regarding finance and spending choices, Barna found that gambling and buying lottery tickets produced no differences between the churched and unchurched. The only real difference based on survey respondents' faith commitment was that "non-born again adults were marginally more likely than born agains to have purchased a lottery ticket in the past week (24% vs. 17%, respectively)."[17] In another Barna survey conducted in 2003, 84 percent of American adults claimed to be Christian, while 61 percent believed gambling is "morally acceptable" behavior.[18]

Eugene Martin Christiansen, a gambling industry consultant, believes "there is a general move toward legal casino-type games. It is part of a fundamental change that is irreversible at this point because the country is changing with fewer people going to church, more older people with time and money on their hands, and especially, with state lottery advertising campaigns that make it seem that buying lottery tickets is almost a patriotic duty."[19]

## Lotterizing America

State-sponsored lotteries are the bridge between the gambling of eighteenth- and nineteenth-century America and gambling today.[20] Between 1894 and 1964, no government-sponsored lotteries existed. Now lotteries are legal in thirty-nine states and the District of Columbia, and the legal numbers games don't look much different from illegal numbers games.

Lotteries gradually regained public trust and ushered in a new period of government-sponsored gaming. State lotteries went from biannual three-dollar ticket sweepstakes in New Hampshire to daily lottos and instant winners.

Lotteries keep growing, even with increased competition from legalized casinos and other forms of gambling nationwide. In 1994, state lotteries captured $34.5 billion. Lotteries held 40 percent of the market share of U.S. gambling.[21] By 2003, annual U.S. lottery sales reached $45.3 billion with a per capita expenditure of $174.74.[22]

State lotteries use a variety of marketing appeals, including sports, get-rich-quick jingles, luck, patriotism, and seasonal themes. State lotteries are the greatest purveyors of hope—against astronomical odds—in American commercial gambling. Yet a lottery ticket buyer is 5 times more likely to be eaten by a shark, 7 times more likely to be struck by lightning, 6,000 times more likely to be hit by a car, and 500,000 times more likely to die in an airline crash than to win a state lottery.[23]

*A lottery ticket buyer is 5 times more likely to be
eaten by a shark, 7 times more likely to be struck by lightning, 6,000 times more likely to be hit by a car,
and 500,000 times more likely to die in an airline crash
than to win a state lottery.*

Men generally gamble more than women. But men and women play the lottery at about the same rate. More middle-aged than younger or older individuals buy lottery tickets. More Catholics than nonreligious people play the lottery, who in turn play more than Protestants. Lower-educated individuals are more likely to purchase tickets than those with greater formal education. More blacks and Hispanics participate in the lottery than do whites. More lower-income than higher-income individuals play the lottery. Ed Looney of the New Jersey Council on Problem Gambling estimated that 45 percent of New Jersey adolescents play the lottery, which is meant to be off-limits to anyone under eighteen.[24]

Many state lotteries pay out 60 to 65 percent of gross revenues, but most pay out less than 50 percent. Compared to other forms of gambling, state lotteries offer some of the lowest payouts and are, therefore, the worst games in town. Consequently, state lotteries are the fastest growing source of state revenues.

State lotteries are monopolies, and they do what monopolies usually do—make exorbitant profits. By 2003, payouts hovered in the 45–55 percent range of the amount wagered. Casinos, by comparison, work with payouts of 90–93 percent across all games.[25] That's why it is such good advice to say, "If you must gamble, at least don't gamble in the lottery. It's the worst odds out there."

With more than three-fourths of American states and the District of Columbia, all Canadian provinces, and more than 100 foreign countries offering lotteries, they are arguably the most locally accessible form of legalized commercial and/or government sponsored gambling in the world. In the United States, only eleven years after New Hampshire reopened the door to state sponsored lotteries, federal law was amended to allow state lotteries to advertise on television. One year later, in 1976, state lotteries surpassed the $1 billion mark for the first time. Some countries, like Mexico, Japan, and France, now even sponsor national lotteries.[26] The primary challenge to the lottery's supremacy as the most accessible gambling in the world is rapidly expanding "e-gambling" on the Internet.

## Dancing with the Wolves

Native American-owned casinos are, along with state lotteries, a central driving force of the nation's renewed gambling craze. It all began in 1987 when the U.S. Supreme Court handed down a decision recognizing Native American tribes' right to own and operate gambling enterprises on reservations.[27] This judicial allowance became law on October 17, 1988, with the passage in the U.S. Congress of the Indian Gaming Regulatory Act.

The act permits "Indian tribes [to] have the exclusive right to regulate gaming activity on Indian lands if the gaming activity is not specifically prohibited by federal law and is conducted within a state which does not, as a matter of criminal law and public policy, prohibit such gaming activity."[28] In addition, the act created the National Indian Gaming Commission to provide federal oversight for the expected new industry.

The act was not intended to be pro-gambling, but it certainly has become that. States made casino compacts with Native American tribes in order to preserve revenue for their economies. The tribes, in turn, did not hesitate to gamble with their futures.

To date, 224 tribes in 30 states are operating newly legal gambling establishments on reservation lands. From one bingo hall in Florida in 1980, there are now more than 89 casinos and 170 high-stakes bingo operations with more opening almost every month. Half of the nation's 562 federally recognized tribes with a total of 1.9 million people are trying to get into gambling. Native American gaming represents about 21 percent of all gambling in the United States.[29]

In 1988, about 70 Indian gaming facilities existed in 16 states with a total revenue of $184 million. By 2002, some 348 gaming facilities had been established in 30 states with gambling revenues of $14.5 billion and more non-gaming revenue of $1.6 billion. Indian gaming now operates some 206,000 gaming machines and 4,600 table games nationwide. Since 1988, Indian gaming has burgeoned by 8,000 percent with an annual growth rate of 37 percent. The number of Indian gaming facilities grew by 400 percent from 70 in 1988 to 348 in 2002.[30]

The National Indian Gaming Association, established in 1985, represents 168 Indian nations, with other non-voting associate member organizations, tribes, and business engaged in tribal gaming. In 2004, there were no federally recognized tribes in 17 states, while tribes operated Class III gambling facilities in 22 states, and tribes in the remaining 11 states operated some form of gambling.[31]

The gambling link with Native American groups is an intriguing one. If casinos are operated by tribal nations, they are not taxable. So state legislatures and city councils have been considering ceding parcels to tribal reservations so that they can make money from these enterprises via contractual arrangements called "compacts." Governments agree to protect Indian gambling monopolies in return for contracted "voluntary contributions" like the $100 million Connecticut receives annually from the 307 members of the Mahantucket Pequot tribe.[32] Other states receive revenue from Native American gambling operations that amounts to a tax but is part of a negotiated contract.

There's no question that Native American–owned casinos make money—lots of it. Reservation gambling is now a $14.5 billion per year industry for federally recognized tribes.

In Michigan, the Chippewa tribe put two casinos in operation in 1990, welcoming 11,000 customers. By 1994, the tribe owned five casinos, handled 3.5 million customers, and took in $100 million. In 1995, the tribe hosted 4 million visitors, an average of 11,000 per day.[33]

Michigan casinos raked in $452 million in 1995, not counting auxiliary business profits. That's about five times as much as fans of the Detroit Tigers, Lions, Pistons, and Red Wings spent on tickets in 1994. In the fall of 1996 in Mt. Pleasant, Michigan, Native Americans opened the second largest casino outside Las Vegas. By 2004, there were twenty casinos in Michigan operated by eleven tribes and three casinos operated by non-Indian owners.[34] Michigan now ranks seventh among states for gaming revenue, bringing in $2.7 billion in 2003.[35]

A Harris poll indicated that 70 percent of Americans favor Native American gaming.[36] Native American pro-gambling arguments are based on recollections of stolen land and broken nineteenth-century treaties. That together with the fact that as a people Native Americans have enjoyed something of a popular revival in the past few years has made tribal-owned gambling seem like poetic justice. Whatever the political context, the new buffalo in town is the casino.

## Casino Mania

Casinos may be Arizona's fastest growing industry. Colorado legalized limited stakes gambling in a November 1991 referendum. More than sixty casinos followed quickly in old gold mining towns like Cripple Creek—the new gold rush.[37]

*By the year 2000, 95 percent of Americans lived within a*
*three- or four-hour drive of a casino.*

Six states allow riverboat casinos, and Mississippi permits unlimited dockside casino operations. Mississippi's 1992 Dockside Gaming Law encouraged riverboat-style gambling. Mississippi Beach, twenty-six miles of oceanside, has been turned into a gambling mecca. Dockside casinos are more lucrative than floating casinos because the cruise is costly and maintenance is higher for floaters.[38]

By the year 2000, 95 percent of Americans lived within a three- or four-hour drive of a casino. The Bible Belt is turning into the Blackjack Belt.[39] In 2004, casinos had become so accepted and successful they had their own online directory at www.A-2casinos.com.

## Win, Place, or Show

The rapid increase of legalized gambling has not created a windfall for all gambling enterprises. In the last ten years, horse racetrack attendance has declined by 41 percent, and wagering has dropped from $7.6 billion to $4.3 billion. With attendance and total wagering dropping, horse racetracks keep losing money, despite the fact that 95 percent of horse-race gamblers still lose money at the track.[40] In Michigan, for example, horse-track betting dropped 37 percent in 2004 from its peak in 1997.[41] Most wagering on horse racing now occurs at offtrack betting parlors, while actual attendance at tracks continues to decline.

Horse races are still considered part of an ongoing effort for the improvement of the breed. With the loss of the military significance and economic importance of the horse, however, one might well say, "Improved for what?"[42]

Horse racing was for decades the game of the aristocratic set—a glamorous hobby—and it still is. Dog racing, however, has always appealed to lower-income groups. Rich man, poor man, beggar man, thief—they all gamble. Dog racing just never appealed much to the rich man.

Dog racing and horse racing are suffering from the expansion of legalized commercial gambling. Due to economic decline, sixteen dog tracks closed between 1981 and 2004.[43] Dog tracks in Wisconsin are seeing lower receipts due to Native American gaming. In Michigan, racing is the one gambling activity experiencing decline.[44] Horse racetracks in Michigan were already losing 30 to 35 percent due to Native American casinos and are predicted to lose another 5 to 15 percent with further casino expansion. A Michigan governor's report concluded that

> the horse-racing industry already has suffered significant economic harm, largely because of Indian-owned casinos and the Windsor, Ontario casino. Limited expansion of gaming in Michigan could contribute to the decline in attendance and handle that has afflicted the industry over the past twenty years, a decline that started even before casino gambling was introduced.[45]

The racetrack cannot compete with the casino primarily because many people have an insatiable desire for instant gratification. Lotteries, slot machines, and other casino games not only offer quicker turnarounds but are also easier to understand than racetrack betting. Consequently, more people can gamble with lotteries or in casinos without a long initiation period.

While there has been some modest growth in revenues at the tracks in the past decade, the racing industry is desperate. It has not been able to attract younger crowds, so it's attempting to develop a new national marketing campaign to reach the gambling public. So far, that campaign has not materialized.[46]

Many racetracks are petitioning states to authorize expanded gambling options at the tracks, including adding slot machines or other casino gambling, creating "racinos." Other racetracks are seeking permission to open additional offtrack betting facilities around their state, thus increasing their total take from a larger daily handle, or total amount of money bet on a race.

In December 1995, Michigan's state legislature voted to allow racetracks to install year-round simulcasting, televising races from the nation's top horse tracks.[47] Still other racetracks are considering combining casino-style gambling with family theme parks located next to tracks.

Iowa gave its horse and dog racetracks tax rebates, loan guarantees, and less restrictive extended loan repayments. Texas started its lottery in 1992, and racetrack business dropped 35 percent. The Lone Star State then lowered the horse-race betting state tax rate from 6.5 to 2 percent in order to shore up flagging profits. Other states have also had to subsidize their racing industry, including South Dakota, Nebraska, Wisconsin, Illinois, New Jersey, and Massachusetts.[48]

Whether these efforts will ensure the continued health and longevity of thoroughbred racing remains to be seen. Jockey Jerry Bailey, winner of all three races in the Triple Crown, believes that only 20 of the 128 thoroughbred racetracks in the United States will be running a decade from now.[49]

Pari-mutuel gambling opportunities focus the sport of racing entirely on gambling. A sport that began as an admiration of beautiful and powerful animals has become just another means to an end. Dobbin no longer matters as much as the daily double.

### Heads I Win, Tails You Lose

Sports betting is big business in the United States—$20 billion in 1975, $80 billion in 1990, and $200 billion in 2000—with the NFL Super Bowl the single biggest wagering event of the year.[50] It generates an estimated $2.5 billion in illegal wagering alone. Some 25 percent of adult Americans make at least one bet on a sporting event each year.[51]

Nevada's sports books handle more than $2 billion per year. The National Football League and college football account for about 40 percent of the sports betting action, and major-league baseball comes in at 25 percent.[52]

Nevada has 142 sports books, source of the famous "point spreads" or "Las Vegas line," which are published in newspapers across the country. "Although point spreads technically pertain only to legal sports betting in Nevada, bookies everywhere in the country use them in their own illegal betting operations. Critics of gambling claim that the line contributes less to the popularity of sports than to the popularity of sports betting."[53] One of those critics, Neil David Isaacs, said, "Sports betting comprises the bulk of the illegal action in the culture of gamblers. . . . Point spread betting, along with the preeminence of football as a TV-friendly event, made NFL football the vehicle of choice for American gamblers (with college football second, though in the last couple of years the NCAA basketball tournament has come close to displacing the Super Bowl as the major single betting proposition on the sporting calendar)."[54]

A survey by the Freedom Forum of the nation's 50 largest newspapers found that 48 publish odds or point spreads on professional and college games. Only the *New York Times* and the *Wall Street Journal* did not. Former NCAA executive director Walter Byers said that the thing that concerned him most about the future of organized sports was the threat of gambling.[55] Betting interests among fans, coaches, officials, and even players change the dynamics of the game, subjecting it to greed and corruption.

Parlay card operations can be found in most metropolitan areas. Cards contain lists of sports events and point spreads on which gamblers wager set amounts. If the bettor's team wins with a score that beats the spread, the bettor wins.

Gambling is a major threat to the integrity of sport, or at least that is the conclusion of leaders within the NCAA. Since 1996, William Saum has worked for the NCAA as its Director of Agent and Gambling Activities. In this role he oversees staff members whose task is to promote awareness of NCAA policies and ensure compliance with those policies, all in the interest of protecting fair play in intercollegiate sports. This leadership has helped establish the NCAA as one of the first and most vocal national agencies addressing concerns regarding the potentially negative impact of gambling on their interests. NCAA By-Law 10.3, "Gambling Activities," positions the NCAA against all forms of legal and illegal sports wagering by collegiate coaches, athletics staff, or student-athletes.[56]

To develop an accurate understanding of the problem, a 2004 press release announced, "The NCAA has commissioned a first-of-its-kind sports-wagering task force to examine the recently released National Study on Collegiate Sports Wagering and Associated Health Risks and to devise recommendations for addressing the problem of wagering by student-athletes." The 2003 report (involving responses to questions designed by Dr. Durand Jacobs, a nationally known researcher in youth gambling, from almost 21,000 male and female student-athletes) was published May 12, 2004, and found that almost 35 percent of male student-athletes have engaged in some kind of sports gambling in the past year. If the study's percentages are extended to the total student-athlete population, an estimated 49,000 student-athletes wagered on college or professional sports within the last year. The twenty-six member task force was chaired by Rev. Edward A. Malloy, president of the University of Notre Dame.[57]

Myles Brand, president of the NCAA, said, "Sports wagering is a double-threat because it harms the well-being of student-athletes and the integrity of sports."[58] The 2003 study found that the proportion of males who have ever wagered on sports stands at 68.9 percent, while 47.2 percent of female student-athletes have gambled on sports at some time.[59] Since 1993–1994, gambling scandals at Arizona State University, Boston College, Bryant College, Columbia University, Northwestern University, and University of Maryland have threatened the credibility of football and basketball programs, which is why President Malloy commented, "If sport loses integrity, then everything becomes professional wrestling with a predetermined outcome and with, I believe, a huge diminishment of interest."[60]

Perhaps of even greater concern, sports gambling has crept into the ranks of collegiate athletics officials. Five of the six NCAA Division I football and basketball game officials answering a University of Michigan survey admitted they gambled. Some 84.4 percent of all Division I game officials have gambled since becoming a college official, 40 percent gambled on sports, and 22.9 percent gambled using a bookie.[61] The NCAA, the NFL, and NHL, and Senator John McCain (R-AZ), who has made a ban on collegiate-sports betting one of his causes, remain virtually alone among national leaders decrying gambling and warning against its potentially devastating side effects.[62]

The NCAA's Sports Wagering Task Force worked during 2004 and reported to the NCAA national convention in January 2005. Among the task force's conclusions are recommendations for increased education to improve awareness of the risks and the penalties associated with sports wagering, as well as recommendations for alliances with other sports agencies to encourage anti-sports wagering policy and appropriate compliance. The Task Force also developed two quick-response initiatives, working with the American Football Coaches Association to sponsor a "National Sports Wagering Awareness Day," October 30, 2004. More than 150,000 blue wristbands, imprinted with "NCAA Don't Bet On It," were distributed for coaches and their support staffs. February 26, 2005, another "National Sports Wagering Awareness Day" was sponsored by the NCAA and the National Basketball Coaches Association and the Women's Basketball Coaches Association.[63]

Betting is now a regular focus of jokes on national sports telecasts. Jimmy the Greek may be gone, but betting is as much a part of game day as soda pop and pizza.

## Hyperbole Hotel

Gambling is family entertainment, no more threatening than Mickey Mouse. Or, at least, that's what Las Vegas hoped. For a while, gambling met the theme park. A sort of sanitized Las Vegas—"Desert Disneyland," "Orlando West"—is the image the Las Vegas gambling tycoons wanted the American public to see.

Despite its high crime and municipal woes, the city of "Lost Wages" is an increasingly popular vacation spot. It features top name entertainment, shopping, glitz, and, of course, gambling. Due in part to the climate, Las Vegas has become the fastest growing urban area in the country. Approximately five thousand people per month move to Clark County, which encompasses Las Vegas.[64]

The Las Vegas Convention and Visitor Authority (LVCVA) markets the city as "Las Vegas: Open 24 Hours." LVCVA is attempting to appeal to adults while being child-friendly. According to LVCVA, among 1995 visitors

- 68 percent were married
- 79 percent were white
- 68 percent were over forty years of age
- 52 percent had household incomes of $40,000 or more
- 11 percent had children with them[65]

To lure families to what was once considered an environment unfit for children, for a time many resorts offered nongambling alternatives. Family theme park and casino packages were vogue. In the 1980s, corporate gambling interests applied mass merchandising techniques to market gambling as recreation, free of moral and financial worries.[66]

Now there's something for everyone. Thanks in part to longtime Las Vegas gambling magnate Steve Wynn, the age of the mega casino arrived. Wynn is the casino king of Las Vegas, the mastermind of the gaming revolution in America. He's the one who frankly said if you want to make money in a casino, you'd better own it.[67] He's also the person most responsible for Las Vegas's continuing gambling evolution.

Fiery volcanic explosions take place at the Mirage, a pirate ship and a British frigate battle outside Treasure Island Hotel, and the River Nile can be found inside the Luxor Hotel.

In late April 1996, the Stratosphere Tower complex opened in Las Vegas, featuring a 1,149-foot tower—the tallest building west of the Mississippi River. Billed as "world-themed casino excitement," the complex contains three themed casinos in a 97,000-square-foot gambling center, including a revolving restaurant, observation decks, and three wedding chapels atop the tower. Attached is a 120,000-square-foot mall. A 70-foot-tall growling mechanical gorilla scales the tower pulling a cage behind it filled with paying customers.[68]

Beginning in 1985, some 35,000 new hotel rooms were added in a Las Vegas accommodations "room boom," and another 12,000 were opened by

1997. By the end of 2003, the number of hotel rooms topped 124,000. Hotel owners in Las Vegas enjoy an incredible 90 percent occupancy rate.[69]

Seventeen of the world's twenty largest hotels are found in Las Vegas. The largest hotel in the world, the MGM Grand, cost $1.03 billion to build and has 5,005 rooms, including 744 suites with up to 6,000 square feet of living space. It also has more ATM machines than any other single building in the world.[70]

More than thirty-five wedding chapels are open around the clock. Over 100,000 marriage licenses are issued in Las Vegas every year, an average of one wedding every five minutes.[71]

The hotel New York, New York features the Empire State Building, Statue of Liberty, and Central Park, including a water flume ride, motion simulation rides, and a Coney Island-style roller-coaster. At this and other hotel casinos, like Bellagio located behind a fifty-acre lake with a huge fountain display, attractions include outdoor activities such as water skiing, parasailing, and wind surfing. The Paris Casino Resort, which opened in 1997, features replicas of the Eiffel Tower, the Champs Élysées, the Seine, and the Arc de Triomphe.[72]

In late 1996, Hilton and Paramount Parks added a forty-thousand-square-foot center: "Star Trek: The Fantasy Experience." Patrons sample image projection and virtual reality stations.[73]

An expansion of Forum Shops, an upscale mall associated with Caesars Palace, focuses on "Atlantis Odyssey," portraying humans and animatronic figures. Unlike its counterparts elsewhere, the Hard Rock Hotel of Las Vegas includes a casino along with assorted rock memorabilia.[74]

All this has produced a gambling and entertainment boom in Las Vegas, which recorded 29 million visitors in 1995—double the number from a decade before. That's more than twice the 13.5 million who traveled to Orlando in the same year, evidencing a several year trend earning Las Vegas bragging rights as the number one vacation destination in America.[75]

Las Vegas gambling revenues hit $5.7 billion in 1995, more than double from a decade before. People in the gambling industry trace the boom to the collapse of taboos about gambling. A 1995 Harrah's Casino survey revealed 59 percent of American adults said they consider casino gambling acceptable, up 8 percent from the previous year.[76]

Las Vegas's customer base grew from 18 million in 1989 to more than 35.8 million in 2003, including 4,149 conventions that year, with visitors spending more and staying longer. Only 6 percent of the adults living in

Clark County (greater Las Vegas) were born there, the lowest such figure for anywhere in the country. Some 60 percent of visitors to Las Vegas are women.[77] Visitor spending increased from more than $22.5 million in 1996 to about $32 million in 2003. By 2004, Las Vegas was bringing in gambling revenues in excess of $7.6 billion annually.[78]

The fact that the new millennium witnessed MGM Grand tearing down its largely unused amusement theme park is a signal that Las Vegas's Orlando-like foray into family entertainment has ended. In 2003, only 10 percent of the city's visitors brought children with them, while 85 percent of these visitors gambled an average of four hours per day.[79] The 1990s "nice vice" approach simply had not worked.

Now the city is marketing itself as a leisure destination using a phrase with slightly naughty implications, "What Happens in Vegas, Stays in Vegas." Las Vegas is back to its roots, "booze, sex, and gambling," for "sin is in," including newly developed, large strip clubs, the "corporate sleaze" of The Palms's "bachelor party" guest rooms featuring chrome poles for in-room dancers, the Rio's Bikini Bar with sexually explicit entertainment, and New York, New York's new show "Zumanity," from Cirque Du Soleil, highlighting "provocative exhibition of human sensuality, arousal, and eroticism." The reason "so many women are taking off their clothes inside the casino is that there are so many women taking off their clothes outside the casino. Almost simultaneously with the explosion of gambling around the country, strip clubs have become a major business in the United States."[80] Sin is making a comeback in Las Vegas because moral relativism—and with it a consequent loss of modesty—is dominating American culture generally.

In November 2004, MGM Mirage announced plans for a $4.7 billion hotel, condominium, shopping complex, suggesting the next Las Vegas mega innovation—Strip condominium living. Steve Wynn is also building what he hopes is his masterpiece, Le Reve, as well as a Wynn Hotel and Casino on the Strip.[81] The goal of these new mega-complexes? Integrated, full-service living and a way for gambling entrepreneurs to get into residents' pockets, even if they don't gamble.

Casino "theming is dead," says Paul Steelman, president and COO of Paul Steelman Design Group. "Dramatic architecture is taking over." The idea is to "empower" customers with a feeling they can win, while at the same time creating a feeling of comfort. The erupting volcano at The Mirage and the computer-guided dancing fountains at The Bellagio are examples of the pizzazz that makes people want to come back. Whatever

Las Vegas does, it somehow relates to finding ever more profitable ways to seduce gamblers to give up their money.

## Croupier, Inc.

Gambling is now just another service provided by "diversified leisure conglomerates. Gambling is no longer a pariah. It is a legitimate business." Owners and operators are publicly held corporations and state and local government. Casino executives have MBAs, avoid mob activity, and work to fit into the corporate mainstream.[82]

American Gaming Association president Frank Fahrenkopf said,

> An overwhelming majority of today's gaming companies are owned by publicly held corporations regulated by the Securities and Exchange Commission, employing directly or indirectly over one million people, and contributing billions of dollars to state and local treasuries by way of taxation.[83]

Gambling establishment owners are typically no longer local people. Outsiders representing huge corporations own and operate most gambling concerns.

Gambling casinos can now be found joined with hotel chains like Radisson, Clarion, Hilton, and others. In what sounds almost quaint today, when Holiday Inn authorized its first casino in Atlantic City, the president, L. M. Clymer, and two board members resigned on moral grounds. That was September 1978, and it's a lot different now.

According to journalist David Johnston, author of *Temples of Chance*, that vote marked a significant turning point for Holiday Inn and for the country. From that time forward the line distinguishing legitimate business from gambling (what most up to that time considered illegitimate business) was blurred.[84]

It's a lucrative business. Hilton's four Nevada casino hotels bring in twice the revenues of its 264 franchised hotels combined. One author provides an explanation for these enormous profits: "The level of betting practiced today by high rollers was never allowed when mobsters controlled the casino business in Nevada."[85]

MGM Mirage Company, owned by casino mogul Kirk Kerkorian, controls the Mirage; T.I. (Treasure Island); Bellagio; MGM Grand; New York, New York; Golden Nugget; 50 percent of the Monte Carlo; and more than a half dozen other casinos in Las Vegas, other parts of

Nevada, Mississippi, Michigan, New Jersey, Australia, and South Africa. The Park Place Entertainment Corporation, an offshoot of the Hilton Corporation, controls Ballys, Caesars Palace, Paris, the Las Vegas Hilton, and the Flamingo, as well as other gambling operations internationally in Canada, South Africa, and Uruguay. Mandalay Resort Group runs casinos in Mississippi, Illinois, and Michigan, and controls the Luxor, Mandalay Bay, Excalibur, Circus Circus, and the other 50 percent of the Monte Carlo, along with half-a-dozen other casinos in Nevada. These three publicly held, MBA-managed mega-corporations, along with Harrah's Entertainment, form the backbone of the Las Vegas gambling industry.[86]

Gambling establishment owners don't gamble, at least not with their own operation. They offer the public an opportunity to lose money by creating a house "edge" with highly sophisticated research and technology enabling gambling entrepreneurs to sweeten their take and maximize their "hold" (net revenue). Add to this an attitude that disrespects the public, and you have a recipe for financial disaster: "Give me a player for six days and I guarantee he'll leave a loser," said a Mandalay Bay pit executive.[87] A slot machine research technician for International Gaming Technology of Reno ("I.G.T. is to the slot industry what Microsoft is to computer software") spoke of "cherry dribbler" slot machines that dispense lots of small payouts while they nibble at a gambler's wallet rather than biting off large chunks at one time. "You want to give the newbie lots of positive reinforcement," he said, "to keep 'em playing."[88] Perhaps this is why nearly 40 million Americans played slot machines in 2003.[89]

A whole industry has developed supporting state lotteries, including computer corporations and ticket printing firms. These companies form a powerful new lobby that pressures state legislatures to approve additional statewide gambling.

Scientific Games, Inc., is the biggest corporation in the market of printing lottery tickets and manufacturing lottery supplies. In 1984, Scientific Games invested $2 million in the California lottery campaign. They also actually wrote the ballot proposition. After the campaign, legislators and state officials discovered that the only company that could meet the specifications established in the proposition was Scientific Games. Although the officials extended bidding deadlines, they found no alternative, and Scientific Games won a first-year contract of $40 million.[90]

In 1995, the American Gaming Association was started in Washington, D.C., as a lobbying arm of the gaming industry. Such agencies, along with gambling industry entrepreneurs, help create a public demand for more legalized gambling through shrewd marketing and classic political deal making. In 1994, the industry contributed $3.1 million to candidates and parties. It's not surprising that gambling corporations are now listed among the top five interest-group contributors to political causes.[91]

Today the power to shape the dimensions of the gambling market is shifting from consumers to suppliers. Because of what Abt, Smith, and Christiansen call the "institutionalization of the business of risk," commercial gambling owners and operators can expand their market geometrically and profit in previously undreamed-of dollars.[92]

The growth of legalized gambling follows what is known as the "economic imperative." There is much money to be made off a willingly gullible public.

**More Than We Bet On**

The so-called third wave of gambling in the United States is now beginning its fifth decade. The lottery movement, begun tentatively in 1964, has merged with the casino craze that began enthusiastically in 1989. Gambling owners and operators have been bullish on the future because investments in gambling enterprises have produced ever greater returns and seem more shrewd than silly. Indeed the rediscovery and decriminalization of commercial gambling were accomplished with limited resistance and even less thoughtful evaluation. Gambling has gone mainstream.

The third wave of American gambling is interesting business history. But it is much more than that. America's embrace of gambling says something about American values—what we consider right and wrong and what we believe we ought to do with our time and resources. Gambling is not an amoral activity. How we ascertain the moral content of gambling is the subject of the next chapter.

# 4

# GOD, GAMES, AND THE GOOD LIFE

## *Is Gambling a Sin?*

"When I was much younger, I gambled on horse and dog racing," my Christian friend said. "I wanted to get more money. I lost more than I could afford. For me, I believe it was sin. I don't think God was pleased with my use of resources."

On second thought he said, "There was also a type of addiction that took over. When you get behind, you feel like you have to 'get even.' Bets become larger—until no money is left. At this point, one is really not in control—the game is. Yet, I believe I could go to a night of dog races right now, maybe place one two-dollar bet for the fun of it, and leave it at that. The motivation is entertainment, but maybe I lose two dollars. Is this sin? That's a tough one."[1]

It is a tough one. Americans have never been of one accord on the question: Is gambling a sin? Among religious people, however, particularly avowedly Christian people, the weight of opinion is heavily to one side of the argument.

### No Eleventh Commandment

There is no eleventh commandment in the Bible saying, "Thou shalt not gamble." Nowhere in Scripture is gambling even extensively discussed. Yet the early church and the medieval church firmly and consistently opposed gambling.

St. Augustine said, "The Devil invented gambling." John Calvin outlawed gambling in Geneva under penalty of fines. Martin Luther said, "Money won by gambling is not won without self-seeking and love of self, and not without sin." John Wesley occasionally used lots to determine God's will, but he did not gamble. In his sermons, the Puritan Cotton Mather condemned gambling as theft. In the 1690s and early 1700s, Mather preached against lotteries as productive of nothing.[2] In 1699, Boston clergy called lottery agents "pillagers of the people." A colonial poem wryly summarized the common view: "The name of Lott'ry, the Nature Bewitches. And City and Country run Mad after Riches." Other religious groups wavered between toleration of and active opposition to gambling; none endorsed or promoted it. This continued throughout the eighteenth and nineteenth centuries.[3]

Despite early attacks on gambling by church fathers, questions about the morality of gambling persist even today among people within the Judeo-Christian tradition.

## The Church and Games of Chance

The American Catholic Church has never been too disturbed about gambling. In the Catholic Church's eyes, gambling is recreation, not a sin, unless it's abused. In Roman Catholic moral theology, gambling may or may not have attendant evils, depending on the circumstances in which it is conducted and the behavior of the participants.

The *New Catholic Encyclopedia* states:

> A person is entitled to dispose of his own property as he wills . . . so long as in doing so he does not render himself incapable of fulfilling duties incumbent upon him by reason of justice or charity. Gambling, therefore, though a luxury, is not considered sinful except when the indulgence in it is inconsistent with duty.[4]

Gambling is also considered in the *Catechism of the Catholic Church*:

> Games of chance (card games, etc.) or wagers are not in themselves contrary to justice. They become morally unacceptable when they deprive someone of what is necessary to provide for his needs and those of others. The passion for gambling risks becoming an enslavement. Unfair wagers and cheating at games constitute grave matters, unless the damage inflicted is so slight that the one who suffers it cannot reasonably consider it significant.[5]

In Roman Catholic thought, the *act* of gambling is not evil, only losing more than one can afford is evil. Freedom to gamble involves a fair and honest contract for play. Cheating is condemned, unless the damage is slight.

Many Roman Catholic leaders, however, still resist expanded legalized gambling. They believe the negative socioeconomic impact that typically results offsets any luxury produced by gambling. Consequently, the Roman Catholic Church has supported some referenda while opposing others.[6]

Catholic Church authorities in Michigan warned that expanded gambling is not all it may seem. "As a microcosm for the state, the Catholic Church's experience with gaming shows that it *is not* the panacea for the economic ills of a society. Despite the revenues bingo brings in, the Church must still close schools, consolidate parishes and scale-back important programs. There is little reason to expect that the state's experience with gaming will differ significantly from that of the Catholic Church."[7]

Referring to bingo and raffles, one Catholic bishop wrote in a letter to his people, "I am convinced that we will never teach our people the stewardship of money as long as any of these means are used for the purposes of church support."[8]

Judaism does not consider gambling intrinsically evil but forbids it for personal gain or for funding synagogues. Professional gambling and compulsive gambling are also condemned. The occasional gambler is tolerated as long as he maintains his vocation and meets his financial responsibilities. Gambling at festive occasions or for purposes other than self-gain are permitted but not promoted.[9]

Protestant churches, with some notable exceptions, have a long history of opposition to gambling in just about all of its forms. The American Baptist Convention's 1959 statement captures the essence of the religious anti-gambling feeling at that time:

> Gambling is essentially the redistribution of a people's wealth according to chance, rather than according to the receiver's contribution to society. . . . The presence of widespread gambling is a symptom of economic decay and an indication that industrious, thrifty, and responsible living has failed, and people in their despair are throwing away what they have today on the chance that it might bring returns tomorrow.[10]

The Southern Baptist Convention has consistently opposed gambling, as has the Presbyterian Church (USA) and the Seventh Day Adventist Church. The Assemblies of God has a long history of opposition and it adopted an anti-gambling statement in 1983.[11]

Methodists have historically offered strong resistance to gambling, fueling both nineteenth- and twentieth-century reform movements. In its "Social Principles," the United Methodist Church calls gambling "a menace to society, deadly to the best interests of moral, social, economic and spiritual life and destructive of good government."[12]

However, just as the Catholic Church has not been unified in its attitudes toward the advisability of gambling, neither have some Protestant groups. Neither the Anglican Church of England nor the Episcopal Church in America has assumed a clear anti-gambling position.

For those religious groups that have opposed gambling, the common theme of anti-gambling resistance has been that gambling is a threat to personal character and social morality. Gambling is blamed for family poverty, is considered an act of selfishness and stealing, and is a distraction from the pursuit of excellence and purity. It undermines the work ethic and encourages wanton feelings and materialism. It ignores God's disposition of human life. To make matters worse, gambling centers seem to attract a host of other carnal pleasures, which tempt the unfaithful into greater depravity.[13]

In a 1951 statement, the National Council of Churches of Christ in the U.S.A. said, "The so-called 'innocent' forms of gambling—such as legalized racetrack wagers, betting on athletic events, lotteries, bingo, and the like—contribute to the weakening of the moral fiber of the individual and lower the moral tone of the community."[14]

A 1966 statement by the National Association of Evangelicals (NAE) called gambling "a parasite feeding on both the individual and society." In 1985, the NAE added that gambling and lotteries "are socially, morally, and economically destructive . . . are rooted in covetousness and violate the biblical work ethic . . . and undermine the economic base of a nation."[15]

Whatever the disagreements among Christian and religious moralists, historically they all condemned addiction, commercial exploitation, and government participation in gambling.[16]

## Gambling as a Christian Concern

Questions about whether gambling is right or wrong, however, remain. Is gambling a sin or isn't it? Is it a sin in some circumstances but not in others? Is gambling harmless entertainment that just sometimes gets out of hand? Should Christians oppose the expansion of legalized commercial gambling?

All of these questions can be answered, but not without reference to the Bible. Christian understanding of gambling (or any other social issue) is based on an interpretation of biblical principles.

Conservative Christians believe that God gave us his Word in propositional form so it can be read reasonably and applied rationally. The Christian task is to apply God's moral will to the questions and challenges of the world in which we live. Gambling—like drugs, pornography, or prostitution (all of which have been called victimless crimes)—is one of those questions.

Gambling is often justified by pointing to the biblical practice of casting lots. So we turn to the Bible and ask: Is this comparison defensible? Gambling assumes a belief in luck and chance. Are these concepts biblical? Should Christians embrace or promote these ideas?

Gambling uses human resources—time, talent, treasure—and distributes these resources, particularly treasure, from one individual to another. Does this action contradict biblical commands, or is it biblically acceptable?

To understand gambling biblically, we must wrestle with questions related to the casting of lots; luck, chance, and the sovereignty of God; stewardship of time, talent, and treasure; covetousness and theft; and Christian liberty. Once we grasp what God says about these behaviors, we will be able to determine whether gambling is a sin.

### Thus Saith the Lord?

Some people think that casting lots was just an ancient way of shooting craps. Physically, this isn't too far off the mark. Lots were made of a sheep's knucklebones and functioned very much like modern dice. In the ancient world, sometimes those bones were rolled in gambling, and sometimes they were used for nongambling play, but the association with gambling was fixed. Any study of gambling and the Bible, therefore, must examine the practice of casting lots and must seek to answer two key questions: (1) Is casting lots an example of gambling in the Bible? (2) If so, did God ever condone the use of lots for gambling?

The Israelites used lots to determine the divine will. The Urim and Thummim (meaning "yes" and "no") were used in the Old Testament to make decisions (Exod. 28:30; Lev. 8:7–9), select Saul as king (1 Sam.

10:20–21), choose soldiers for battle (Judg. 20:9–10), divide the land (Num. 26:52–56; 33:54; 34:13; 36:2; Josh. 13:6; 14:2), and select animals for sacrifice (Lev. 16:7–10). Lots were used to identify the man, Jonah, who caused the storm (Jonah 1:7). In the New Testament, lots were cast to choose Matthias to replace Judas (Acts 1:21–26) and to distribute Christ's clothing (Matt. 27:35; Mark 15:24; Luke 23:34; John 19:23–24).

Lots were also used to determine who had committed a sin (1 Sam. 14:42), identify the holder of loot (Josh. 7:13–21), distribute the sons of Aaron into the priesthood and guide priests' rotations in office (1 Chron. 24:5; Luke 1:9), and decide privileges of living in Jerusalem (Neh. 11:1).

Proverbs 16:33 says, "The lot is cast into the lap, but its every decision is from the Lord." No fate, chance, or luck is involved in the casting of biblical lots. It was an ancient practice used in decision making. That decision recognized the sovereignty of God in all things, including the lay of the lot.

Cotton Mather said that "lots, being mentioned in the sacred oracles of Scripture as used only in weighty cases and as an acknowledgment of God sitting in judgment . . . cannot be made the tools and parts of our common sports without, at least, such an 'appearance of evil' as is forbidden in the Word of God."[17]

After Pentecost, the casting of lots was never used again as a means of determining God's will. God had sent the Holy Spirit, and he gave us his written Word as a source of his moral will. The practice of casting lots was no longer needed.

One thing is clear. Casting lots was not gambling, nor can the practice be used to justify the idea of gambling.

Even the soldiers casting lots for Christ's robe at the foot of the cross were not gambling. No soldier had paid to play. No soldier was taking any risk. No one was going to win at another's expense. They were simply trying to determine who got to keep the robe. This example of casting lots is similar to what today we'd call "drawing straws."

Even though the word *lottery* comes from the word *lot*, casting lots and contemporary lotteries are qualitatively different activities. The former is based on an understanding of God's providence, the latter on a hoped-for luck of the draw.

## Divine Luck

A forgotten sage once said, "Good luck is the lazy man's estimate of a worker's success." He was right. Both luck and laziness are nonbiblical, non-Christian ideas.

God has a plan for the universe. Good fortune is a blessing of God. In Isaiah 65:11–12, God said,

> But as for you who forsake the LORD
> and forget my holy mountain,
> who spread a table for Fortune
> and fill bowls of mixed wine for Destiny,
> I will destine you for the sword,
> and you will all bend down for the slaughter.

*Fortune* comes from the Hebrew word *Gad* and means "luck" or "good fortune." *Destiny* comes from the Hebrew word *Meni* meaning "bad luck, the god of fate." *Gad* and *Meni* were pagan gods of good and bad luck.

*Gad* combined as Baal-Gad means "Lord of Luck" and was an integral part of ancient pagan worship of the idol Baal (Josh. 11:17; 12:7; 13:5). In Numbers 13:10, *Gaddiel* means "God of my luck." Faith in luck and faith in God are mutually exclusive ideas. Isaiah 65:11-12 promises judgment for those who worship or honor the false gods of luck.

To believe in luck is to believe that God does not exist. For if God does exist—an all-knowing, all-powerful, Creator God—then luck makes no sense. Things don't just happen. Nothing happens outside of God's will and disposition. So belief in God not only dispels any idea of luck, it also rejects any idea of chance.

*Faith in luck and faith in God are mutually exclusive ideas.*

Chance stands in direct opposition to a purposeful creation, ordered and directed by the sovereign God of the universe. Chance is the person-ification of anarchy and nihilism. God controls, not chance (see Amos 3:6).[18] "Chance is only another word for human ignorance. So far as the use of the word 'chance' is justifiable, it is justifiable as a reminder of the infinite and unknown region that lies beyond our ken, in which, however as the discoveries of science tend to prove, law and order reign just as certainly as in the limited field within human horizons."[19]

Gambling is a kind of "secularized divination,"[20] which is based upon chance. The idea that events are disposed merely by chance is akin to superstition. Fyodor Dostoyevsky reminded us in *The Gambler* that gambling and superstition go hand in hand.[21] From the lucky shirt and a certain way of holding the dice to the lucky lady standing at one's shoulder, gamblers look to unknown forces to guide their play. But "a lucky day in gambling is an illusion that does not exist. There never is a lucky day in gambling whereby money is permanently won."[22]

All of life is a gamble, or so the saying goes. That may be pop culture *c'est la vie*, but it is not biblical theology. Life is not a gamble. God is in control of the Christian's life, of the non-Christian's life, of life itself (see Luke 12:6–7). Christians understand the universe as a purposeful creation in which they "will take the odds of life and transform them into response to the will of God."[23]

"Depending upon luck and chance is a philosophy which deifies an impersonal view of life and of reality." It is a form of idolatry.[24] Our God is a sovereign God, and he reigns in heaven above and earth beneath. Pagan superstition is a violation of God's will. Worshiping the gods of luck and chance is an offense to his character.

God gives with an expectation of accountability. We live with an anticipation of responsibility.

### What's Mine Is Thine

The *things* in our lives may be either toys or tools. Whichever they are, we're responsible to God for their use. It took me awhile to understand this.

When I was a child, I struggled with the idea that gambling was wrong, because I associated my parents' injunction against gambling with the device. Later on I learned that the device is not intrinsically evil. Cards, dice, dollar bills, horses, and greyhound dogs have all been used as instruments of gambling, but they are no more evil than baseball, basketball, or golf, which are also periodic instruments of gambling.

The things God created are not evil. How we use them may be evil. Our values and our motives are what matter to God.

I also thought that I could spend my money any way that I wanted, answering to no one. What I hadn't yet grasped and what my parents were trying to teach me was, "It's not *your* money. God put this money in your care, and you're responsible to him for its right uses." I didn't understand responsibility for time, talent, and treasure, not just in gambling but in life in general.

God owns all things (Pss. 24:1; 50:10–12; Matt. 25:14–30; Luke 12:42–48; 1 Cor. 10:26). As Christians, we are responsible for all that God places into our care, including our time, talent, and treasure. This is called *stewardship*. He places these things into our hands only for a season. In that time, we are responsible to him for their right uses. We are not permitted to destroy wantonly or develop excessively. We are keepers of a sacred trust for which we will someday be held accountable. With our time and talent, we are to work for our treasure as unto the Lord (Eph. 4:28; 2 Thess. 3:10–12). This is the root of the well-known and rightfully well-regarded Protestant work ethic.

*As Christians, we are responsible for all that God places into our care, including our time, talent, and treasure.*

God says, "He who works his land will have abundant food, but he who chases fantasies lacks judgment" (Prov. 12:11). "A good man leaves an inheritance for his children's children" (Prov. 13:22).

There is no better definition for *chasing fantasies* than gambling. Gambling encourages people not to work and to throw their money away on blind wishes. By gambling, people attempt to avoid God's principle, "By the sweat of your brow you will eat your food" (Gen. 3:19).

Gambling masquerades as a surrogate for work. It undermines work, rationality, and responsibility. But work is both a command and a gift of God (Exod. 20:9; Eph. 4:28; 2 Thess. 3:6–12; 1 Tim. 5:8), and reason is an essential part of being human. "Irresponsibility is man's abdication of his humanity. We are made to be moral decision-making creatures."[25]

God's world is not a place of undefined chaos. It is a place of order and purpose. God said for us to work and that we would be blessed by that work. He said for us to use our reasoning capability and that we would be blessed through this capability. God said that he would meet all our needs "according to his glorious riches in Christ Jesus" (Phil. 4:19). Meeting our needs includes not only our physical sustenance but also our emotional well-being. God will provide for our work and our play.

Americans are good at play. In fact, Americans *demand* to be entertained. We believe we have the *right* to be entertained, and there's much to entertain us. The United States now offers the most highly developed leisure economy that ever existed. "American pop culture is the single most powerful force on the globe."[26] In the midst of all this, gambling is offered as a legitimate form of entertainment. It's the fastest growing element of the leisure economy.

Comparing gambling to other forms of entertainment, though, is problematic. Clearly there are some people who participate in gambling for its recreational benefits. And gambling may honestly be considered pleasurable to some people in some ways.

Does gambling offer any positive benefits? Maybe. Genuine leisure or play, an escape, the enjoyment of circumscribed risk are a few possibilities. Spontaneous and voluntary pleasure in making a decision under conditions of uncertainty with immediate and definite results and the intellectual stimulation of handicapping or card counting are a few more.[27]

An activity's pleasure quotient, however, does not determine its moral legitimacy. As George Brushaber put it, "I have no right to my 'fun' if it undermines someone else's morality, modesty, or spiritual welfare."[28] Entertainment that harms oneself or others is not legitimate entertainment. It is morally unacceptable and in its worst forms is called sadomasochism.

Unlike other forms of entertainment, gambling costs are not known. It has a habit-forming quality. It creates social consequences not associated with entertainment.

If both our work and our leisure time are gifts from God, then we are responsible to him for how we use them. "Gambling is a waste of time and is unwholesome recreation."[29] I could not have said it better.

Wholesome recreation contributes to mental, emotional, and physical well-being. Gambling only debilitates. A biblical theology of recreation understands rest and relaxation pursuits as those that restore the body, mind, and spirit. Gambling debases.[30]

Christians who wish to be good stewards of their lives must evaluate all forms of entertainment carefully, not just gambling. Wasting money or time, filling our minds with nonbiblical philosophies, eating unhealthy foods or eating to excess, or participating in immoral behaviors all qualify as sinful stewardship.

Gambling also violates our stewardship of others. In Scripture we are told to love our neighbors as ourselves (Lev. 19:18, 34; Matt. 19:19; 22:39; Mark 12:31). Winning at gambling, no matter how distantly removed by the economics of enormous jackpots, always comes at the cost of others. Winners always win less than losers lose. The winner's gain is always at the expense of many other people's pain.

You cannot gamble while arguing that you are being a proper steward of your God-given resources. It's impossible. This is the primary fallacy in the Roman Catholic position on gambling, as well as those pro-gambling positions that contend that gambling is a healthy and harmless pursuit.

Gambling in any form is a violation of God's moral will. First, we hold all our resources in trust, and we are accountable to God for their use. Gambling ignores this biblical principle by staking money on chance or luck.

Second, the amount of money wagered does not change the essential nature of the gambling transaction. Whether we gamble with a little or a lot, we still gamble. Small stakes gambling is a difference of degree, not kind.[31]

Third, whether we can afford to lose the money wagered is not a very sound test. This seems to suggest that it is morally acceptable for the wealthy to gamble but not for the poor to do so. This is a morally inconsistent position and one that is biblically indefensible.

Gambling is only one violation of biblical stewardship. Pastors need to preach total stewardship. It's more than tithes and offerings. Stewardship summarizes a Christian worldview. "So whether you eat or drink or whatever you do, do it all for the glory of God" (1 Cor. 10:31).

### Easy Street

In D. James Kennedy's words, "gambling is institutionalized covetousness." Gambling violates the tenth commandment of God. It is, Kennedy contends, "the Devil's delusion."[32]

People who gamble chase fantasies. They yield to the lure of quick riches, the something-for-nothing enchantment. Gambling is bred by the sin of covetousness, and it masquerades as harmless fun while it sucks the dollars and sometimes the life out of everyone it touches (see Exod. 20:17; Deut. 5:21; Matt. 6:21; Mark 7:21–23; Luke 12:15; Rom. 1:29; Eph. 5:5; Col. 3:5; 1 Tim. 6:6–10).

"The persistent appeal to covetousness is fundamentally opposed to the unselfish, which was taught by Jesus Christ and by the New Testament as a whole. The attempt (inseparable from gambling) to make a profit out of the inevitable loss and possible suffering of others is the antithesis of that love of one's neighbor on which our Lord insisted."[33]

The basis of all anti-gambling legislation is the necessity of curbing or controlling covetousness, the selfish desire to get something for nothing.[34] Greed, materialism, and the love of money all come alive in a gambling venue.

"You shall not steal" (Exod. 20:15). Gambling also creates a condition in which one person's gain is always another person's loss. Gambling takes from the loser, and stealing is immoral (Matt. 19:18; Eph. 4:28). As such, gambling curtails brotherly love, justice, and mercy (Lev. 19:18;

Micah 6:8; Matt. 7:12; 22:37–40; Luke 6:31; Rom. 12:10; 14:21; 15:1; Heb. 13:1–2; 2 Peter 1:7).

We are commanded not to steal, and we must consider gambling robbery by mutual consent. Someone always loses, and it is generally those who are least able to afford it, financially or emotionally. Because people agree to do something does not make it moral.

Gambling is a classic example of Satan's use of worldly allurements to tempt people to sin. Ornate casinos, graceful horses, exciting gaming tables, easy slot machines—gambling is a spiritual and financial time bomb in a pretty package.

Samson fell victim to these allurements in Judges 14:12–20. Some say he gambled with a riddle but was beaten by cheating and broken relationships. Ultimately he turned to murder and theft as the solutions to his inability to pay his gambling debts.

Gambling feeds covetousness, the opposite of God's call for contentment (Phil. 4:11–12). Gambling goes to the heart of human nature: No matter how much people have, they want to possess more.

### Snake Eyes

George Washington is often quoted as saying, "Gambling is the child of avarice, the brother of iniquity, and the father of mischief." But he kept a detailed account in his diary of his winnings and losses in card games.[35] Perhaps Washington was like a lot of the rest of us. He sometimes said one thing and did another. Or maybe he was simply giving a warning about what he recognized from experience could be a very bad habit. Either way, he had a discerning eye.

*Gambling goes to the heart of human nature: No matter*
*how much people have, they want to possess more.*

To serve God faithfully in a sin-tainted world, Christians must develop their spiritual discernment (Phil. 1:9–10). They must be able to choose between good and bad, better and best. Christians need to understand how gambling fits into this decision-making grid.

Gambling may be understood in the context of what Bible scholars call "Christian liberty." In the Bible, God gave us principles, not detailed laws for every eventuality. His principles are true for all times and all peoples, and he commands Christians to make life choices based on those principles. In other words, God gives spiritually mature

Christians a freedom to choose within the boundaries of his moral will. That's Christian liberty.[36]

In 1 Corinthians 10:23–24, Paul tells us, "'Everything is permissible'—but not everything is beneficial. 'Everything is permissible'—but not everything is constructive. Nobody should seek his own good, but the good of others." If something is not beneficial and not constructive, it is not allowed.

Paul also says that "'Everything is permissible for me'—but not everything is beneficial. 'Everything is permissible for me'—but I will not be mastered by anything" (1 Cor. 6:12). We are not to participate in or partake of anything that would surrender the rational and reasonable control of our own actions.

Gambling is potentially habitual, what Pascal called a "fatal fascination," like a moth for the candle.[37] Gambling is so potentially habit-inducing that we have developed terms like *obsessive, compulsive,* or *pathological* to describe the problem. Some even label the problem an *addiction*.

Whatever we do, we are to do all to the glory of God (1 Cor. 10:31), and we are to "avoid every kind of evil" (1 Thess. 5:22). So while something may be permissible, it may not be beneficial or constructive. While it may be permissible, it may be dangerous in that it can potentially master us.

The early church father Tertullian understood this biblical injunction and applied it to gambling: "If you say you are a Christian when you are a dice player, you say you are what you are not, because you are a partner with the world."[38]

Some Christians argue that gambling is only threatening in its abuse, and therefore, one may participate in some form of social or casual gambling without detrimental effects. Gambling is just a matter of Christian liberty.

Perhaps that is true. A few dollars here or there may not destroy a person's solvency or character. But given gambling's history, the burden of proof for this argument lies with the Christian gambler.

Gambling may be permissible, but it is not beneficial. It may be permissible, but clearly it can potentially master the gambler. Gambling is not like any other form of entertainment; its seductive power can take a person from harmless to harmful in seconds.

## Serving God, Not Mammon
Is gambling a sin? Yes. Why? Because gambling is a biblically indefensible activity.[39]

While we will examine other moral objections and socioeconomic questions in later chapters, it is possible to reject gambling based on biblical teachings alone:

1. No justification for gambling can be found in Scripture, including the practice of casting lots.
2. Gambling appeals to luck and chance, disregards the sovereignty of God, and promotes pagan superstitions.
3. Gambling violates Christian stewardship of time, talent, and treasure, and it violates our stewardship of our relationship with others.
4. Gambling undermines a biblical work ethic and human reason and skill.
5. Covetousness, not godly contentment, is the chief end of gambling, which encourages greed, materialism, and the love of money.
6. Gambling is a form of theft.
7. Gambling is potentially addictive.
8. In most cases, gambling is associated with a host of social and personal vices, thus violating God's command to avoid every kind of evil.

Gambling is a sin because it misuses God's creation. Gambling maximizes covetousness and minimizes stewardship. It separates us from God with the idolatry of luck and chance, the love of money, or the worship of self.

Stanley Hauerwas said, "Tell people who are involved in gambling that as Christians they can't do it. Otherwise, you're just caught in pluralist politics that will ultimately destroy the church."[40]

While the intrinsic evil of gambling may be debated, the extrinsic effect of gambling may not. Gambling produces negative effects.

*Bad gambling* is redundant. *Good gambling* is an oxymoron.

# 5

# GOVERNMENT'S WHEELS OF FORTUNE

## *Paying the Bills with Gambling Profits*

Mark Twain shrewdly observed that "the best throw at dice is to throw them away."[1] Apparently Walter Cronkite would agree. In a March 1994 Discovery Channel program titled "The Dice Are Loaded," Cronkite indicated that the collapse of moral resistance against gambling is among the worst things that could happen in the United States. He believes it is the destruction of "who we are as Americans."[2]

What was the dean of television news talking about? Well, for one thing, for the first time in history, state governments are in the gambling business. Governments facing budget deficits and anti-tax sentiment see lotteries and revenues from other forms of gambling as a painless panacea. States promote gambling, then use the revenues as a substitute, "voluntary" tax.

Gambling interests sell commercial gambling as a way of salvaging Rust Belt industrial cities. Then they lure legislators and voters by associating gambling with some noble purpose like providing more money for public education or better roads. Such arguments provide a politically palatable moral justification that helps dilute or mute opposition to gambling.

In practice, however, state legislatures time and again have refused to stick to promises of earmarked funds, whether for education, parks, roads, or whatever. Instead they let gambling revenues pay for promised public works and use the general funds originally set aside for these programs for other purposes. The schools or parks don't get *more* money as the public is led to believe. Gambling revenues become just another part of the state's giant budgetary pie.

There is a lot of money at stake. In 1994, casinos paid states and localities $1.4 billion. State lotteries garnered $34.5 billion more. That's not a small piece of change.[3] In 2003, on gross revenues of just over $27 billion the eleven states with commercial casinos were paid $4.32 billion in tax revenues with tax rates ranging from 6.75 percent in Nevada to 70 percent in Illinois.[4] Total lottery sales in 2003 were $45.3 billion, producing a profit for the states of $14.1 billion.[5] By 2003, in Michigan alone, the state lottery produced $586 million, earmarked for education, while Indian casinos paid $14.6 million in state taxes and another $8.2 million in local taxes. In 2004, the Michigan State Legislature approved a 33 percent tax increase on three non-Indian Detroit casinos in order to aid the state's projected $1 billion budget deficit.[6] In California in 2003, candidate Arnold Schwarzenegger made casino payments to the state an issue in his successful run for governor. The governor is seeking to negotiate deals with Indian gaming establishments to pay the state more money to assist in California's estimated $10 billion budget deficit.[7]

While legalization of gambling may produce more funds, it's also a way to avoid electoral responsibility. "Lotteries are adopted by politicians who lack the will to tax people with the ability to pay. It is politically easy for a state legislature to create a lottery." But lotteries are no money miracle. Lottery revenues typically account for less than 5 percent of the budget in most states that have them.[8]

Why then do we keep expanding legalized commercial gambling? Robert Goodman, author of *The Luck Business: The Devastating Consequences and Broken Promises of America's Gambling Explosion*, points out that he did not find a single popularly based organization lobbying for more gambling. In fact, the last state-wide public referendum approving high-stakes gambling was in 1976 when casinos were legalized in Atlantic City, New Jersey.[9]

The public usually rejects gambling, but legislators promote it. Politicians adopt what Goodman calls a "hold-your-nose-and-legalize-it-position."[10] It's go for the green—more money, any way we can get it.

Campaigns for legalized gambling generally revolve around four considerations: economics, crime, compulsive gambling, and Native American politics. Legalization campaigns have usually been politically leveraged with promises of benefits for "the three big *e*'s": education, environment, and economic development. Some campaigns add a fourth *e*—the elderly.[11] Economics drives them all.

## Gambling as Economic Salvation

Economic arguments for and against the legalization of gambling have been around since the colonial period and are fairly clear and easy to understand. Economic arguments favoring the legalization of gambling include:

1.  As an alternative to increased taxation, gambling is a politically feasible way to raise revenue.
2.  Gambling receipts, while a relatively small percentage of government revenues, still enable new programs to be established and existing ones to be improved.
3.  It is a voluntary, neutral, and nonregressive tax.
4.  Legalized gambling preserves for states revenue that would have been drawn off by other states.
5.  Legalized gambling cuts the cost of government by eliminating major sources of corruption and reducing law enforcement activity.
6.  Legalized gambling provides employment and stimulates the economy of depressed areas.

Economic arguments against the legalization of gambling include:

1.  Gambling revenue is insufficient to offset the cost of its administration and regulation.
2.  Gambling increases law enforcement and welfare costs.
3.  It is a regressive tax because it weighs more heavily on lower income groups.
4.  Gambling competes with consumer dollars, returns little to the economy for what it takes out, and is a disincentive to industry.
5.  Gambling lowers productivity and erodes the community work ethic.
6.  As a form of revenue, gambling rises and falls on the whims of consumers, competition from other states, and general economic conditions. Its revenue-raising potential is limited by a saturation point.
7.  Instead of luring consumers from illegal gambling, it creates new customers.
8.  It simply postpones a state or local government's need to raise sufficient revenue through taxation.[12]

Politicians think in terms of immediate need. Gambling provides quick cash. Politicians look longingly at Nevada, which has no corporate, estate, inventory, personal state income, franchise, or unitary taxes.[13] Arguments about the negative impact gambling has on society are somebody else's problem.

Some groups may have supported the expansion of commercial gambling reluctantly or at least inadvertently. Many cities and states feared loss of revenue to other political jurisdictions nearby. Restaurant owners feared loss of business to casinos and consequently lobbied for slots. Racetracks have pointed to similar concerns. Educators thought gambling revenues might help schools.[14] Hotel owners who do not want to offer "casino packages," paying Native American casinos a cut, have been ostracized in the local marketplace.

Legalized gambling is what Robert Goodman calls the hope for the "magic-bullet cure."[15] But both historical and recent evidence paint a different picture. Financial gains are often concentrated in the hands of casino owners. Jobs become available primarily within the casinos, not elsewhere. Only limited success is enjoyed in addressing public works needs. Increased road maintenance, police protection, and a tremendous increase in local social problems all cost the public more over time.

William Safire believes states and particularly casinos are "cannibalizing local economies."[16] As the casinos prosper, neighboring businesses begin to die for want of funds siphoned into the gaming industry. Why? Casinos create no new wealth.

> With tourists for customers (like Las Vegas), it does not really matter that many players go broke, a mathematical certainty known as "gambler's ruin." However, when the casino is located in a closed community, it acts like a black hole, sucking the money out of the local population. Around the world, and throughout history, every society that has allowed casinos to cater to local customers has eventually outlawed gambling.[17]

There are only so many discretionary consumer dollars in a community. Either those funds go toward consumer goods and services produced by businesses for area families, or they go to gambling operations that take but do not produce.

Nor does the idea of casino operators, including Native Americans, buying or establishing area nongambling businesses necessarily signal an economic boom. Total discretionary dollars spent in a community do not always go up with the arrival of a casino. Indeed, the total goes down. Businesses owned by casino operators are more often a symbol of a massive redistribution of wealth in a community than they are of general economic prosperity.

*As the casinos prosper, neighboring businesses begin to die for want of funds siphoned into the gaming industry*

Author David Johnston said, "Casinos are to Atlantic City as factories are to a Third World country, thrown up at a distant location, served by a highway designed primarily to obtain raw materials and ship out finished products." In 1990, 98 percent of Atlantic City casino gamblers were day-trippers who came on a bus and stayed less than six hours.[18] Other area businesses profited little.

"Casino gambling is a shell game, attracting dollars from one person's pocket to another and from one region to another," says Earl Grinols, a University of Illinois economics professor. "The more people there are who gamble to acquire money, the poorer society is. If everyone gambled to acquire money, we would all starve."[19]

Robert Goodman points to the "myth of casino coattail economics." Casinos just rearrange dollars. "Convenience gambling" in bars, restaurants, racetracks, and so on relics on a local clientele. This kind of gambling does not add to the local economic base or create jobs. The experience has been the same in the wake of riverboat gambling in Illinois, Mississippi, South Dakota, and Wisconsin.[20]

Something similar happens with lotteries and other forms of electronic gambling promoted by state governments. When governments promote convenience gambling, which is largely patronized by local citizens, government is playing robber baron. The state government has entered the entrepreneurial marketplace and is competing directly with area businesses for the dollars of citizen consumers, and state governments are doing this with the distinct advantage of monopolistic powers, something not available to area businesses. This only drains local economies and contributes to future financial problems.

## American Roulette

Bad business drives out good business. Trading "morality for dollars," gambling robs communities of talent, treasure, and time.[21]

In December 1995, the *Detroit News* reported that in the eighteen months following the opening of Casino Windsor across the river in Canada, gambling-related bankruptcies in metropolitan Detroit increased an estimated fortyfold. In the Detroit area's Wayne County, prosecutions for writing checks with insufficient funds increased 67 percent in the months after the casino opened its doors.[22]

Some argue for casinos in their state or city so that they can keep money from draining away to other states or to Native American casinos, which federal law prevents states from taxing. Consequently, if states do not authorize non-Native-American-owned casinos, they lose revenue.

The 1995 Governor's Blue Ribbon Commission on Michigan Gaming cautioned that "gambling as a means of solving social and economic problems has a checkered history, and the committee warns it should not be regarded as a 'quick fix' for society's problems."[23]

In Nevada, gambling produces 42 percent of state revenues, while in New Jersey the figure is 6 percent. Other state totals are lower, most ranging from 1 to 3 percent. Gambling taxes make a major difference only in Nevada. As a source of government tax revenues, gambling assessments must be evaluated like any other tax: by its revenue potential, reliability, efficiency, and equity.[24]

The past few years have yielded a phenomenal gambling revenue potential. The problem is that one cannot bank on the continued increase of gambling revenues. While the potential is sometimes great, it is also unreliable (except in Nevada). As other states and communities add legalized gambling, competition increases sharply and revenues at given gambling locations may decrease. Nothing is excepted from the law of supply and demand.[25]

In 1974, Illinois authorized a state lottery and began an instant game the next year. Sales went from $129 million to $163 million. State legislators then developed the next state budget with these figures and projected increases in mind, but the novelty wore off and lottery sales fell 60 percent over the next three years. A similar scenario occurred in California in 1992 where lottery sales fell 17 percent from the previous year.[26] In cases like these, states typically do not cut budgets, they promote lottery games more vigorously.

As a consequence of the pressure of competition and the ever-insatiable desire for more funds, state lottery agencies are driven by a mandate to maximize revenues. In Arizona, revenues are to be maximized "consonant with the dignity of the state." In Michigan, "the lottery shall produce the maximum amount of net revenues for the state consonant with the general welfare of the people." Washington and Vermont mandate a combination of "dignity" and "welfare."

> *Clearly, money matters, and now that state legislatures*
> *have gotten a taste of lottery funds, it is difficult for them*
> *to consider anything but how to get more.*

What these legislative parameters mean are anyone's guess. Delaware is perhaps more straightforward if less concerned with ethical limits, saying that lottery commissioners are expected to "produce the greatest income for the state." Clearly, money matters, and now that state legislatures have gotten a taste of lottery funds, it is difficult for them to consider anything but how to get more.[27]

The efficiency of gambling revenue taxes varies dramatically from one state to the next. In New Jersey, thirty-five cents is spent for administrative overhead for every casino tax dollar collected. In Nevada, it is six cents. State-run lotteries also vary. Maryland spends eighteen cents per tax dollar raised. Colorado, Montana, and Kansas spend more than a dollar for each dollar raised. Canada spends forty-three cents.[28]

Measuring a tax's equity impact is another concern. Does the tax unfairly assess or burden one income group relative to others? Clearly and perhaps logically, legalized gambling, particularly lotteries, tends to attract more lower-income individuals than higher-income citizens.

A 1995 Wisconsin study directed by University of Nevada Las Vegas professor William Thompson found that Wisconsin casinos generated $326.7 million in revenue but that related social costs had reduced that amount to about $166 million. It is possible that the state even lost money. Thompson said, "What we found is that it's a transfer of money really from the lower-middle-income and poor to the casinos' operators."[29]

One study demonstrated that 65 percent of lottery tickets were purchased by 10 percent of the population.[30] This is not surprising given states' vigorous promotion of lotteries to lower-income groups as a ticket out of their economic circumstances.

Some states have also placed more lottery ticket purchasing stations in poor neighborhoods than in wealthier communities. One Delaware study found almost no purchasing stations in wealthy areas outside of Wilmington, with one ticket dispenser for every 17,714 people. In lower-income areas machines were available for every 5,032 residents, and in the poorest areas there was one machine for every 1,981 people. Other studies have demonstrated similar lottery ticket machine distributions in Maryland and Detroit.[31]

## The Bottom Line

Legalized gambling brings not only increased revenues but also increased costs, what economists call "negative externalities." Administering and policing gambling operations require huge capital investments. States assume responsibility for regulating the gambling industry. They must hire more police and incur additional social costs in the form of marital stress, alcoholism, and job absenteeism.

Gambling attracts and stimulates a number of social pathologies, including alcohol and drug abuse, prostitution, violent crime, and pornography. Add to this list an increase in suicides and family poverty. In William Safire's words, "The yen to gamble is a personal weakness, but state-sponsored gambling is a banana-republic abomination that undermines national values."[32]

John Warren Kindt, a commerce professor at the University of Illinois at Urbana-Champaign, estimated that a one-cent increase in local sales tax will raise more net revenue than legalized gambling. He says that for every dollar gambling contributes in taxes, taxpayers spend at least three dollars fixing streets, increasing police patrols, and treating compulsive gamblers.[33]

Privatization—the act of shifting ownership and responsibility of a government service into individual or corporate private hands—is now being discussed for state lotteries. The idea is that somehow this will result in substantial state government savings even as lotteries continue to provide states with windfall profits.[34] The problems with this suggestion are many, not the least of which is that privatization was tried in the nineteenth century only to end years later in a national scandal of graft, greed, and corruption.

It is true that gambling makes money for casino or lottery operators. It is not true that casinos and lotteries come without costs or that they are in some way an unmitigated economic blessing to states and communities.

As a tax, gambling offers revenue potential but is economically unreliable. Gambling taxes vary in efficiency, and they are inequitable in their impact.

## Miracle or Mirage

Gambling is often advocated as a source of new jobs and dollars, but it's an illusion (or delusion). For its gamble nearly twenty years ago, Atlantic City lost jobs in retail, wholesale, and manufacturing, and gained more homelessness and crime . . . and the mob. Most of the new forty thousand jobs went to people from outside Atlantic City.[35] Glass palaces, "mausoleums" some have called them, are surrounded by dilapidated neighborhoods.

Some jobs are created by gambling operations, but many are simply transfers from other closing industries. Some new jobs, like those in the construction industry, may be transitory. Many jobs that are created are lower paying, even minimum wage, unskilled jobs that do not appreciably change the economic picture in the community.[36]

As for dollars, ten dollars gambled is ten dollars *not spent* on consumer goods or services. This is different from business where both the buyer and the seller gain value and the community is benefited. In gambling, who gains besides the game owners?

The expected increases in tourism dollars also prove to be more mirage than miracle. Casinos do not always attract tourists. They attract day-trippers who spend all their money in the casino and not in area businesses. Casinos do not always attract stable, ancillary businesses.

Gambling is a siphon. It sucks money away from other legitimate businesses, and the only thing it produces is a host of hidden costs. Gambling comes with a promise of growth but fails to explain that the growth is an economically and morally cancerous one.

## One-Armed Bandits

Wherever it is practiced, gambling is closely associated with increases in crime: robberies, embezzlement, credit card fraud, suicide, abused wives and children, prostitution. Despite all this, the American public has maintained a strange ambiguity toward gambling, and consequently, anti-gambling law enforcement has risen and fallen in cyclical fashion with public whim.

During the early and middle part of the twentieth century, gambling was the heartbeat of organized crime, a major source of wealth and influence. It was not until 1950 that the federal government finally focused on illegal gambling, launching a U.S. Senate select committee investigation that became known as the Kefauver Commission. The commission weighed in heavily against gambling and promoted continued federal and state enforcement of anti-gambling laws.[37]

In 1962, Robert F. Kennedy published what was to become a

well-known anti-gambling piece in the *Atlantic Monthly* titled "The Baleful Influence of Gambling." Kennedy reflected the majority perspective of his times, castigating gambling as a vehicle of organized crime, the domain of loan sharks, bootleggers, and white-slave traders, and as an activity "weakening the vitality and strength of [the] nation."[38]

The heat Kennedy put on gambling kingpins lasted only for a few years. While the rest of the country tolerated gambling or looked the other way, the 1967 President's Commission Report on Law Enforcement and Administration of Justice recommended that gambling not be legalized.[39]

In 1970, the U.S. Congress passed the Organized Crime Control Act in which it created the Federal Gambling Commission for the purpose of conducting "a comprehensive legal and factual study of gambling in the United States." The Federal Gambling Commission made its report in 1976.[40] The commission concluded that gambling was inevitable, that state and local governments should control it, that legal winnings not be taxed, and that casinos should be privately operated and located in remote areas.

More recently, Michigan's Oakland County prosecutor, Richard Thompson, resisted the introduction of off-reservation gambling in Detroit, saying, "I believe it will result in the largest increase in crime and corruption in the history of the State of Michigan. It is moral insanity."[41]

Even charity gambling is suffering from an image that it's controlled by organized crime. Rip-offs, scams, and skimming have always been problems, but now the numbers are reaching into the millions. Gambling becomes a front for criminal activities, and only a fraction of the funds raised actually go to the charity.

In Maryland, one local volunteer fire department raised $4.1 million in 1992 and spent $3.3 million to run the event. In Tennessee, a charity bingo effort generated $50 million in 1988; only about $1 million went to charities. "We are no longer talking about bingo in church basements," Prince George's County Executive Parris N. Glendenning told the *Washington Post.* "We are talking about a multi-million dollar industry that has as much potential for evil as it does for good."[42]

Not all professional charitable gambling agencies are dishonest, but some are. The dishonest agencies *use* charities. They use the charity's good name and worthy cause to attract gamblers, then they take home the lion's share of the amount gambled.

Enforcement of charity gambling laws is invariably lax. This is because the total amounts gambled in local charities are generally rather small compared to other white-collar crimes to which police must respond. And tracking such crimes can be incredibly tedious and expensive.

Even when a professional charitable gambling agency is honest, the amount that ends up going to the charities is usually quite small. Usually 50 to 80 percent of the amount gambled goes to winners; 30 to 40 percent may go as fees to the group operating the games. The charity might get 5 to 10 percent of the take.[43]

State governments put their hand in the till also. In 1991, Minnesota collected $55 million in fees and taxes related to charity gambling, two-thirds as much as went to the charities. South Carolina collected six times as much as charity bingo games kept.[44]

Legalized lotteries create crime problems too. Legal lottery numbers games may strengthen, or at least not weaken, illegal numbers games. States promote gambling and thus encourage it generally. Legal state-sponsored games and illegal games have developed demographically distinct markets. Illegal games use state number drawings for their purposes, make higher payoffs, draw more people into illegal games, and undermine legal ones.[45]

Illegal numbers games have actually gained advantages from the inception of government lotteries:

- Customers of illegal games now have a source of honest and random numbers.
- Winning numbers are quickly aired via media.
- Illegal operators can lay off bets when customers bet heavily on particular numbers. Illegal operators reduce risk of losing by placing wagers legally on the same numbers their customers have chosen in illegal games.[46]

It should not be surprising that gambling attracts crime. The criminal element follows the money. In a thriving gambling environment, money changes hands at a mind-boggling and intoxicating pace. People arrive with large amounts of cash. A few leave with large amounts of cash. They become easy marks for pickpockets, gambling cheats, thugs, prostitutes, and smut peddlers.

*In a win-or-lose environment,*
*the criminal element is the only one winning.*

When gamblers lose—and most do—they also become easy marks for the same loan sharks, the same thugs, and the same prostitutes and smut peddlers. In a win-or-lose environment, the criminal element is the only one winning.

The gaming industry today is controlled more by corporate America than by organized crime, but the syndicate need not be present for crime to flourish. Wherever there is gambling, crime increases.

## Economic Racism?

A 1995 Harris poll indicated that 70 percent of Americans supported Native American gaming.[47] The reason for this support is unclear but may stem from the public's belief that tribal gambling establishments produce social benefits.

Native American gambling revenues support scholarships; construct health clinics, day-care centers, and teenage runaway and halfway houses; build new schools and hospitals; open hotels, restaurants, gas stations, and flower shops; fund retirement programs; and invest in hydroelectric plants. This is all done for the benefit of a previously impoverished Native American community supported by the federal welfare system.

Statistically, however, it can be demonstrated that only a small percentage of Native Americans derive benefits from casino operations. A recent report by Native Americans in Philanthropy found that gambling on reservations has not yet significantly lowered high poverty rates among Native Americans nationwide, and that poverty has instead risen in the last decade. This finding seems to contradict both public perception of Native American casino ownership and arguments promoting reservation gambling.[48]

It's not difficult to understand why Native Americans have so quickly embraced the casino culture. Some 24 percent live in poverty on reservations. The suicide rate is two times higher than for other nonwhites. They claim the highest high school dropout rate among nonwhites, and unemployment among Native Americans averages 45 percent.[49]

However, the Native American windfall is not all that it appears. Non-Native Americans comprise up to 75 percent of the workforce in the 354 United States tribal gambling centers and claim most of the management positions.[50] Tribes have lost millions to dishonest gambling consultants. Most of the money generated each year by tribal casinos goes to the large corporations that manage them. Some estimates indicate that as much as

65 to 85 percent of the profits at some tribal casinos ultimately goes to non–Native American, off-reservation sources.[51]

In 2001, "just 39 casinos generated $8.4 billion. In short, 13 percent of the casinos accounted for 88 percent of the take. All of which helps explain why Indian gaming has failed to raise most Native Americans out of poverty." Revenues in five states with almost half the Native American population, Montana, Nevada, North Dakota, Oklahoma, and South Dakota, accounted for less than 3 percent of all casino revenues.[52]

The Native American gaming experience involves the rich getting richer; influence buying; legal gymnastics that prevent some with claims to Native American heritage from being recognized as tribal members; chicanery; and continuing social problems like alcoholism, high rates of teen pregnancy and divorce, low education, and third generation welfarism among many tribes. "More than 90 percent of the contracts between tribes and outside gaming-management companies operate with no oversight."[53] Some 25 percent of gaming tribes distribute profits to tribal members, perhaps a few thousand dollars per year. "The big winners are non-Indian investors, some of whom pocket more than 40 percent of an Indian casino's profits."[54]

Keeping casino management in Native American hands has been a problem. A small program has been started at the Menominee Nation reservation in Wisconsin to teach Native American students how to manage gambling establishments. In 1995, the first class in a two-year associates program with a certificate in Indian gaming studies began at Deganawidah-Quetzalcoatl University, an Indian college near Davis in western Canada.[55]

Tribes are also beginning to fight over who really is a Native American. It seems that many long-lost relatives are showing up at tribal councils and casinos attempting to claim "their rightful piece of the pie." In nearly every tribe involved in commercial gambling, infighting has increased. In resulting lawsuits, claimants have had to prove that their bloodline is at least 25 percent Native American. In some instances, people have become tribal members with far lower percentages of documentable bloodline, and politics has played a much larger role.[56]

In 1986, the Mashantueket Pequots built The Foxwoods Resort in Ledyard, Connecticut, with a 2,100 seat bingo hall. By 2001, the operation had grown into one of the largest casinos in the world with more than $7.5 billion invested in a 1.3 million square foot complex including 2 hotels and 15 restaurants serving some 60,000 plus guests per day.[57]

But the Pequots have had their problems, because they were organized around federal recognition and money, not an authentic culture and traditions. Tribal member Bruce Kichner said, "We are the first tribe in American history to be formed around money." An observer said, "What makes the new Pequots so remarkable is that they have achieved the American dream by redefining themselves as an American Indian tribe. Led by talented lawyers, they managed to leverage the barest trace of Indian descent into a fortune akin to the Rockefeller family."[58]

However, by 2001, tribal members worried about a cash crunch, crime, violence, and general mayhem. More than 200 tribal members had been arrested since 1984, a period of time when the average tribal population was about 400. "Increasingly, Pequots were afraid of other Pequots." Other social problems plague the wealthy tribe: a high percentage of unwed mothers, teen pregnancy, drug abuse, domestic violence, absentee fathers, child neglect, child abuse, and child sexual abuse. "Marijuana and cocaine use by tribal members had been rampant on the reservation for years." Author Brett Duval Fromson noted that overwhelming cash led to a desire for instant gratification and spending sprees.[59] It is an old story writ anew that money cannot buy happiness, nor can it guarantee success in life.

Tribal casinos typically return about 8 percent of revenues to states, while privately owned casinos return as much as 20 percent. Consequently, states eagerly consider off-reservation gambling. Meanwhile, Native American groups argue that they alone have the experience to run casinos and that tribal casinos benefit communities rather than just enrich the owners. When their operations have been opposed, some Native Americans have accused opponents of economic racism. Such is the case with the so-called National Indian Lottery. This is a proposed toll-free operation run by Native Americans in Idaho. Several states have petitioned telephone companies not to carry it. The economic racist charge comes because states do not prevent callers from gambling via foreign lotteries, just the newly proposed National Indian Lottery.[60]

Not everyone has been happy with states' willingness to authorize Native American casinos. Donald Trump, who owns interests in three Atlantic City casinos, filed a constitutional challenge in Newark, New Jersey. His primary concern, as might be imagined, is with their tax-free status—a significant financial advantage over competitive enterprises. Innumerable other politicians, citizens, and private casino operators have also initiated or threatened court action nationwide.[61]

State governors have found themselves in the awkward position of negotiating with Native American tribes in a manner that conflicts with the laws and culture of their states. Members of the National Governors Association have said that they support economic development for tribes but believe gambling is a states' rights issue. Governor Roy Romer of Colorado said, "We remain very concerned about the spread of casino-style gambling in states where those activities are not allowed on non-reservation land. To have a federal mediator force a fundamental change in the culture of a state is very serious. It is not right."[62]

Not all Native Americans are enthused about the "new buffalo."[63] Tribal law for the Salt River Indian community, just east of Scottsdale, Arizona, has prohibited gambling for more than ten years. The tribe generates income from farming, sand and gravel, shopping center and golf course businesses, and leases land to an area community college.[64]

Some Native Americans are concerned that legalized gambling is a short-cycle financial boom with limited potential for long-term positive impact on Native American populations. When the social and criminal problems associated with gambling are added, gambling's contributions to tribal culture appear grim.[65]

In Michigan as elsewhere, the monopolistic position granted to Native American tribes as sovereign nations means that they enjoy a distinct market advantage over neighboring businesses. Indian casinos are not regulated by states, and they do not have to purchase state liquor licenses. Area businesses are not permitted by law to give out free drinks, while Native American casinos may do so as they wish.

Political struggles are emerging as tribes use gambling revenues to buy more local land and take it off tax rolls. Reservation land is becoming a national issue. Indian tribes argue that they are simply participating in the local free enterprise system. Area politicians contend that government services to nontaxed tribal lands increase the local financial burden. The potential for civil disobedience or even violence is great.[66]

## Crapped Out

State attitudes toward gambling are replete with internal inconsistencies and hypocrisies. Some states say no to gambling yet sponsor state lotteries. States and the federal government allow reservation gambling, in essence guaranteeing tribes a monopoly if the state gets a cut.

Native Americans want the right to own and operate casinos, but they don't want the state to legalize other forms of gambling, which in turn has resulted in an increasing number of lawsuits asserting that tribes are illegal monopolies.[67] Gambling is seen as a new state revenue source, an easy tax that is not called a tax.

As noted before, Americans evidence a cyclical pro and con attitude toward gambling. Consequently, gambling has followed an approximately seventy-year boom and bust cycle since colonial times. A period of intensive and extensive gambling is followed by a period of reform, which in turn is followed by more gambling.

I. Nelson Rose, the Whittier Law School gaming expert, says that legalized gambling tends to self-destruct. He believes that a cheating or corruption scandal will trigger the next gaming industry crash in about thirty-five years.[68]

Something of a backlash against legalized and expanded commercial gambling may have begun in 1994. Elections for new casinos failed in at least seven states. In state legislatures that year, only one of seventy-one proposals related to casinos passed. In 1995, citizen groups began fighting back even more vigorously with "CasiNO" and "NO DICE" campaigns. But the fight is only beginning. Pro-gambling proponents in nine states placed initiatives on the November 1996 ballot but won in only two states—Arizona and Michigan.[69]

A put-the-casino-somewhere-else attitude characterizes much of the new toleration of gambling. If this view grows, anti-gambling forces may be able to use it to defeat local proposals even while failing to defeat gambling outright.

Opponents of gambling do not have any personal financial incentives for their cause, at least not like pro-gambling forces. Opponents typically operate with shoestring anti-gambling campaign budgets compared to the millions available to pro-gambling forces. But it is yet possible that virtue may win a few from vice.

Recent citizen reaction to gambling does not mean that a full-fledged anti-gambling uprising is necessarily beginning. It may mean, though, that citizens are realizing that in a number of cases they've purchased an economic pig in a poke.

Gambling creates so many negative side effects that businesses will eventually look for nongambling environments. Economist John Warren Kindt predicts that long-term, gambling-free states will experience proportionately fewer personal and business bankruptcies, stronger financial institutions, more vibrant business economies, and better tourist, business, and community environments.[70]

Gambling is not the best means of pulling people out of economic deprivation. Real keys to economic growth include strong, intact families; lower taxes, a responsive bureaucracy, and reduced red tape; safe neighborhoods, good schools, and a confident citizenry working together.[71]

While economics has been the driving force behind the expansion of legalized commercial gambling, economics along with moral concerns work both ways. Economics may yet be the principal reason that further legalization and growth of commercial gambling begins to slow down or even reverse itself. Political backlash may be built upon economic dissatisfaction with the failed promises of the gaming industry.

Sooner or later, Americans are going to learn once again that "there ain't no free lunch."

# 6

# To Gamble or Not to Gamble

## Moral and Economic Arguments

He was confused, dejected, and even a little feisty. Being backed into a corner makes you feel that way.

"The tribe wants to buy my hotel with casino funds. I don't want to support casino gambling," the hotel owner explained. "But what am I supposed to do? I'm being offered an amount at which I'd sell under any other circumstances."[1]

The hotel owner's dilemma illustrates the impossibility of separating moral from economic concerns. Yet this is exactly what American state legislators and city and county council members have been trying to do with commercial gambling.

But gambling's about luck, not morality—at least that's the gambling industry's message. Anyone offering moral objections to gambling in today's cultural environment comes off sounding like Cotton Mather. Even *U.S. News and World Report* observed that "moral outrage has become as outmoded as a penny slot machine."[2]

Arguments favoring gambling have tended to ignore moral concerns and have focused more on practical and economic concerns:

- legalization as a source of government revenue
- legalization as an alternative to illegal gambling
- legalization in the face of seemingly futile efforts to uphold anti-gambling laws

Without question the number one reason for the expansion of legalized

commercial gambling is the economic incentive—the financial imperative. Governments are looking for easy money, so we've sold our soul for
a promise of riches. So far, except for a few scattered anti-gambling victories, money has bested morality in most contests for legislative hearts.

Renewed legalization of commercial gambling appears to be the result,
not the cause, of changes in public morality, although it may also ac-
celerate such changes. Some studies of the effects of legal gambling on
society have been conducted, but not many. One study concluded that
commercialized gambling offers a means of enhanced self-esteem and
gratification in a culture in which satisfactions are increasingly found
in enterprises of consumption rather than production. Another study
concluded that people gamble to "buy hope on credit" or for what's been
called "elderly life-seeking"—an opportunity to make decisions in an
increasingly regulated world.[3] Both of these studies attribute gambling
behavior to the psychic angst of the gambler.

Some people consider gambling a pleasurable form of recreation. They
may take part in casual gambling or social gambling, such as office pools
or bets over golf or card games. Gambling is seen as a means of harmless
escape from the pressures of everyday life. Unfortunately, the escape may
be from ongoing frustrations, stresses, and real-life problems, none of
which are resolved by gambling. In this case, gambling can easily move
from entertainment to addiction.

States, therefore, are capitalizing on the emotional vulnerabilities and
weaknesses of their residents, and are tampering with the character and
future of the American public.

Whether government should enhance its revenues with gambling
money—the losses of its citizens—is a moral question, not just an economic one, no matter what reason is given for why people gamble. Casino
games, for example, are more than twice as likely to attract problem gamblers as other forms of gambling. Legislators know this, but money wins
out over morality.

## Government's Golden Goose

Taking money from citizens is one thing, but states are doing more than
just collecting gambling revenues. Whether governments should own
and operate gambling establishments and promote gambling activity are
also moral questions. Government-sponsored gambling turns state government into a huckster. It makes a one-time social evil into acceptable
social policy. Government becomes a gambling pusher.

In this respect, recent American gambling policy distinguishes itself from policies in most other industrial countries. Social researcher Vicki Abt and her colleagues observed, "There is a fundamental difference between allowing gambling to the extent of satisfying unstimulated demand and actively promoting gambling, using all the resources and advertising techniques of modern commercial enterprise, as though it were soap or some sort of passive entertainment, like movies or television." The British Gaming Act of 1968, for example, allows unstimulated gambling: no advertising, no entertainment, alcohol only at meals and not at gambling tables, and no credit. *Unstimulated gambling* is gambling as a conventional leisure activity.[4]

*Gambling is not a victimless crime.*

In the United States, gambling operations vigorously promote their games, and states are counted among the owners and promoters. There are no restrictions on advertising, entertainment, free alcohol, or credit. *Stimulated gambling* is the American pattern of legalized commercial gambling.

This is why gambling is *not* a victimless crime. What appears to be harmless play with one's own money has a destructive and costly impact on the person and the community. Sooner or later, people dip into their discretionary income, assuming they have any. Sooner or later, the gambler's circle of friends and relatives is drawn into the gambler's habit, sometimes in codependent fashion. Everyone loses at gambling—except the game owners.

Even winning may not be what everyone thinks it is, particularly for high-dollar lottery winners. Their new notoriety produces long-lost relatives asking for handouts, lawsuits from complicated marriages and divorces, loss of privacy, harassing or threatening phone calls, and tax problems. Anecdotal evidence suggests that many higher dollar lottery winners spend all of their winnings in five years and some even declare bankruptcy. Many winners try to continue in their jobs but eventually quit because they are the subjects of greed and jealousy.[5]

States glean funds from contract agreements with Native American casinos, from profits on state-owned-and-operated gambling enterprises like the lottery and racetracks, and from taxes on a few privately owned gambling operations. In each instance, whether or not the state owns the gambling operation, the state's compelling interest is no longer to protect the welfare of its citizenry. Instead the state government's vested interest is to work through any legal means possible to increase the state's financial take, to maximize state profit.

States encourage fantasy, yet supposedly they're interested in the general welfare of the people and the education of children. This is why the question of state gain from citizen loss and the question of state-owned-and-operated gambling enterprises are moral, not just economic, issues. States do not just accommodate people's desire to gamble; states encourage gambling.[6]

## Buy a Ticket, Your Patriotic Duty

Henry Fielding said, "A lottery is a tax on all the fools in creation."[7] He was right. Lotteries seduce every class of people, but especially those on the lower end of the economic ladder. Offering the hope of quick riches, lotteries tax the people least able to afford losing money from limited household budgets. In this way, lottery games are transformed into regressive state taxes. They charge or cost the lower-income public, ostensibly in the name of public gain.

Lotteries are especially suitable for state control. Their profitability is increased by monopoly power and wide coverage.[8] Consequently, the state government-as-entrepreneur moves into the marketplace with distinctive advantages not available to private ownership.

Studies indicate that lotteries draw people into other gambling. State-owned-and-operated lotteries mix the state's role as regulator with a traditional private role of entrepreneur.[9] States succumb to the financial imperative and become aggressive lottery promoters. States become financial predators. State governments use lottery gambling revenues to promote more gambling. New York State spends $30 million annually on advertising state lotteries alone. All states combined spend $400 million per year advertising lotteries and claim some $40 billion in revenues. In George Will's words, "Big government now depends on big gambling."[10]

Robert Goodman notes that this is *not* like the end of Prohibition, when the government responded to popular demand. There has been virtually no popular demand for more legalized commercial gambling.[11] It has been created and promoted by state governments, the gambling industry, and Native American tribes. Worse, government is promoting the most easily accessible form of gambling.

State-sponsored gambling advertisements promote everything but rational inquiry. A potential ticket buyer is just one ticket away from the wealth he or she deserves. "Play Today, Cash Tonight." Play this game and impress your friends with your good luck, material goods, and status. "Turn Your Friends Green [showing pictures of money] with Envy. Be the Next Big Winner." Apparently there is no ethical limit to which state-sponsored lottery advertisers will not go.

Valerie Lorenz, director of the National Center for Pathological Gambling in Baltimore, said, "You have state governments promoting lotteries. The message they're conveying is that gambling is not a vice but a normal form of entertainment." This comes in a country in which thirty-six states outlawed lotteries in their constitutions during the nineteenth century. "Alchemizing vice into virtue, state lotteries glamorize the same activities that could get you five years in the slammer—if you had the misfortune to get caught running a numbers racket."[12]

Lottery games are soon boring, so there's a built-in dynamic for faster action. Consequently, state lottery commissions are forever seeking more instant games with larger and larger jackpots, something that computer technology has allowed them to do.

Fifteen percent of the hot-line calls to the National Center for Pathological Gambling are from people who say they are hooked on lotteries.[13] Insofar as this is true, the government's support for gambling is contributing to the moral and financial degradation of its citizenry.

### Itch to Be Rich

Karl Wallenda, the great high-wire patriarch of the Wallenda family, once said that "to be on the wire is life; the rest is waiting."[14] Habitual gamblers feel like this. Gambling becomes their life.

People's desire to gamble results from a variety of motivations. They include a desire for:

- wealth
- entertainment
- escape
- status or materialism
- social interaction
- satisfaction of neurotic needs

Casino owners are as adept at appealing to people's innate desires as the marketing wizards on Madison Avenue. They know, and so do state gambling commissioners, that people itch to be rich. They hunger for something more, so the casinos provide.

Casinos are a study in imagery and imagination, fantasy and fiction. Gilding, oversized mirrors, plush material trappings, everything new and shiny, the smell of liquor and tobacco, and glittering lights all combine to make the casino atmosphere a world unto itself.

Casino owners and operators know that the longer they can keep people on the wagering floor, the more money they will bet—and the more the casino owners will win. So casinos are constructed without windows or clocks—hermetically sealed environments, the better to create a sense of suspended time. One observer called it "elaborate unreality."

Soft seating in hotel lobbies, typical anywhere else in the country, is virtually nonexistent in hotel casinos. Hotel pools close at an early 7:00 P.M., and hotel room televisions omit movie channels. All this is corporate policy designed to encourage visitors to move into the casinos.

Use of chips rather than money contributes to the unreality. Slot machines give more credits than money. They pull gamblers in, causing them to spend more money in the process of using their credits.

"Shills"—people hired by the casino to gamble and create gambling excitement—are strategically placed on the casino floors. Periodic winners excite and incite other gamblers to more gambling.

Free food is available on the casino floor. Big gamblers are given free hotel rooms, free show tickets, free limousine rides, and liberal play now/pay later policies. Free prostitutes can also be arranged—call girls for the high rollers or street hookers for the regular gamblers.

Hotel casinos will send corporate jets anywhere in the world to fly big gamblers to high roller suites. These rooms feature up to six thousand square feet of space, palatial decor, private balcony pools, twenty-four-hour maid and butler service, and free everything. *If* you gamble—a lot.

"Alcohol is the grease that makes the wheels turn."[15] Alcohol and gambling are inseparable. Free liquor is a mainstay of the gambling industry. Liquor loosens people's inhibitions and makes them forget.

Credit markers account for nearly one-third of the gambling activity in Las Vegas. Easy credit does not make people gamble excessively any more than a department store charge card produces uncontrolled spending, but it does make it easier.[16] Credit gambling creates a fantasy atmosphere. People gamble more when they never actually see money leave their hands.

Government, through its support of legalized commercial gambling, takes advantage of people's natural desire for wealth to create new sources of revenue for government spending rather than protecting the economic well-being of its citizens. The owners of gambling operations also prey on the weaknesses of people. In both cases, the people lose.

### Risky Business

All gambling involves risk, but not all risk is gambling. Risk is a necessary and defensible part of a stewarded life in a fallen world.

Phil Satre, president of Harrah's Hotels and Casinos, said, "Americans have a philosophical drive, an instinct for achievement, and that includes taking risks. They have an inbred tendency . . . to gamble."[17]

Charlotte Olmsted said, "Risk taking is a necessary activity in any society, and there are elements of risk in practically any human undertaking."[18] Gambling, however, is an artificially contrived risk. The possession of money depends on luck, with the gain of the winner related to the loss of the loser.

Life involves risk, but such normal risks are not the artificial risks of gambling and are not morally equivalent. Gambling risks taken for hope of great gain do not involve creative efforts and skill. There is no value-added intellectual or physical capital produced. In this sense, "gambling is bad theology."[19]

Comparing gambling to any other business transaction is inaccurate and misleading. Work has intrinsic value, and the value of money is tied to the value of work. Gambling diverts people from useful labor.[20] Money changes hands but with no exchange of material goods or services. Business, however, rests on the principle of fair exchange, value for value.

While business transactions promote reason and reduce risk, gambling celebrates chance and irrationality at the expense of reason. Business produces gain for the buyer and the seller, and the community benefits. Gambling produces nothing; the gambler loses, and the community is forced to absorb social costs. Only the game owner wins. In legitimate business, the total community benefits.

"Gambling produces no new wealth. Put 100 people together, legalize gambling, and let the action begin. When you return a week, a month, a year later, there will be no products created, no source of new wealth, only a redistribution of currency on an inequitable basis."[21]

Virgil W. Peterson observed that gambling as business is wrong and injurious to the morals and welfare of the people. Arguments against gambling may be founded not only in morality but also on the hard-headed fact that gambling withdraws money from the regular channels of trade vital to the well-being of a nation or community. Gambling is parasitic in nature.[22]

Gambling is sometimes called the "poor man's stock exchange." Comparisons of gambling with the stock market or the insurance business, though, are deceptive. Gambling is destructive. The stock market and the insurance business are socially constructive. Business persons exercise a social trust unavailable to gamblers. The stock market and the insurance business use probability as a means of dispersing and accounting as much as humanly possible for risk. The market and insurance are rational. Gambling is irrational.

> *Gambling withdraws money from the regular channels*
> *of trade vital to the well-being of a nation or community.*
> *Gambling is parasitic in nature.*

Business transactions, when guided by honest principles, contribute to society. Gambling, though it has produced a multibillion dollar contemporary industry, is still an opportunity lost. Gambled dollars represent money squandered, not invested.

There are only three ways to legitimately acquire property: (1) as a gift, (2) as payment for labor, and (3) in fair exchange. Gambling fits none of these criteria.[23]

However, it is possible to gamble in the stock market or in insurance. "Taking a flier" in the stock market is to invest wildly. Speculators who invest funds hoping for a quick return are in some sense gambling. They have no control of the outcome; sometimes they invest more than they can afford and look for a speedy personal gain, irrespective of the good of the community.

In the market, though, unlike in gambling, when a speculator loses, the marketplace typically still gains. The same is not true for gambling losses. In that case, only the game owners gain. Interestingly, though, compulsive gamblers only rarely play the stock market.

The argument that there is no moral difference between gambling and business transactions or investments is specious. Gambling takes from the gambler and the economy. Legitimate business gives to the investor or consumer and the economy. While the moral difference between gambling and business risk may be difficult to ascertain, the consequences for individuals and society are not.

## Economic Immorality

Gambling feeds on human weakness, contributes to the debasement of character of a population, and destroys community self-respect. Sometimes nongaming corporations help. H & R Block, for example, opened offices in Nevada casinos offering gamblers same-day "refund anticipation loans." Pawn shops are everywhere apparent in gambling communities offering "cash for stash."

The American culture has developed a new formula for success. A 1984 Gallup survey found that 20 percent agreed that the only way to get ahead was the lottery. That number is growing. Instead of the tried and true equation of hard work plus skill plus time, we've developed a bias toward fate and luck. If people really believe the way to get ahead is luck, then why work? Americans no longer work for future earthly or spiritual rewards. They only consume and take less and less satisfaction from it.[24]

*Gambling feeds on human weakness, contributes to the debasement of character of a population, and destroys community self-respect.*

Gambling tends to create a new and unimproved philosophy of life. It undermines a positive work ethic and the productivity that comes from it. Gambling also undercuts a person's ability and desire to defer gratification in order to accomplish a goal. Individual enterprise, thrift, effort, and self-denial are set aside for chance gain, immediate satisfaction, and self-indulgence. In this sense, gambling exemplifies a reversal of American values.[25]

A Connecticut lottery television commercial shows a man thinking about his youth: "I suppose I could have done more to plan my future, but I didn't. I guess I could have put more money aside . . . or I could have made some smart investments. But, I didn't. . . . Heck, I could have bought a one-dollar Connecticut lottery ticket, won a jackpot worth millions, and gotten a nice big check in the mail every year for twenty years." (Huge smile.) "And I did! . . . I won millions—me!"[26]

Lottery researchers Charles T. Clotfelter and Philip J. Cook believe the perverse education being offered by lottery agencies may have the ironic effect of reducing lottery revenues in the future. If such values as hard work, saving, and investing do indeed encourage economic growth, then the absence of such values will erode prosperity and thus reduce the income people spend on lotteries.[27]

Economists sometimes point out the potentially destructive results of gambling. They note that the addition of one thousand dollars in winnings to a person's income may give less benefit than the harm caused by the subtraction of one thousand dollars, owing to the law of diminishing returns.[28] Over the long haul, gamblers lose more than they gain. Their activity steadily dwindles resources faster than they can be replenished.

## Playing the Odds

America is playing the odds. We're gambling that our embrace of legalized commercial gambling will somehow pay off more economically than it will cost us morally.

Serious questions about public morality go unasked and unanswered:

- Should government promote gambling?
- Should government use its unique position to create a monopoly for state owned-and-operated gambling enterprises?
- Should government participate in the marketing of a fantasy philosophy to its citizenry?
- What price is paid when government uses patriotism to sell lottery tickets?
- What does it say about a people when their government promotes gambling rather than legitimate business?
- What will be the future cost to a generation robbed of the philosophic heritage of the American workplace?
- If the economy suffers periodically now, when people still understand what a work ethic is, what will economic times be like when only a few people practice a genuine work ethic?

These are not idle questions. They get to the heart of what it is to be a free government of a free people. What is that government's purpose? What are its ideals?

These questions remind us of the collapse of moral resistance against the juggernaut of decriminalized commercial gambling. If we don't answer these questions, and answer them correctly, we will lose an essential characteristic of what it means to be an American.

We'll lose our work ethic and our respect for individual initiative. We'll lose our ability to think rationally, to see goals clearly, and then to achieve them. We will have sold our soul to the Devil, and he will come to collect. He always does.

# 7

# CHARITY GAMBLING
# STRIKES IT RICH
## *Gambling as a Means of Fund-Raising*

Harriet plays church bingo three nights a week, sometimes even five. "I'm a bingo fanatic," she says cheerily, sitting in her favorite chair at the church bingo hall. She's wearing her lucky shirt.

Harriet likes the social interaction she has at bingo, what her church group calls "fellowship." Playing bingo with friends is a lot more fun than watching evening television alone. Harriet is a widow who lives on a fixed retirement income, so regular nights on the town are not an option. They're too expensive.

But bingo costs too. The diminutive, gray-haired lady prefers not to think about the amount of money she loses. It's not a huge sum, but then again she doesn't have huge sums to risk. Toward the end of some months things get a little tight. Harriet knows she's into bingo deeper than she ought to be, but she feels good about the money her church bingo club raises for church operations.

"It's more money than is probably smart, and it's even more time. But what else am I going to do with my time? And the money, well, I get by. It's for the church, right? That's the good part. At least it's going for a good cause."

Harriet is worried, though. In the last couple of years since the new casino was built in the next county, fewer and fewer people have been coming to the church bingo hall. Revenues have gone down. Church leaders are considering phasing out a couple of programs and closing the doors on one bingo night.

"I always thought we were lucky to have bingo here at the church," Harriet said. "I mean, how else could we keep our doors open? Now it looks like our luck's running out. I hope God'll understand."[1]

## Pair-o-Dice for Paradise

Virtually every category of nonprofit charity organization has its gambling enthusiasts. Charity gambling is a staple of nonprofit organization fund-raising. Some organizations claim that they could not exist without charity gambling. Gambling brings in the bucks that people won't otherwise give. Gambling is entertaining. *Everybody* wins. Others see it as a supplement to more traditional approaches to philanthropic support.

Charity gambling is a new growth business. It's one that is ostensibly nonprofit, but one that makes mountains of money for the corporations and individuals involved in the industry. In 1993, charity gambling yielded an estimated $10 billion. Yet the average earnings for most charities is only about 10 percent of the take.[2] The amount gambled in charity gambling is far more than the charities ever see.

From 1982 to 1994, charitable gambling, excluding bingo, grew 321.16 percent, an average annual growth of 12.73 percent. Charitable bingo grew in that same period 41.78 percent, an average annual growth of 2.95 percent. Total charitable gambling of all types in 1994 again exceeded $10 billion.[3]

But charity gambling has fallen on hard times. Players are being lured away to glitzy casinos and faster action with higher payouts and other nearby entertainment. Overall consumer spending on bingo has not changed much since 1982, but charitable gaming revenue has fallen from an estimated $1.12 billion in 1998 to $974 million in 2001. Annual attendance is down from 10.4 million in 1984 to 3.7 million in 2001. Among the reasons are an aging player population and an increase in the number of working women who have less time to give to bingo gaming.[4] In 2003, gross revenues for charitable games rebounded to $1.56 billion, up 3.4 percent from the previous year. Charitable bingo declined 4.6 percent from the previous year to $1.1 billion in 2003.[5] Still, "bingo draws one of the more loyal followings in gaming."[6]

Charity gambling is legal in all states except Arkansas, Hawaii, Tennessee, and Utah. Some 46.2 percent or $3 billion of charitable gambling receipts is generated by charity game tickets, also known as pull-tabs, jar tickets, breakopens, instant bingo, Lucky 7s, and pickle cards.[7]

Besides the well-known bingo, charity gambling comes in many forms.

Nonprofit organizations schedule casino nights (also known as Las Vegas Nights, Monte Carlo Nights, and Millionaire Parties). There are also raffles, crane games, fishing derbies, dog mushers, and more. Maryland allows some fraternal, veteran, and other social groups to run slot machines, provided half the proceeds go to charity.[8] Las Vegas Nights are now permissible in thirty-one states.

In 1991, net proceeds to charities varied from as low as 4.81 percent in Florida to as high as 35.82 percent in Washington, D.C. In 1994, charitable gambling in Michigan yielded $317 million in revenues and $64 million in profits. Total revenue has risen an average of 2 to 3 percent for the state in each of the last ten years.[9]

More charities are initiating gambling fund-raisers in part to compensate for reductions in state and federal support and in part due to declining private donations.[10] But the biggest competition for the charity dollar has been the rapid introduction of legal casinos. The faster action and bright lights of casinos have begun to threaten the take if not the existence of some forms of charity gambling.

To fight the new competition as well as to take advantage of America's growing acceptance of gambling in mainstream life, the charity gambling industry created its own lobbying and boosters group. The nonprofit National Association of Fundraising Ticket Manufacturers is located in St. Paul, Minnesota. The association publishes "A Report on Charity Gaming in North America" found at www.naftm.org.

At more than $10 billion per year, charity gambling is a healthy percentage of the $144 billion Americans gave to charities in 1995.[11] What puts it all in perspective, though, is the fact that while Americans gave $144 billion to community, religious, and educational organizations, they gambled a total of $482 billion. In other words, Americans gambled 335 percent more than they gave to charities.

"Charity" gambling is ostensibly about giving to a nonprofit organization. But the nonprofit organization rarely raises more funds than it otherwise might if supporters simply contributed directly. In 2002, of all charitable gambling, 71 percent of revenues were returned to participants in the form of prizes, 3 percent went to taxes and fees for the events, 16 percent of revenues covered other operational expenses, leaving only 10 percent of all revenues for the sponsoring nonprofit organizations.[12]

In one in-depth Virginia investigation of charitable gambling in 2003, some 115 bingo games in Hampton Roads reported receipts of $100 million. The investigator's question was, "Where did the money go?" The answer was: not to the charities. "Only a dime of every reported dollar was put back into community good works. The actual amount is almost certainly much less. Through indebtedness or dishonesty, state auditors found that nearly half of the community organizations low-balled the amount wagered in their games. Even the most scrupulously managed games rarely return 15 percent to their civic activities because jackpots and expenses have gotten so high. Fewer than half of the 115 games gave back as much money as they were required to."[13] The moral of this story is that charity gambling can be as much of a racket as any form of illicit gambling.

Gambling increased in 1995 at a rate more than three and one-half times faster than increases in personal income and at a rate two times faster than personal philanthropy.[14] This is good news/bad news for charity gambling. The good news is that gambling increased in all categories, including for most charity gambling events. The bad news is that Americans are learning to care more about risking their dollars to chance than they are about investing it in social betterment.

## Bingo!

In 1935, police in Grand Rapids, Michigan, jailed a woman who organized bingo games for Catholic charities.[15] From a vantage point seventy years later, this police action seems like overkill. The punishment hardly seems to fit the crime. One thing is certain, though—we've come a long way from the moral perspective that motivated the criminal justice system back then.

Beginning in the United States just after World War I, charity bingo is now legal in forty-seven states. It claims about 45 percent of the total charity gambling handle in recent years.[16] Sometimes called housey-housey, beano, or the corn game, bingo is no longer the sole province of the Catholic Church—if it ever was. It can be found at Little League fund-raisers, local school districts, firefighters' associations, and ladies' civic clubs. Bingo halls even attract professional bingo players.

Bingo's early association with religious enterprises and its image as a game played by the elderly for a few nickels helped it survive both law enforcement and political reform. Even after it became a multimillion-dollar racket linked to New York organized crime figures, bingo thrived.[17]

With bumper stickers like "Legalize Bingo—Keep Grandma off the Streets," bingo has become something of a national joke. At worst, it's considered silly but certainly not threatening or harmful. Many bingo players don't even consider bingo gambling. It's just a game that happens to use money. But for the nonprofit organizations that depend on bingo, the money is the motive.

## Gambling for Jesus

In Walter Cronkite's 1994 Discovery Channel special on commercial gambling, he not only decried the collapse of moral resistance against gambling, but he laid the blame for it right at the door of the church. Not all charitable gambling is for religious purposes of course, but the portion of the take going to religious organizations is increasing. Many church groups have developed a more tolerant attitude toward gambling generally. Consequently, more religious organizations are sponsoring charity gambling events.

"The biggest things we have to help people are churches and temples and the government. And now they're all in the gambling business," said anti-gambling activist Arnie Wexler.[18] He could have added schools. Virtually all public agencies have at least dabbled in charity gambling, and some churches have led the way.

As demonstrated earlier, many denominations have historically opposed gambling in all of its forms, including charity gambling. For some denominations, gambling is anathema—it's bad no matter how you slice it.

But in classic democratic fashion, church groups clearly do not all agree that charity gambling is morally questionable. Rev. Stephen J. Sidorak Jr., executive director of the Christian Conference of Connecticut, believes church-sponsored gambling and commercial gambling are qualitatively different. According to Sidorak, charity gambling meets social needs, whereas commercial gambling benefits only a few. So charity gambling is acceptable, even laudable.[19]

The Catholic Church is among the best-known organizations sponsoring charity gambling, usually in the form of bingo. While some Catholic followers oppose gambling, or at least the continued legalization of commercial gambling, the official position of the Catholic church allows it. Several other denominations regularly use bingo and raffles to help fund operations or specific events, but the Catholic church has been the most prominent.

## Fleecing the Flock

This raises several moral questions concerning whether churches (and other nonprofit organizations as well) should be sponsoring gambling-based events, even if gambling revenues are dedicated to worthy causes. Does the commitment of gambling funds to a legitimate social enterprise change the nature of the activity? Are luck, chance, greed, or covetousness a problem at the casino but not at the church?

Are churches feeding compulsive-gambler addictions? In the church at least, is this an appropriate form of stewardship? Does church gambling, as Walter Cronkite suggested, pave the way for other cultural gambling?

More than thirty years ago, Ross Coggins pinpointed two problems in church gambler rehabilitation and anti-gambling activity:

1. "Churches have done little in a practical way to help the gambler to overcome his illness. By and large he has been condemned or ignored."
2. "Some churches sponsor gambling in terms of raffles, bingo, and the sale of chances on some item for charitable causes. Under the guise of religion such churches not only provide incentive but set the seal of public approval on gambling."[20]

Sadly, his observations are still true today.

More than thirty years ago, David L. McKenna, former president of Seattle Pacific University and Asbury Theological Seminary, said that "it can be expected that gambling will be reintroduced to the American public through the door of the church." He argued that charitable gambling set a precedent for other forms of gambling. McKenna believed that it was less defensible for churches to use gambling as a substitute for responsible stewardship than it was for states to use gambling as a substitute for responsible taxation.[21]

Those who argue that it is morally defensible for the church to support charity gambling are those who want charity gambling to support the church. They say that the end justifies the means. But does it? "How can the church, even in the name of supporting the Christian mission, justify an enterprise which contributes to social, economic, and psychological deterioration of people?"[22]

Gambling activity always causes social disruption and evil. There's no historical evidence to the contrary. In David McKenna's terms, "gambling is a corrupting yeast that contaminates the loaf from core to crust."[23] So the gambling practices of institutions whose purpose is "moral betterment" is a curious one.

Nowhere in the Bible does God condone the idea of doing something bad or morally debatable in order to do good. An end-justifies-the-means argument is never biblically sound. The good causes of charity gambling cannot displace biblical principles condemning greed or covetousness. Gambling in any form provides a context in which greed and covetousness can flower.

Nor does charity gambling for a worthy endeavor escape the biblical doctrine of God's sovereignty versus the idolatry of belief in the impersonal forces of luck and chance. Both luck and chance personify anarchy and nihilism, not biblical Christianity. As such, charity gambling is poor stewardship of motivations and resources.

> *Gambling in any form provides a context in which greed and covetousness can flower.*

While the gambling action is typically less intense, charity gambling is as able to encourage compulsive gambling behavior as any other form of gambling. Christian financial advisor Larry Burkett believed there was already at least one compulsive gambler in every church and that some churches have several. "All too often," he said, "they are supported out of the church benevolence fund without the benevolence group even knowing about the gambling."[24] If he's right, church-based gambling is even more likely to stimulate destructive habits.

People argue that charity gambling is a necessary form of philanthropic support for nonprofit organizations. It's an odd position. If people wish to support the charity, why not just give to the organization directly? Why is it necessary to provide games, prizes, and chance in order to get people to give? The biblical pattern of 2 Corinthians 9:7 commands loving responsibility: "Each man should give what he has decided in his heart to give, not reluctantly or under compulsion, for God loves a cheerful giver."

Nonprofit organizations that use gambling as a form of fund-raising send the message that they're not effective at raising money by other means. If they must resort to gambling, they're saying something rather loudly about their programs and their constituency.

The Salvation Army, the charity receiving more donations than any other in the United States, has refused to accept donations from the gaming industry. This is a very visible and admirable step by a well-respected religious humanitarian agency. Others should follow. "Charities should never allow casinos or other gambling industry businesses to hold an event in the charity's name.... Gambling businesses are not just any ordinary corporate sponsor.... Charities must never align themselves with, support, or accept money from the gambling industry. It is money lost possibly by some of the same folks whom the charity is trying to help."[25]

Churches that promote gambling fund-raisers are in even greater jeopardy. Churches that gamble lose the moral high ground in dealing with a culture enamored by money and materialism. People ask, "If it's good enough for the church, why isn't it good enough for me?" The church that accommodates or acculturates to the point of embracing morally debatable or biblically indefensible activities has lost its prophetic voice. It no longer has anything to say to a needy culture. Or when the church does have something to say, it lacks credibility. Soon, people stop listening.

Clearly, no church or denomination is unanimous or even unified in its support of or opposition to gambling, so these comments are not intended as an attack on any particular church or denomination, including the Catholic Church. Rather, the purpose is to disagree respectfully with those who promote charity gambling among nonprofit organizations and in particular in the church.

Gambling for Jesus is still gambling. It violates all the biblical principles that any other kind of gambling violates. Financial stakes are usually lower in the church than in the casino, but the moral stakes for the church are greater.

## House of Prayer, House of Cards

Charitable gambling statistics are notoriously incomplete. Most experts believe the total gambled is much higher than the evidence suggests. Volunteers keep poor records, charity gambling behavior is not well regulated by states, and abuses have contributed to a less than trustworthy reporting. Cheating in the form of skimming is a continuing problem.

The same economic arguments against other forms of gambling may also be applied to charity gambling. It is a regressive tax or assessment on the people least able to afford it. Charity gambling attracts crime and aids the increase of a plethora of other social costs. It robs people of economic incentive. It produces nothing of value for the community. It undermines people's philanthropic motive, thus hurting other charities.

With the rapid rise of legalized casinos, charitable gambling has felt the pinch. In England, for example, where a national lottery began in

1994, contributions to charities have fallen by 14 percent.[26] Early returns suggest a similar possibility in the United States.

In Michigan, the governor's commission estimated that charitable gambling could lose 3 to 5 percent, with bingo (the largest charitable gambling operation) losing very little and Millionaire Parties losing significantly. In point of fact, though, bingo profits in Michigan dropped $10 million between 1992 and 1994.[27]

In the 1980s, Native Americans began operating bingo parlors to offset reductions in federal aid. Since they pulled players and therefore funds from other nonprofit bingo ventures, some states attempted to regulate the rapidly increasing Native American bingo. Those states were rebuffed in 1987 by the U.S. Supreme Court in *California v. Cabazon Band of Mission Indians.*[28]

In New Jersey, casino operators were forbidden by law from offering bingo and raffles, thus protecting these games for nonprofit organizations. Casino operators responded by finding a loophole: not charging bingo players for cards and awarding noncash prizes.[29]

Large numbers of nonprofit gamblers are disappearing into casinos and leaving charitable gambling behind. While it has increased along with the tide of growth in all gambling categories, charity gambling cannot ultimately compete with casinos. The speed and excitement of casino game action, the size of the prizes, and the free drinks and other perks are simply out of reach for most charity gambling.

For now, charity gambling will keep "playing the margin." However, much depends on whether there is any philosophic change in the public's sense of the morality of using gambling to bilk the congregation or the constituency. If that happens, charity gambling's house of cards will come tumbling down.

# 8

# TARNISHED GLITTER
## *The Growing Problem of Problem Gambling*

Baseball great and all-time hits leader Pete Rose served time in prison for betting on baseball games. "Charlie Hustle," as Rose was affectionately known, became a hustler. One of the greatest hitters in the history of the game is barred for life from Cooperstown's Baseball Hall of Fame.

William Bennett, former secretary of education in the Reagan administration and author of the best-selling *Book of Virtues,* was ridiculed as a hypocrite when his binge gambling was discovered. Like most problem gamblers, he denied the evidence and blithely claimed he was not gambling the milk money.

Art Schlicter, Ohio State University star quarterback, was later bounced out of professional football ranks because of his inability to control his compulsive gambling. At twenty-three years of age, he reportedly had gambling debts exceeding $750,000.

Basketball great Michael Jordan, though not accused of any crime, suffered through a spate of bad press when his golfing partner alleged that Jordan had bet and lost enormous amounts of money on golf games.

Former owner of the Philadelphia Eagles Leonard Tose, once a wealthy trucking baron, was forced to sell the team for $65 million to settle gambling debts. Eleven years later, at age eighty-one, he was evicted from his home of thirty years because of continued losses to drinking and gambling. The money is gone. Four marriages are gone. The possessions are gone. Some friends remain, but most are gone.[1]

Problem gambling has gotten a higher profile among counseling professionals in recent years. Dr. Durand Jacobs, a clinical psychologist in Redlands, California, said, "We have an epidemic in America, a little-noticed epidemic."[2]

*The problem gambler is the person sitting beside*
*you on the bus. He's the fellow at the other table in the*
*diner. She's the girl next door.*

Despite its growing profile, problem gambling is difficult to see. Representative Harold Voorhees of the Michigan state legislature described gambling in this way: "With an alcoholic, you can tell it on their breath. With tobacco, you can tell it on their teeth. With a drug addict, you can tell it by the marks on their arms or the glaze in their eyes. But with gambling, it's the stealth addiction."[3]

The problem gambler is the person sitting beside you on the bus. He's the fellow at the other table in the diner. She's the girl next door.

## Coined Personality

The Earl of Sandwich, who is credited for inventing the food that bears his name, was a problem gambler. The earl wouldn't leave the gambling table long enough to eat his dinner, so his servants had no choice but to develop a meal, later dubbed the *sandwich,* that could be eaten while gambling.[4]

This bit of gambling trivia demonstrates the degree to which gambling can alter a lifestyle, even a personality. Gambling frequently becomes a cause, which always has effects.

Problem gambling goes beyond so-called casual gambling or even impulse gambling. Problem gambling begins to take over a person's life. It remakes his or her personality.

The terms *problem gambling, compulsive gambling, obsessive gambling,* and *pathological gambling* are frequently used interchangeably, but a clearer system of usage may be emerging:

- *Problem gambling* is the umbrella term, referring to gamblers who for whatever reasons cannot seem to stop.
- *Obsessive* or *compulsive gambling* tend to be used synonymously and define gamblers who seem involuntarily driven by habit or addiction to the point of personal and financial destruction.
- *Pathological gambling* is sometimes considered a psychiatric problem even more extreme than compulsive gambling, which may result in the suicide of the gambler.[5]

Edmund Bergler was among the first to define compulsive gambling. He listed five criteria:

1. an attraction to gambling that is chronic, highly repetitive, and totally absorbing
2. an inability to stop when winning
3. a pathological belief in the ability to win, usually in the very near future
4. a pleasurable-painful tension felt between the placing of a bet and the outcome
5. neither weak willed nor greedy; obsessed by the action

Lyn Barrow added to the list:

6. a feeling of guilt when away from the tables
7. a progressivity in the intensity of the obsession
8. an unwillingness to seek help
9. the existence of a condition from which gambling is an escape[6]

Contemporary counselors believe compulsive gambling is like alcohol or drug addiction, driven by a complex of hungers and inadequacies, no single one being dominant.[7] It stems from a host of rationalizations:

- My number is overdue.
- Sooner or later my number will come up.
- One big win will cover all my losses.
- I'll quit when I get ahead.
- I can handle it.
- Somebody has to win. Why not me?[8]

Compulsive gambling has been called the "invisible addiction." The composite compulsive gambler is a thirty-nine-year-old male who first bet at age thirteen. He is hardworking, intelligent, a high school graduate, and a white-collar professional. He may be suffering from a depressive disorder or even a tendency toward suicide. He tends to seek help for his gambling problem when his debts range from $36,000 to $43,000.[9]

Compulsive gambling also leads to personal bankruptcies, a financial collapse that soared in the 1990s. Casino-gambling related bankruptcies are particularly pronounced on a local level.[10] After gambling is legalized, communities experience a 100 to 550 percent increase in the number of addicted gamblers. In Minnesota, when 16 casinos were established, the number of Gamblers Anonymous groups rose from 1 to 49. Mean gambling debt of compulsive gamblers ranges from $52,000 to $92,000.

The compulsive gambler is the backbone of the gambling industry. Since 80 percent of the people who gamble wager less than four hundred dollars per year, if the gambling industry is going to make big money, it must be on big gamblers—not just high rollers but compulsive rollers. More than 37 percent of casino revenues comes from people struggling with problem gambling.[11] Carl, a compulsive gambler from Illinois, said, "Casinos are the crack cocaine of gambling."[12] Eighty-five percent of compulsive gamblers bet on horses, 79 percent wager on sports events, 74 percent play cards for money, and 42 percent visit casinos.

As many as ten to fifteen people are typically influenced by each compulsive gambler, including family, workplace associates, and even acquaintances. Gambling counselors estimate that the compulsive gambler costs society an average of $53,000 per gambler per year in lost wages, theft, related substance abuse costs, and legal and health counseling.[13]

The American Insurance Institute estimates that as much as 40 percent of white-collar crime is caused by compulsive gamblers. This affects us all. The same can be said of the correlation between compulsive gambling and rising automobile insurance rates, increased drunk driving, frequent job changes, worker absenteeism, and the growing need for aid to families with dependent children.[14]

Gamblers Anonymous is famous for its "Twenty Questions," a list of queries designed to help a problem gambler identify his or her own problem.[15] If gamblers answered the questions honestly, more of them would admit they already have a problem with gambling. Recovering gambler Stephen Katz, who says he still gets urges to gamble watching television advertisements for gambling, offers what he calls "The Factual Laws of Gambling," all of which illustrate the futility of gambling:

1.  Every bet will lead to a financial loss.
2.  The next bet continues a gambling losing streak.
3.  There is not any such thing as luck with gambling.
4.  Whatever the gambling house edge, that percentage of money bet is lost.
5.  There is not any skill in gambling as far as making money is concerned.

6. Gambling which involves handicapping is betting on random numbers.
7. Being close to winning money is a false perception in gambling.
8. Gambling long enough results in losing all money, credit, and assets.
9. It is impossible to permanently win money on gambling house games.
10. The only way to beat gambling is to never bet.[16]

Compulsive gambling is a major family problem, not just an individual one. In just two years following the introduction of casino gambling in Deadwood, South Dakota, child abuse reports increased 43 percent and domestic violence 80 percent.[17]

Compulsive gambling squanders family resources and creates pressures that frequently lead to divorce. Compulsive gamblers are five times as likely as the general population to have been married three or more times.[18]

One Gamblers Anonymous study found that:

• 67 percent of the Gamblers Anonymous members' household debt was due to gambling.
• 67 percent of gamblers' spouses were harassed by creditors.
• 61 percent of gamblers' spouses become violent toward the gambler.
• 78 percent of gamblers suffer from insomnia.
• 26 percent had been divorced or separated because of gambling.
• 34 percent lost or quit their job.
• 44 percent had stolen from work to pay gambling debts.
• 18 percent had gambling-related arrests.
• 66 percent had contemplated suicide.
• 11 percent had attempted suicide.[19]

When wives and children talk about gambling, they don't mention winnings. In classic codependency terms, spouses begin to question their own sanity. They often wonder whether things would be different if they were better looking or younger or more supportive or more talented. The suicide rate of spouses of compulsive gamblers is 150 times the national average.[20]

Although entertainment is the chief reason that many non-problem gamblers gamble, the motivation is more complex for problem gamblers. Entertainment remains a motive, but it is soon surpassed by a chance to win money and an opportunity for excitement.

The compulsive gambler becomes a victim of the "gambler's fallacy." He or she genuinely believes that a chance event is less likely to occur again if it has just happened. In other words, the fact that the gambler just lost makes it more likely that he or she will win next time. Unfortunately, chance is based on the laws of probability, and the chance of a number occurring is the same with each roll of the dice or pull of the handle.[21] As a result, the compulsive gambler keeps making "just one more bet" until his or her money is gone.

Dr. Henry Lesieur's book, *The Chase: Career of the Compulsive Gambler,* is still the best look at the destructive life of a compulsive player.[22] The "chase" is the gambler's tendency to keep placing bets in the hope of winning back what he or she has lost. In other words, the gambler "chases" his or her losses. Long-term chasing is what gamblers call "plunging."

Lesieur says that "a gambler's life is a continuous stringing together of action." Compulsive gamblers are constantly seeking money, juggling money, stealing from the cookie jar. As they lose, they increasingly engage in more serious behaviors attempting to finance their gambling. And, Lesieur notes, "most gamblers experience little or no moral dilemma regarding the illegal activity they engage in."[23]

Compulsive gamblers gamble on anything anytime, but sports are a major wagering venue. Paul R. Ashe, president of the National Council on Problem Gambling, said, "The Super Bowl is to a compulsive gambler what New Year's Eve is to an alcoholic."[24]

Because of the special knowledge required, the language learned, and the subculture created, horse-race betting is more likely than any other form of gambling to become habitual behavior. Handicapping the sporting event and betting from the odds offered is not an easily learned activity. Handicapping takes considerable time, even away from the track. This encourages obsessive behavior but not necessarily compulsive behavior. In fact, it may mitigate against compulsive behavior because the gambler has time away from the track to think.[25]

State lotteries may seem like harmless excitement, but they harbor hidden dangers. Law professor I. Nelson Rose said, "If compulsive gambling is an addiction, then the state lottery is the gateway drug." Ohio recognized this when it began printing warnings on lottery tickets: "Compulsive gambling can be treated." In Florida, the number of

Gamblers Anonymous chapters more than doubled when the state began sponsoring a lottery.[26]

There are 6 to 10 million compulsive gamblers in the United States, and yet there has been no national study of the problem since 1974.[27]

## Suicide Without Death

George Will calls gambling "suicide without death."[28] It's an apt phrase, especially for those caught in the allure of the game.

More than 85 percent of Americans report that they have gambled at least once in their lifetimes and 65 percent say they have gambled in the past year. Worldwide, gambling is expanding at a rate far in excess of all other forms of entertainment combined.[29] Meanwhile, computer industry sources report that 40–60 percent of cash wagered in casinos is not carried onto the property—in other words, gamblers are going to ATMs or their credit cards to extend their gambling opportunities.[30] Consider that "all customers of the gambling industry have a gambling problem. The problem is only a matter of degree . . . [because] with gambling you have lost, are about to lose, or eventually will lose very important things." Even "choosing to bet on lower versus higher, house edge percentage, gambling games is simply a slower financial demise for a bankroll."[31]

In places where gambling is legal, pathological gambling is also higher. Pathological gambling "is more extreme than problem gambling. Its essential features are continuous or periodic loss of control over gambling; a progression in frequency and amount wagered; and a preoccupation with the act of gambling and in obtaining money to gamble." Gambling expert Henry Lesieur describes it as the "chronic and progressive failure to resist impulses to gamble, and gambling behavior that compromises, disrupts, or damages personal, family, or vocational pursuits."[32]

Ultimately, according to Dr. Lesieur, pathological gambling results in crime, check forgery, embezzling, theft, larceny, and armed robbery. Add to this bookmaking, hustling, con games, fencing stolen goods, loan fraud, tax evasion, burglary, pimping, prostitution, selling drugs, and hustling pool, golf, bowling, cards, and dice. The pathological gambler, "because of established credit, tends to become a master of 'precriminal' behavior." In addition, Lesieur notes that between 47 and 52 percent of pathological gamblers are abusers of alcohol or other substances.[33]

Joanna Franklin, executive vice president of the National Council on Problem Gambling, says that 20 percent of those treated for compulsive or pathological gambling have attempted suicide. Some 80 to 90 percent have considered it. She also says, "Almost two-thirds of non-incarcerated and 97 percent of incarcerated pathological gamblers admit engaging in illegal behavior to finance gambling or payment of gambling related debts."[34]

In Michigan, an increase in the number of casinos was expected "to cause social harm, primarily because problem and pathological gamblers would have easier access to gambling facilities. An increase in crime can be expected. The divorce rate, spousal abuse, and child abuse can all be expected to increase."[35]

Legal costs also increase. A Maryland task force found that pathological gambling is more likely than alcoholism or most forms of drug abuse to drive its victims to crime, and, as part of the net impact of legal gambling, costs the state far more than it generates in revenue. In Minnesota, for every problem gambler addicted to high stakes gambling, the state must pay $13,200 to prosecute the gambler, incarcerate them, and provide restitution to victims. A report by the University of Minnesota found that the social costs of compulsive gambling alone are equal to about one half of a casino's gross revenues.[36]

Estimates of problem gamblers range from less than 1 percent to nearly 4 percent of the population.[37] Whatever the number, the problem is increasing. Further studies need to be conducted to determine ways to deal with this serious problem.

## The Gambling Epidemic

In *The Gambler*, Russian author Fyodor Dostoyevsky speculated that gambling is not a profession but a dangerous neurosis.[38] Dostoyevsky hit on an ongoing nature/nurture debate. Is a propensity for pathological gambling imbedded in our genes, or is it learned neurotic behavior?

In 1980, the American Psychiatric Association recognized pathological gambling as a disorder of impulse control, which in effect defined the problem as a disease and thus promoted a medical model of treatment. By 1987, gambling was reclassified as a pathology similar to substance abuse.[39]

Henry Lesieur observed that sociologists have been skeptical of the "medicalization of deviant behavior" and have debated the matter by focusing on four issues:

1.   placement of people in compartments has a distorting effect on reality

2. the determinism implicit in the medical model
3. the placement of biological and individual factors in a position of prominence, which pushes sociological considerations aside
4. belief in the disease concept gives a veneer of moral and ideological neutrality, which some sociologists say distorts reality[40]

Lesieur further observed that the idea of a deterministic compulsion is being rejected. People still have choices even in the midst of the most oppressive of compulsions. So psychiatrists and others are adopting a "soft determinism" or "limited voluntarism" and use the term *pathological* as opposed to *compulsion* for that reason. Psychiatrists, though, are still using the compulsion model, testifying in courts at times about the "diminished capacity" of compulsive gamblers.[41]

Gambling is seductive. It lures in the weak and the supposedly strong with easy credit and check-cashing policies, loose security on underage gamblers, and above all, the "rush." There is no question that the psychological high or rush that comes from gambling simulates addiction to chemical substances. Gamblers can become virtually mesmerized, in a trancelike state and near hypnotized, in the psychology of the game.

One woman always felt it: "I got a real rush that was beyond any peak experience—including the births of my children—that I've ever had."[42] Losing does not seem to reduce appreciably the gambler's high, and therein is the danger. Win or lose, it's a thrill—but not a cheap one.

The rush may be from high levels of endorphins in the blood. This creates a euphoria similar to the well-known "runner's high." The gambler's emotional state is similar to that induced by drug and alcohol addictions. Gambling is different from alcohol and drugs, though, in at least two key respects—no external stimulant enters the body, and no intense physiological experience (like sex) is induced, although the rush is frequently compared to sexual excitement.[43]

> *Losing does not seem to reduce appreciably the gambler's*
> *high, and therein is the danger. Win or lose, it's a thrill—*
> *but not a cheap one.*

While gambling can become an overwhelming urge in a person's life, it is not a disease, which is implied by the use of the word *addiction*. To date, no one has been able to demonstrate conclusively that there exists some biological tendency or pathological imperative that causes people to gamble. And there is no agreed-on definition of *addiction*.

Physiological imbalances and psychological stresses may weaken people's judgment, but such maladies do not cause people to gamble. That's why it seems inappropriate to call compulsive or pathological gambling a disease. This would also undermine the biblical idea of individual responsibility. Gambling is a moral choice with moral consequences. Gambling is learned behavior. It may become habitual, like many other "besetting sins," but the Spirit of God provides the power to break any sin.

### There but for the Grace of God Go I

No one should misinterpret the arguments of this chapter. Problem gambling is a moral issue, a matter of moral choice, and we must answer to God for our actions. But this does not give us grounds for self-righteous condemnation of problem gamblers. These people need help, not ridicule.

While gambling is not a disease, we still should treat problem gambling like we treat problems with alcohol. Society's experience with alcohol and gambling are similar in many ways. Both have been around since the beginning of time. Both have provided people with an opportunity for excessive and compulsive behavior. Both have been limited by governments.

Since the rebirth of lotteries, however, gambling is now promoted by governments. Thus a mediating agent between gamblers and their problem has been largely removed.

Churches, which have served as moderating influences on the consumption of alcohol and proliferation of gambling, are now less effective on both counts. Many churches promote their own form of gambling in bingo and raffle events. Consequently, few social barriers remain to warn people about problem gambling.[44]

Most treatment programs for problem gamblers have accepted the American Psychiatric Association's medical definition, considering pathological gambling a permanent and irreversible condition. The recommended cure is abstinence—total, complete, and permanent. The addicted gambler must never bet again.

The American Psychiatric Association's criteria for identifying the condition of pathological gambling are:

1. mental preoccupation with gambling
2. increasing amounts wagered in order to achieve the desired excitement
3. irritability and agitation when not able to gamble
4. gambling as a form of relief from negative feelings or problems
5. "chasing" losses, meaning betting more even as the gambler continues to lose, in the hope of winning back the losses
6. deceiving others regarding the extent of gambling
7. gambling causing significant problems in important relationships, marriage, educational endeavors, occupations, or resulting in the loss of any of these social areas
8. engaging in illegal behavior to procure money for gambling
9. requiring one or more persons to give money to remediate a financial crisis caused by gambling—a bailout[45]

People exhibiting at least four of the nine criteria are considered pathological gamblers. The difficulty is in the evaluation. There are apparently people who binge gamble pathologically who do not become pathological gamblers (just as there are heavy drinkers who never become alcoholics).

Gamblers Anonymous (GA) treats gambling as a disease: "once a gambler, always a gambler." But GA also suggests that gamblers need more than willpower. They need spiritual help from a power greater than themselves.

GA offers gamblers hope for ridding themselves of compulsive gambling via "the elimination of character defects and a guide to moral progress in their lives." The compulsive gambler breaks free through "progressive character change within oneself." All this points to the reality that gambling is more than a financial problem. It is an emotional and a spiritual problem.

GA uses group therapy and personal support, especially the support of the gambler's family. Similar to alcoholics, problem gamblers begin their statements with "I am a compulsive gambler, but I haven't had a bet today."

Gamblers Anonymous teaches six truths about gambling:

1. Gambling is a progressive illness.
2. It always gets worse but never better.

3.  It can only be arrested and may never be cured, regardless of the time of abstinence.
4.  It can only be arrested through total abstinence.
5.  It is a baffling, insidious, compulsive addiction.
6.  In its worst form, it can very easily lead to demoralization, insanity, and death.[46]

In 1972, a Gamblers Anonymous chapter in Ohio persuaded a nearby Veterans Administration Medical Center to open the first inpatient program for compulsive gamblers. Brecksville, Ohio, and Loma Linda, California, are now the largest pathological gambling care centers in the country. Their clientele is limited to veterans. Major treatment centers for pathological gamblers in the general public are yet to be developed.

Also in 1972, the National Council on Compulsive Gambling was formed in order to educate the public that gambling is a treatable illness. The council uses a medical model of treatment and has worked with some minimal success in lobbying state governments to fund compulsive gambling programs from gambling tax revenues.[47]

Valerie Lorenz argues that "the role of government is to protect the welfare of its citizens, but the enactment of legal gambling is damaging to every person in the country."[48] Consequently, she believes that at a minimum governments should be obligated to fund research into problem gambling so that the negative fallout of commercial gambling expansion can be addressed.

New Jersey funds its problem gambling program with fines paid by casinos. Iowa supports its problem gambling program with money from a 1 percent tax in casinos. Nevada has only recently responded to problem gambling. The Nevada Council on Problem Gambling's twenty-four-hour hot line is funded in part by $200,000 in support from eight casinos.[49]

Self-help outpatient treatment is still the primary source of help available. Volunteer anti-gambling treatment groups try first to get the compulsive gambler to stop gambling and begin to resolve financial or legal crises. Over the long haul, counselors work with compulsive gamblers to free them from probable coaddictions to alcohol or drugs, care for anxiety disorders, and reestablish personality growth. Compulsive and pathological gamblers are extremely narcissistic.[50]

Self-help groups like Gamblers Anonymous continue to grow in response to rapidly increasing demand. Gamblers Anonymous now has 1,358 chapters operating nationally, double the number of six years ago, but demand for chapters outstrips supply. New chapters are needed in rural areas as well as for women and teens.[51]

Two of the most effective tools used in working with compulsive gamblers have been developed in the past few years. One is the South Oaks Gambling Screen (SOGS), and the second is the Custer Chart, named for the late Dr. Robert Custer, medical advisor to the National Council on Compulsive Gambling.[52] SOGS helps in identifying compulsive gambling behavior, while the Custer Chart aids in understanding the phases a compulsive gambler typically experiences from occasional gambling to hopeless desperation to recovery.

Increasing the availability of gambling increases the number of people struggling with a gambling habit.[53] That has been the repeat story in Iowa where one compulsive gambling clinic went from 30 to 40 clients per year to 200 in the year after riverboats were introduced. That is the story in New Jersey where the number of calls to a gambling hotline jumped from 1,200 per year to 32,000 per year after casinos were introduced. The number of New Jersey calls is now up to 39,000, with 65 percent saying their gambling problem relates to casinos. It's the same in Louisiana following the arrival of riverboats and electronic gambling.[54]

*Increasing the availability of gambling increases the number of people struggling with a gambling habit.*

Valerie Lorenz called compulsive or pathological gambling "the mental health epidemic of the 1990s." The problem is not going to go away. States and localities need to develop reasonable, reliable, and accessible treatment programs. Henry Lesieur insightfully says society will either pay more for treatment facilities or it will pay more for increased prison space, extra guards, and other components of the criminal justice system.[55]

Not only does the gambler lose—society loses.

# 9

# Casino Culture
## Gambling Demographics

It's Sunday morning at 11:00 A.M. People by the thousands from all walks of life are worshiping at the First Church of Hucksterism. They're setting aside the problems of life, looking for hope and a sense of well-being. They gamble religiously. Money goes into slot machines rather than offering plates.

The casino is more economically and racially diverse than the typical church. No one is turned away. Gender doesn't mean much at the roulette wheel. People "pray" together in small groups around the blackjack or poker tables, or they express themselves singly at the slots or sportsbook monitors. The "communion wine" is free and flows freely.

From Atlantic City to the Mississippi coast, from midwestern riverboats to Las Vegas, Sunday morning at the casino is no different from any other daybreak. People are on what one columnist called a "big bender with gaming."[1] We've produced a casino culture in which seemingly everybody gambles.

### Lady Luck

Thirty-five years ago, 95 percent of gamblers were men. According to a 1995 survey by Yankelovich Partners and Home Testing Institute, 55 percent of gamblers are now women. Casino managers know this and are encouraging the trend with more expensive prizes, colorful gaming lobbies, and free child care.[2] Las Vegas visitors in 2003 were nearly evenly split, 53 percent men and 47 percent women.[3]

Professor Henry Lesieur believes there are primarily two kinds of gamblers: action seekers, who want wealth and power, and escape seekers, who are running from personal problems. Dr. Lesieur says most male gamblers seek action, while women seek escape. Women more often than men use gambling as a way of blocking out the pain of the real world. One woman said, "When I gambled I no longer felt lonely. I got caught up in a dream world and forgot all my problems."[4]

> *Women more often than men use gambling as a way of*
> *blocking out the pain of the real world.*

About 33 percent of compulsive gamblers are female. The Council on Compulsive Gambling of New Jersey found that most female compulsive gamblers are closet gamblers and seldom brag about winnings. Some 75 percent of female pathological gamblers describe it as escape gambling— a release from stress, marital problems, financial problems, and so on.[5]

Female pathological gamblers are more likely than their male counterparts to be depressed, to abuse drugs and alcohol, and to be single (unmarried, separated, or divorced). They also evidence a higher percentage of psychiatric needs and suicide attempts than men. The New Jersey Council discovered that most female pathological gamblers are also dependent on another addiction, such as overeating, alcohol, drugs, overspending, or sex. These women tend to begin gambling at a later age than men and to confine their activities to legal gambling.

Like their male counterparts, female compulsive gamblers eventually steal, embezzle funds, and beg and borrow money from anyone they think might respond. In addition, many turn to prostitution. Since children are still most frequently left in the care of mothers, children feel a greater ripple effect from compulsive gambling when mothers overindulge than when fathers do. Divorce, loss of child custody, and suicide are only some of the results of compulsive gambling, particularly among women.[6]

The rapid growth of female gambling is a potent indicator of the casino culture. Gambling is no longer an obscure far-off problem in Las Vegas or Atlantic City. It's in your town and your neighborhood. It robs the children of your local school. If it's not already in the pews of your church, it will be soon.

## Granny Gambling
Casinos are patronized by a considerable number of people who might be characterized as the retired working class. Multiple busloads of retirees roll into casino parking lots daily. They are the "Granny Gamblers."

These gamblers, ranging in age from fifty to seventy-something, are former factory workers, farmers, tradespeople, and shopkeepers. For these folks gambling is a form of recreation, something to do, and escapism. The casinos are a place to spend time with people their own age, smoke freely, and enjoy cheap booze. Once in a while somebody wins; mostly they lose.[7]

Seniors frequently first get involved in gambling via mail or sweepstakes companies. Often socially isolated, "loneliness and boredom are the two conditions that drive seniors to gamble."[8] What follows later in active casino gambling has been called "day care for the elderly."[9]

Professor Felicia Florine Campbell believes elderly people are trapped in rest homes, and that gambling would perk them up. She suggests that slot machines be placed in the rest homes so that seniors would have something to look forward to and dream about. While slot machines cannot be found in rest homes, several casinos in Las Vegas specifically market to seniors: Sam's Town, the Gold Coast, Arizona Charlie's, and the Santa Fe, to name a few.[10] But seniors are found in all casinos and now form a basic foundation to the gambling industry. Visitors to Las Vegas in 2003 averaged 48.3 years of age with 28 percent over age 60.[11] The white-haired casino gambler is a common sight.

Church buses drive into casino parking lots from the inner city offering parishioners a different kind of hope. They offer people deals instead of ideals, casino packages rather than biblical truth. These churches bring the people least able to afford to have their financial and emotional hopes dashed—the poor and the elderly. It's a reverse Robin Hood action. Robin Hood robbed the rich to give to the poor. Casinos rob the poor—and the retired older generation—to give to the rich.

## Casino Kids

Another damaging side effect of adult gambling is a new phenomenon called *casino kids*. They are the children of gamblers. They're left in hallways, hotel rooms, and along the walls of casino lobbies. Some are as young as six months. A security worker at Atlantic City's Taj Mahal says, "On a scale from 1 to 10, the problem is a 10."[12] Ed Looney of the New Jersey Council on Problem Gambling says Atlantic City's casinos evict about 34,000 young people annually.[13]

Unsupervised children are becoming a greater problem for casino security. If security officers do not intervene, children wander through gaming areas where it's illegal for them to be. If security officers intervene, they run the risk of parental displeasure. Consequently, casinos often give parents comps for free meals in a nearby restaurant. Get the kids out of the casino by buying off the parents. It's a cheap fix.

Las Vegas doesn't quite know what to do with children. Casinos have clearly attempted to create an entertainment-centered, family-friendly atmosphere. But still, the kids are an impediment to gambling. Gamblers with children spend an average of four hours at the tables, while those without kids spend an average of five hours at the tables and slots. Circus Circus Casino aims at families, but a Tropicana Casino advertisement takes a different twist: "They Got Strollers—We Got Rollers."[14]

Harrah's and Trop World sponsored a student poster competition to advise youth about gambling. One poster shows the king and queen from a deck of cards. The king says, "Casino gambling is a lot like life. Sometimes you win, sometimes you lose. But most important, it's a game with rules!" The queen answers, "So remember, kids, casino gambling is fun, but you have to be twenty-one." Robert Goodman's concern is worth noting: There's nothing in this campaign about the potentially habit-forming nature of gambling or the reality of lost dollars.[15]

Kids Quest has opened in six casinos, including Boulder Station, a hotel-casino on the Boulder Strip in East Las Vegas. Kids Quest is a drop-in center for children from six weeks to twelve years. Kidz Adventure in Casino Rouge, Baton Rouge, Louisiana, is a similar establishment. Children may be deposited in a day-care center with video arcade games simulating gambling activities.[16]

The "family resort" remains a conundrum for Las Vegas gambling houses. They want more people, and they want to lure younger gamblers, but they really do not want children after all. In a telling omission, the *Las Vegas Insider Viewpoint* does not report statistics for visitors under twenty-one years of age.[17] "The family resort idea soon flopped 'just as soon as the casinos figured out that kids don't really gamble very much.'"[18] This knowledge resulted in two changes at Treasure Island in the new millennium: the casino's name was changed to a more juiced-up "T.I." and the casino's three-times nightly show on a mock ship in the waters in front of the casino morphed from pirates to scantily clad "sirens."[19] It's not a show made for children, and it gives new meaning to being on the Strip.

Aside from concerns about the general well-being of these children, the specter of casino kids raises the obvious question about whether these children will later develop problem gambling habits. So far, research has shown that "extensive childhood involvement with gambling is predictive of later gambling problems."[20]

*Involvement* in this instance means wagering. While many teens are playing the slots, many very youthful casino kids are not yet betting. But it's not too much of a stretch to predict that the behavior is being absorbed. Children are the greatest copycats on earth.

## Joystick Generation

Youth gambling is on the rise worldwide: 80 percent of American high school students reported gambling with money in the last year. Of these, some 4 percent to 8 percent are estimated to be struggling with serious gambling problems. Some 10 percent to 14 percent are at risk of developing serious gambling problems. In 1999, the National Gambling Impact Study Commission reported 7.9 million American adolescents were problem or pathological gamblers (5.7 million problem and 2.2 million pathological).[21]

In one study, significantly higher rates of problem gambling were identified among American Indian youth.[22] In 2002, a Delaware study found that 49 percent of eighth grade youth had gambled (12 percent in the past month) while 44 percent of eleventh grade youth gambled (9 percent in the past month). More Delaware boys than girls gambled, but there was no significant difference among races.[23] The Delaware study found that students reporting gambling were:

- more than 50 percent more likely to drink alcohol
- more than twice as likely to binge drink
- more than three times as likely to use marijuana
- three times as likely to use other illegal drugs
- almost three times as likely to get in trouble with the police
- three times as likely to be involved in a gang fight
- almost three times as likely to steal or shoplift[24]

No demographic group is immune to the social pathologies associated with gambling. According to Gamblers Anonymous, compulsive gambling is increasing rapidly in all population groups, even among teens. Estimates suggest that up to 90 percent of teenagers have gambled in some form by age eighteen.[25]

The fastest growing addiction among high school and college age young people is problem gambling, with as much as 7 percent or 1.3

million teens addicted to gambling. Dr. Durand Jacobs, a pioneer in the treatment of problem gambling, believes the rate of problem gambling among teens is at least 15 percent—about twice the rate of problem gambling among adults. In 2000, Jacobs found that in the past ten years the number of youth reporting serious gambling problems increased by 50 percent (from 10 percent to 15 percent).[26]

The National Institute of Mental Health notes that addiction to gambling is growing fastest among teenagers, many of whom bet sizable amounts on the lottery. Howard Schaffer, director of the Harvard Medical School Center for Addiction Studies, said, "We will face in the next decade or so more problems with youth gambling than we'll face with drug use."[27]

Teenagers are nearly two and one-half times as likely as adults to become compulsive gamblers. Suicide rates are twice as high among teenagers with gambling problems.[28] Even though this is a serious problem, no national studies exist. Only Texas, Minnesota, and Washington have conducted studies of teen gambling.

Teen gambling is an epidemic, the "least reported, least scrutinized, and least confronted problem of adolescence." Valerie Lorenz of the Center for Compulsive Gambling said, "We never saw a teenage gambler 10 years ago. Now we see them regularly."[29]

It is increasingly easy for teenagers to gain access to gambling venues. Even though states prohibit sale of lottery tickets to minors, for example, teen lottery gambling continues to grow. *U.S. News and World Report* predicted casino gambling would be "the teen vice of the 90s." Nearly thirty thousand underage youth are turned away from Atlantic City casinos per month. This does not count the number who slip through the gilded doors.[30]

Gambling is considered a respectable leisure behavior. The Washington State study of teen gambling identified three activities that provide teens with betting opportunities and that can lead to problem gambling: pool, board games with family and friends, and sports events.[31]

Youth gambling begins early and often with the endorsement of parents or family members—afternoon poker games, sports betting, participation in sweepstakes, casino nights, lottery tickets purchased for youths by adults or tickets purchased with a promise to youth for "a piece of the winnings," 50-50 drawings, availability of gambling options, dice and board games played for money with family and friends, bingo—all provide a "stamp of approval." "Like alcohol and drugs, young people see people they respect engaged in these activities and deem them to be acceptable."[32] "Yet for most parents and teens, gambling is viewed as an innocuous behavior with few negative consequences."[33] Keith Whyte, executive director of the National Council on Problem Gambling, said, "We've had a number of parents say, 'Thank God, it's just gambling.'"[34]

In a misguided effort to steer teenagers away from alcohol-based social events, adults have organized casino nights in school gymnasiums. "Compulsive gambling counselors cringe at the idea. They say some teens face just as high a risk from gambling as from drinking. 'The attitude is that gambling isn't that big a deal,' (said Edward Looney of the Council on Compulsive Gambling of New Jersey), 'Let me tell you it is a bigger deal.'"[35] Dr. Durand Jacobs, a nationally known expert on youth gambling, says, "There is not a high school in the U.S. where kids are not making book on sports events."[36] In 2003, a Kansas City casino made news for having a "delegation" visit an elementary school in the city, passing out casino T-shirts, and then leading "the children in singing the casino song."[37] Most school personnel obviously have not yet grasped the threat gambling presents to children of all ages. "Clear school policies, analogous to those in place for drug and alcohol use, must be written concerning youth gambling." But unfortunately, "issues surrounding youth gambling problems have been greatly ignored."[38]

Problem gamblers come in all ages, and the behavioral pathologies that beset them are all too familiar. "Their behavior is the same as that of older gamblers," says psychologist Michael Frank of Richard Stockton College. "They lie, they deceive, and they steal. They're just younger."[39]

Teenagers are growing up in a time of legitimized gambling in which the state has become the biggest bookie in town. "Today's high school seniors are unique in American history because they are the only generation to have experienced gambling as a state-sponsored and culturally approved activity during their entire lifetime."[40]

"High school and college-age youths represent a large and growing group of pathological gamblers. These individuals do not remember (or have never experienced) a period when some form of gambling was not legal. They, therefore, do not share the same trepidation toward gambling common among much of the older population."[41]

Teenagers and college-age students think gambling is just another form of entertainment. They don't understand gambling's allure or its sucker punch—until it's too late. Arnie Wexler, New Jersey anti-gambling expert, knows the story too well: "First of all, gambling gets you high, like drugs or alcohol. Second, college kids are smart, and I've never met a dumb compulsive gambler. They think they can pick winners, and in the beginning they do. There's always an initial period of success."[42]

"Gambling is an equalizer among youths just as it is among grown men. When teenage boys gamble, whether it is on sports they play, on cards, on pool, or on bowling, it puts them on the same footing. The class brain and the athlete are equal. The tough kid and the Milquetoast are equal. The lady's man and the shy kid are equal. Everyone is as good as the next guy, yet 'When I win the bet,' for the moment I am better and am envied."[43]

Listen to what youth gamblers say about their problem. One student gambler poignantly said, "If my life were a tree, one branch would be that I'm a thief, another branch is that I'm a liar, another being that I'm no longer in school, and another being that I no longer have my parents' trust and respect, and I'm not permitted to live in their home. But if you cut off each of the branches, you still haven't gotten to the root of the problem, which is my gambling."[44] Another young man started a hard-core hockey-watching pool in which twenty friends each participated with $20. At the end of the season, the player whose team scored the most points won the pot. "It's not that I can win nearly $400," he said, "I also did it for fun and for bragging rights."[45] Still another young man named Gary said, "Gambling, gambling, gambling your life away . . . you might as well have put it down the drain. You've got to face the truth that you're having a love affair, and it's with a machine whose lights takes your money, and kills your soul."[46]

Maybe Ben Franklin knew what he was talking about when he said, "Keep flax from fire and youth from gaming." Gambling is not a sport, but youth more than anyone else think of it that way. In their naïveté, it's just a game. But it's a game that turns into a moral and financial vampire, sucking out their life before it has really begun.

Youth don't always know that you can't serve God and money. And their elders aren't doing much to teach them.

### From X-Appeal to Millennial Zeal

Generation X is a label social researchers generally apply to that generation of Americans born in the mid-1960s through the late 1970s. The generational title was a way for researchers to describe the cultural differences between this generation and their parents, the so-called Baby Boomers, and their parents, the "Greatest Generation." Now Generation

X's children are in elementary school through college, and this generation is evidencing cultural differences from its parents, so today's youth
are being called Millennials—the first generation that is or will come
of age in the new millennium. Each generation seems to differ in attitudes toward work, family, marriage, sexuality, political philosophy, and
much more. What does not seem to be different is their attitudes toward
gambling. As Generation Xers have matured, they have increasingly
embraced legalized commercial gambling, spurring America's headlong
rush to make gambling its leading recreational past-time. Millennials
gamble differently, more of them online, more of them playing poker,
more of them gambling on sports—but all-in-all, just like their parents,
they are gambling, and at an increasingly alarming rate.

In a 1994 survey on gaming attitudes conducted by *Casino Journal*,
Generation Xers were asked to evaluate gambling. More than two-thirds
of young people between ages 18 and 25 said they favored gaming, in comparison to less than 30 percent of people over 65. The researchers rightly
observed that this change in attitude signals "a shift that should have a
dramatic effect on the success of future gaming initiatives." Generation
Xers "have no negative moral perceptions with casino gaming. For a majority of them, gaming is an acceptable form of entertainment."[47]

Gambling on college campuses (the hangout of budding Millennials)
is both rampant and ubiquitous. *Pandemic* is the word being used to
describe this new phenomenon. Since most college-age gambling is illegal, realistic statistics are difficult to find. Most police and academic
leaders believe the numbers are far higher than the ones generally
quoted. A 1991 study headed by Henry Lesieur found that 23 percent of
the students gambled at least once per week.[48] Sports events provide the
primary entree.

"A kid finds a bookie on campus, he learns about gambling, he gets
hooked," says Wexler. "For every college kid who derives nothing but entertainment from his betting, there is another who cons his parents to get
money to cover his gambling losses, another who becomes so consumed
with betting that he tosses away an education and another who plunges
into gambling addiction. It is far from harmless recreation."[49]

If anything, sports betting is even more dangerous than other forms.
One student summarized it like this: "I could just pick up the phone and
bet. I didn't need the money up front, and I never thought I'd lose. But
at casinos I go in with the cash and will only lose a certain amount."[50] In

the end, they always lose—first their money, then their self-respect, and then, in the worst cases, their futures.

Youthful problem gamblers experience the rush just like adult gamblers. Money is the medium, the tool, the means; it's not necessarily the end of their gambling activity. Consequently, it's relatively easy for students to get deep into their pockets before they realize they're in trouble. Then they finally go to their parents, and bookies know when that point comes.

Bookies on the street shake down their patrons when the monthly welfare and social security checks arrive. Bookies on campus consider payday the beginning of the semester when students get and have more money.

*Sports Illustrated's* two months of research on gambling in 1995 "found that it was nearly impossible to visit a campus in search of organized gambling and not find either (1) sophisticated on- or off-campus bookmaking operations with a large student clientele or (2) legal casinos within a short distance of the schools, easily accessible to underage students—or both." For example, on weekends, hundreds of college students from New England and New York head for Verona, New York, where the Oneida tribe runs the only casino on the East Coast where eighteen-year-olds can legally gamble.[51]

Wexler notes that gambling is "such a hidden thing on college campuses. But if you saw what happens when I go to a college campus and do a presentation and then ask the audience how many of them gamble, it would blow your mind. One hand goes up, and then another, then another."[52]

Generation Xers were the first to grow up without moral condemnations of gambling. Now, Millennials are building on their parents' foundation, participating in gambling as if it were another meaningful career choice or harmless form of entertainment. Gambling is pervasive, so it must be OK. Wexler wonders, "How could a college kid think there's anything wrong with gambling? There's legal gambling everywhere: lotteries, casinos, racetracks. Forget it."[53]

It does not help when universities jump on the gambling industry bandwagon. Central Michigan University, near Native American–owned Soaring Eagle Casino, has developed a new gaming entertainment management program. The program is the second in the country, similar to the one offered at the University of Nevada Las Vegas. Students take at least six courses in casino management and complete an internship at a casino.[54]

*A 1990 St. John's University study concluded that students were four to eight times more likely than adults to develop gambling problems.*

This is the same campus where a recent random survey of students indicated that 33 percent of students said that they knew someone with a gambling problem. Some 4 percent said that they had lost money intended for essentials—rent, food, etc.[55] If these statistics are accurate, several hundred students of the more than fourteen thousand on campus could have developing gambling problems.

A spokesman for the Native American owners of the Mt. Pleasant, Michigan, Soaring Eagle Casino near Central Michigan University admitted that college students comprised a good portion of the casino's clientele. While he characterized student gambling as entertainment, a 1990 St. John's University study concluded that students were four to eight times more likely than adults to develop gambling problems.[56]

American culture is sinking deeper into a gambling mentality. First, men are seduced, then women, then the elderly generation, finally our youth. The casino culture is complete, and we continue on the path from seduction to destruction.

# 10

# JACKPOT JUNKIES

## *Controlling the New Gambling Drug*

Cecil Fielder no longer lives in Detroit. He no longer lives in his own house. Since his glory days as "Big Daddy," the Detroit Tigers' homerun king in the 1990s, he's lost his considerable millions, lost his substantial possessions, including his fifty-room Florida mansion, lost most of his friends, and possibly lost his family. With career earnings of $47 million in salary alone, one would think that Cecil Fielder was set for life, and he was—until he started gambling.

Lines of credit at Atlantic City casinos in one forty-hour gambling binge alone yielded a total loss of $580,000. Debts mounted at Las Vegas casinos and other gambling enterprises, yet somehow, Fielder kept his habit hidden from family, friends, and the public, until financial collapse forced the facts to the surface. Fielder's wife said, "I never knew anything about any of this until I started noticing things when I was doing the finances. I'd be going over the bills with the accountant, and I'd be like, 'Hey, there's $35,000 gone from this account. What happened to it?' Then these gambling people just descended on the house one day and started just taking things out of it. They took my truck." Fielder's life became a series of lawsuits, process servers, bounced checks, and liens on his property. Whether he ever gambled on his sport is not yet known, but in a rerun of the Pete Rose story, another athletic hero has lost his reputation.

"Gambling caused Cecil Fielder's empire to collapse," said the real-estate agent who sold the Fielders their 19,500-square-foot home in Melbourne, Florida. "The biggest losers are the Fielders themselves. They have lost a great dream home, a wonderful life, and now it's all gone." Fielder wants to make things right: "I'm going to be a man about it. I'm going to take care of all my responsibilities." In the end, gambling hit harder than "Big Daddy" Fielder.[1]

Lisa is not a famous athlete with millions to blow and a mansion to lose. Lisa is a nurse, a wife of sixteen years, and mother of two. She also was a gambler—horse races, casinos, the lottery, whatever. It started innocently enough playing bingo. But video poker was her main temptation and the gateway to her downfall. In just a year and a half she gambled and lost more than $30,000, and she almost lost it all—her husband who threatened to leave her, her children. She hocked her jewelry, she spent her children's savings account of $10,000 that their grandmother had created, and she even lied to God. It was her mother's mastectomy surgery that got her and her mother's attention. You see, Mom had been gambling right along with Lisa. When they faced death's door, they knew their lives must change, and they sought God's deliverance. God did forgive and he did deliver both of them. Now Lisa says, "My life has changed more than I can ever tell you. I am so happy now. . . . My marriage has never been better. . . . Satan is not the only one who knows how to fish. I am now a fisherman of men and I want everyone to feel the happiness that I have."[2]

In 1990, Americans bet $286 billion. By 2004, the total legal wager jumped to $650 billion, and it is still climbing. For the gambling industry, "The future looks so bright every bookie in town ought to be wearing shades."[3]

We are becoming a nation of jackpot junkies. The question is, what do we do about it?

### Hot Slots

Americans have always had an ambivalent love/hate relationship with gambling. Anti-gambling laws have been put in place, but Americans have generally tolerated the many loopholes.

Today gambling is no longer just a periodic if questionable leisure activity fulfilling the purposes of a few individuals. Gambling is being changed into routine behavior that serves the economic ends of casino operators and state governments. It is now a transformed set of more aggressive, commercially profitable games aimed at a mass public.

The United States is not yet as fully immersed in gambling as Canada, where virtually all forms of gambling are available in every province and a cliché is "There is no one more 'addicted' to gambling in Canada than our provincial governments," but the United States is clearly moving in that direction.[4]

State-sanctioned gambling has become a collection of stimulated responses to programmed experiences designed to produce maximum losses from the maximum number of people. Government has a vested interest in the losses of consumers. This together with the fact that no wealth is created by gambling means that state governments are no longer acting as representatives of the public interest.[5]

David D. Allen noted that in European, Asian, and American society, history teaches us that the introduction of gambling always eventually produced a corresponding action to eliminate or control it. Did all these societies make the same error of judgment in seeking to eliminate or control gambling? Not likely.

These governments had some foundation for their actions other than puritanical desires to live virtuously. Few governments, if any, have ever acted out of simple idealism.[6]

In America today we think we're different. State governments have joined the gambling industry in mass civic exploitation. "State Looteries" are a nearly invisible part of the fabric of virtually every community.

Vigorous pursuit of commercial gambling is itself a gamble with both the economy and the character of a state or locality. It's a bet that a casino culture will bring more pleasure than pain, but it's a poor bet.

Based on the experience of innumerable localities, we know that gambling associates itself with a number of social problems and pathologies including alcohol and drug abuse, prostitution, violent crime, embezzlement and bankruptcy, theft, spouse and child abuse, and pornography and obscenity. What may appear to be harmless play with one's own money has a destructive and costly impact on the person and the community.

Gambling is parasitical and predatory. Gambling begets gambling. It always brings social disruption and corruption. It is a fiscal shell game. "The practice of the gambling industry is to take as much money, credit, and assets from their customers as quickly and often as possible. They acquire huge profits from this practice. The huge profits from this practice are in direct proportion to the huge losses suffered by their customers."[7]

Economist Earl Grinols has demonstrated that on a national basis, the social costs of problem and pathological gambling are between $32.4 billion and $53.8 billion. On a per adult basis, this translates to $165 to $274 per year or a $219 per person average. Costs of gambling outweigh benefits by a factor of 3:9:1 and 6:3:1. The long-term cost to benefit ratio to introduce a casino to a region that did not have one previously is 3:1. As a device for raising taxes, casinos are more socially costly than a conventional tax. In 2003 dollars, roughly half the social costs are publicly borne and 37.5 percent require tax dollar support. Grinols observes, "The evidence indicates that casino gambling fails a cost/benefit test by a wide margin." In 2003 adjusted dollars, benefits per adult were $46 while costs per adult ranged from $180 to $289. In the year 2000, the average per adult cost was $181.

The social impact of gambling is immense, if largely ignored. In July 2000, South Carolina used court action to ban slot machines. At the time, the state had thirty-two active Gamblers Anonymous groups with a typical meeting size of forty. Six months later, there were only eleven groups, with the size of the meeting decreased to as few as one or two per group.[8]

So it's something of a social and political disgrace to see American state and local governments buy in and promote gambling with the enthusiasm of pit bosses. It further gambles away the credibility of state and local governments at a time when Americans' doubts about the efficacy of political institutions are already high.

## Gambling in the Public Interest

"In the past century, gambling has undergone a profound transformation. From being regarded as an economically marginal, politically corrupt, and often morally dubious activity, it has, at the start of the twenty-first century, become a global player in the economies of North America, Europe, and Australasia." However, "the net result of gambling expansion is not so much a dramatic *increase* in wealth as a *transfer* of existing wealth."[9] While this latter point is fundamentally true and eminently demonstrable, governments soldier on toward ever greater expansion of legalized commercial gambling, whether or not such expansion is really in the public interest.

Legalized gambling continues to spread for several reasons. Gambling expert I. Nelson Rose lists eight:

1. The moral argument is dead.
2. Government has said it is "OK."
3. The outrageous becomes acceptable if taken in small doses.
4. The domino effect.
5. The easy money is not so easy; states are hooked on gambling revenues.
6. Gambling begets gambling.

7. Competition for the gambling dollar is fierce.
8. Operators push the limits.[10]

We would argue the categorical comment, "the moral argument is dead," but religious people generally and Christians specifically are admittedly no longer mounting much of a fight—which with a few exceptions has been the pattern during the past nearly twenty years of gambling's elevation to mainstream acceptance.[11] Rose noted that "once churches started running bingo games and governments began selling lottery tickets, gambling opponents lost their main moral spokesmen. With no one to say what is right or wrong, everything has become a cost/benefit analysis."[12]

When economics is all that's valued, you get the kind of reasoning Peter Collins offers. Collins believes that in the great scheme of things what government does about gambling is of rather limited moral and social importance. Interestingly, he still draws moral lines in the sand, comparing gambling to sexual morality and opting for what he terms "moral and cultural relativism," while rejecting things like slavery, child prostitution, or gladiatorial contests as threats to human rights and purveyors of suffering.[13]

Collins does provide a service with his list of the general positions governments have historically adopted as gambling policy:

- Gambling is a vice. It is the business of government to promote virtue and to eradicate vice. Therefore it is the business of government to stamp out gambling.
- Gambling is undesirable. However, the moral and material costs of enforcing the prohibition of gambling are unacceptably high. Therefore government should do what it can to contain and discourage gambling.
- Gambling is a harmless pastime for most people. Government should therefore treat it as a normal part of the entertainment industry except to the extent that special measures are needed to keep the industry crime-free and to deal with the dangers of addiction.
- Gambling is a good way for governments to raise money for public interest projects. Therefore an abnormally large share of gambling revenues should accrue to government, and gambling should either not be discouraged or should be encouraged.

- Gambling is a good way for a jurisdiction to earn money from foreigners. Therefore gambling should be treated as an export business—like tourism.[14]

The first view has been the policy of most of the civilized world for most of history. It's still the policy in China, Islamic countries, and states like Utah and maybe Hawaii (although this state probably fits better under the second view) and a few localities in the United States. What's interesting about the other common policy views is that they fly so blatantly in the face of accumulated evidence to the contrary demonstrating that "gambling is a failed economic model for funding state governments."[15]

Under the category of "easy money . . . states are hooked on gambling revenues," we'd have to say that the likely future of gambling in the United States is continued expansion. "As long as cities face weakening economies tied to the long-term weakening of the manufacturing sector, casinos will supply an attractive alternative for urban revitalization." It is difficult to roll back gambling because states are hungry, the gambling industry can frame the discussion (i.e., promoting jobs, helping education, etc.), gambling interests are the primary source of data on the industry, and citizens no longer see gambling as an activity "requiring great public vigilance."[16]

Under the general category of "operators push the limits," gambling interests are becoming more politically influential than they were in years past. In the early part of the 2004 congressional and presidential campaigns, casinos and other forms of wagering contributed through individuals and political action committees more than $2.8 million. For the 2004 campaign, "gambling is on a pace . . . to outspend the lodging and tourism industry, HMOs, big mining, the savings and loans, and the aerospace and electronics sectors of the defense industry." In 1990, gambling was seventy-fifth in order of campaign spending among eighty industries tracked by the nonprofit, nonpartisan Center for Responsive Politics. "Since then, contributions soared 500 percent, peaking at $14.9 million in the 2002 congressional election, when the industry finished just behind the automotive industry in total dollars and actually outspent it in terms of soft money by a margin of almost 3:1."

## NIMBY—Not In My Back Yard

Yet the rapid legalization, which is to say decriminalization, of commercial gambling in recent years is not an irreversible process. The Netherlands has reversed its earlier enthusiasm and greatly restricted gambling.[17] So did the United States in response to waves of legalization-followed-by-corruption experiences in the last century. Why can't we do it now?

American federal, state, and local government agencies have been involved in a number of publicly encouraged efforts to curtail the negative effects of commodities like alcohol, narcotics, and tobacco. Gambling should be added to the list.

Citizens are not without recourse in the fight to slow down gambling expansion, to stop gambling from being established in one's hometown, or to roll back a form of gambling entirely. Historically, citizens have involved themselves in a whole list of what some have called "morality policy," including abortion, spousal rights, spousal abuse, child neglect or abuse, gay marriage and associated issues, euthanasia and other forms of biomedical ethics, drug and alcohol policy, prostitution, pornography, and child pornography, to name a few. The questions in a free society always are, "Should the state be making policy in this area? Should the state ever profit from the 'sin' of its citizens?"[18] To the first question, we say yes, and to the second, we say no.

While the continued near institutionalization of legalized gambling makes its resistance difficult, citizens have gradually begun to exercise the "NIMBY" principle—"Not In My Back Yard." Now, rather than "sin" or "morality" being the primary argument used to fight gambling expansion, the anti-gambling movement has most often attempted to educate the citizenry on the economic arguments favoring rejection of gambling.[19]

In the decade of the 1970s, 5 gambling measures were placed on ballots in 5 states. All the measures failed. In the 1980s, 16 gambling measures were placed on statewide ballots in 12 states. Nine of these measures passed, a significant change from the previous decade, including the one that approved the now well-known casino in Deadwood, South Dakota. During the 1990s, 28 gambling measures were placed on 16 state ballots. Of the 28 measures, only 6 passed. Since 2000, 74 measures have been placed on statewide ballots with only 15 moving in the direction of gambling expansion.[20]

In 2003, 45 gambling expansion proposals (bills, referendums, etc.) were placed on the ballot in 29 states. Of the 45, only 3 measures were passed. The remaining 42 measures failed. Among the defeated measures were 19 proposals to add slot machines to existing racetracks, 6 proposals for new casinos and 6 to expand existing casinos, 5 lottery proposals, and 6 efforts to increase "convenience gambling" (VLTs in stores).[21] In other words, citizens rejected all types of gambling expansion in all parts of the country.

In 2004, six states placed thirteen gambling expansion measures on the November ballot. Only in Oklahoma, where all three ballot measures passed, did gambling expansion proponents run the table. Six measures in other states failed. Supported by gambling opponents, an innovative measure in Michigan passed, requiring the question of all future non-tribal gambling expansion proposals be placed on a statewide ballot for a vote. An additional measure in Missouri proposing the expansion of riverboat gambling failed in an August 2004 ballot. Two other Nebraska measures passed, changing how gambling revenues and taxes are handled, which could be counted as a type of victory for gambling opponents.[22] This means that in 2004, gambling opposition garnered ten of thirteen measures, continuing the anti-gambling reaction begun in 2003.

The odds are not in favor of unlimited gambling expansion in the United States. One leading gambling economics consultant, Eugene Martin Christiansen, CEO of Christiansen Capital Advisors, LLC, said, "The golden goose of casino gambling cannot lay an infinite number of golden eggs. I have never seen any place where dollars dried up, but I have seen growth stop." In Michigan in 2004 gambling interests wondered about a "saturation point," for nearly all forms of gambling revenues remained flat or declining.[23]

"The truth was, and is, that gambling contains the seeds of its own destruction. States, like individuals, cannot gamble themselves rich. But they can, and have, gambled themselves poor, as demonstrated by Nevada's $870 million budget deficit in 2003. Expanding gambling is a futile exercise in chasing one's existing gambling losses! Gambling continues to demonstrate its failure to solve states' budget problems."[24]

## No Dice?

While gambling is morally suspect in all of its forms, this is not an argument to recriminalize all forms of gambling. Not all *sins* should be *crimes*. A total ban on gambling is both unnecessary and impractical.

What is called for is an honest evaluation of the negative impacts of gambling. State and local governments should take action that will protect their citizenry, not harm them. Neither of these suggestions is unworkable or especially threatening to individual liberty, as can be attested by how gambling laws have worked in Great Britain, the Bahamas, or the United States in the past.

Short of a total ban, a variety of regulatory approaches is available to state governments that desire to contain or curtail legalized commercial gambling. They include:

1. Restrict gamblers in some way involving voluntary self-choice or family-choice mechanisms for exclusion from the ability to play.
2. Ban credit gambling. In Iowa, players can charge chips to bank cards and lose money for which they will be charged 19.8 percent interest.
3. Make gambling debts uncollectable and attempts to do so a crime.
4. Restrict or ban advertising.
5. Require casinos to close at least a few hours weekly so people can get a grip on their pocketbooks.
6. Restrict or ban free alcoholic drinks.
7. Fine, suspend, and ultimately revoke the license of any casino that allows juveniles to gamble.
8. Destroy old slot machines because many end up being purchased and used illegally.
9. Send unannounced auditors to casinos.
10. Make casinos liable for return of embezzled money lost by any rated player (a regular player whose gambling is recorded by casinos so he or she can qualify for complimentary perks) who received extensive comps.
11. Draft casino laws not to legalize gambling but to grant limited and specific exemptions from the criminal law.[25]

Some of these regulatory approaches are more drastic than others. None of them calls for an elimination of commercial gambling. They suggest a more responsible approach to the legalization of commercial gambling that acknowledges and accounts for some of the personally and socially detrimental spin-offs of gambling.

States can also earmark state gambling revenues for treatment of compulsive gamblers. While compulsive gamblers represent a small percentage of the population, they cost the public in a variety of ways far beyond the costs of any reasonable treatment program. Funding compulsive gambling treatment is not so much another government program as it is a financially prudent investment recouping dollars in the future.

On the national level, gambling policy is founded upon another commission study. On March 5, 1996, the U.S. House of Representatives passed Representative Frank Wolf's (R-VA) bill mandating a three-year, bipartisan National Gambling Impact Study Commission. The nine-member commission was charged with reviewing:

1. state lotteries and their advertising practices
2. the effects of casinos on local businesses
3. gambling addictions and related crime
4. the influence of the gambling industry's political contributions
5. computerized gambling on the Internet

Representative Wolf's House bill had more than one hundred cosponsors, which suggests that legalized gambling was at least a politically hot topic.

President Bill Clinton supported this study and is on record as saying, "Too often, public officials view gambling as a quick and easy way to raise revenues without focusing on gambling's hidden social, economic, and political costs." On the other hand, in April 1994 President Clinton told a group of more than two hundred tribal leaders at an unprecedented gathering in Washington, "I want the tribes to continue to benefit from gaming."[26]

In 1995, the Clinton Administration proposed a 4 percent federal gaming tax—something it quickly dropped when thirty-one governors and several gambling industry tycoons protested.[27] Apparently the Clinton Administration was not quite sure what it thought about legalized commercial gambling.

The national gambling commission was opposed by the American Gambling Association, the industry's lobbying arm. Frank J. Fahrenkopf Jr., former chairman of the Republican Party, believed the commission would be an attack on the gaming industry by "a greedy federal government and moral crusaders."[28]

Fahrenkopf is also on record as saying, "We don't agree that Tom Grey [executive director of the National Coalition Against Legalized Gambling] and his supporters have the right to force their morality on others." To which Grey replied, "If we based our opposition on personal morality, we would lose. After all, a majority of Americans gamble. But we're not for prohibition. People can go to Las Vegas or play poker in their homes. We are just saying, let's stop the expansion of gambling."[29]

The National Gambling Impact Study Commission (NGISC) met from 1997 to 1999 and submitted its completed report June 18, 1999. The report detailed the political, social, and economic effects of gambling and offered generally favorable, or at least not for the most part antagonistic, observations about commercial gambling and its associated industry. The NGISC report concluded that casinos generally created jobs, increased state revenues, and reduced unemployment, but the study found that problem gambling was growing, was devastating to those involved, and that problem gambling should be evaluated and new treatment programs developed. Overall, the study recommended support and further study rather than prohibition. The NGISC also concluded that "destination style resorts" were responsible for most of the presumed social and economic benefits traced to gambling expansion, while "convenience-style" gambling like VLTs and Internet gambling could yield huge social ills.

The NGISC effected a major change in federal policy toward commercial gambling. The 1950 Kefauver Committee considered gambling a social and moral evil backed by the criminal underworld. The 1999 NGISC looked upon gambling kindly, even though the Commission had been chartered partly out of anti-gambling sentiment.[30]

National gambling commissions, or for that matter most national commissions, have not enjoyed a history of significant political impact. Studies are completed, public money are spent, and lengthy reports are waved at press conferences and then put on a shelf. Whether the national gambling commission helps to direct public gambling policy or turns out to be just another political sideshow remains to be seen.

### Play Less, Win More
The previous section listed some of the ways American governments could (rather mildly) contain or curtail the negative individual and social effects of easily accessible commercial gambling, but there is more that can and should be done. Most of those suggestions pertained to casino gambling and not lotteries, bingo, or other forms of commercial gambling. Even if some of those suggestions were adopted, states and nonprofit organizations would still be in the gambling business, which is reprehensible.

The economic, political, and moral consequences of expanded legalized commercial gambling are in the long term detrimental to society, robbing individuals of their liberty and the public of its welfare. States must return to their constitutionally established roles as protectors of the liberty and general welfare of their citizenry.

*The economic, political, and moral consequences of expanded legalized commercial gambling are in the long term detrimental to society.*

State governments could once again act in the public interest if they would take the following four steps:

1. *Eliminate state government sponsorship and promotion of all forms of gambling.* This can be accomplished in one of two ways.

First, states could privatize state lotteries, thereby getting states out of the ownership and advertising of gambling activities. Although this is not the preferable approach, it is better than the present dominant policy of state ownership. Privatization would still require state regulatory commissions for gambling oversight, but states would no longer be laboring with the clear vested interest of gambling operators. If the corruption of the nineteenth century's experience can be avoided, privatization would be a step in the right direction.

Second, states could suspend state lotteries, lottos, and other forms of state-sponsored gambling, including racetracks. Legislators would be required to replace revenues currently generated by state gambling enterprises through astute state budgeting. In most cases, other state programs would either need to be eliminated or taxes raised because states have become dependent on gambling revenues. This, of course, can be politically painful, but it is no more so than the stressful political maneuvering and consensus necessary to change or eliminate any other program already in the budget.

*Eliminating lotteries and state-sponsored gambling is a far better and more fiscally and morally responsible action of a government in a free society than the support and promotion of games that pilfer money from the electorate.*

Even raising taxes is more acceptable than maintaining state lotteries and other gambling operations, and it's certainly more equitable. Eliminating lotteries and state-sponsored gambling is a far better and more fiscally and morally responsible action of a government in a free society than the support and promotion of games that pilfer money from the electorate.

*2. Cease state-approved expansion of legalized commercial gambling.* The now easy accessibility of casino gambling to most of the American population is a long-term threat to the health of state and local economies. The point here, however, is not so much to argue for a recriminalization of commercial gambling or its elimination as for reduction or maintenance of current casino compacts.[31]

At a minimum, state legislatures should appoint state gambling commissions charged with evaluating the impact of gambling, in particular casino gambling, on the state population and economy. Such commissions should seek independently generated data, not just information readily provided by the gambling industry. Out of these studies state gambling policy can be developed that is more reflective of the public interest.

A state ban on further approval and development of casino gambling would provide time for public and private agencies to study the economic and social impact of gambling on communities. It would also protect communities from the unrepresentative and unfair legal leverage available to Native American tribal groups under the 1988 Indian Gaming Regulatory Act. As it stands, some communities have found themselves host to casino gambling after virtually no input into the legalization process or with little or no authority to stop it.

*3. Work with the U.S. Congress and Department of the Interior toward legal clarification of the 1988 Indian Gaming Regulatory Act.* States should work toward preserving state and local authority as well as Native American citizens' rights to free and fair access to the state and local political process. Casino gambling discussions too frequently become entangled in a threefold cultural and legal combination. One part is political correctness. A second is the legal morass enveloping Native American tribal sovereignty. And a third is latent public guilt for the sins, real and perceived, of three hundred years of "American Indian policy."

Gambling arguments pro and con can logically and morally be separated from any direct reference to any ethnic or racial group, including Native Americans. Regardless of the wrongs, even barbarity, perpetrated against or by Native Americans in the past—and there were many on both counts—none of that has anything directly to do with whether commercial gambling should be permitted on Native American reservations today.

An anti-gambling position or an anti–casino gambling expansion position are not ipso facto anti–Native American.[32] Of course it is entirely possible for either opponents or proponents of commercial gambling to be racist in their motivation and action. But it's not a given, and for either camp to suggest it without clear evidence is to be guilty of using the race issue for personal advantage.

The frequently heard argument that somehow commercial gambling is the last chance for Native Americans is itself an injustice to Native Americans. It sells them short. This view focuses on limited natural resources on reservations and fails to acknowledge the most precious natural resource of all—people. This argument ignores the many Native Americans who are already pursuing successful lives and professions of their choice.

Many examples can be cited worldwide of people groups with limited natural resources who have, nevertheless, developed dynamic economies. Taiwan is one; Hong Kong and Singapore are others. The dynamism of their economies is based on *intellectual* capital.

I am not suggesting that Native Americans do not need or deserve help, nor am I suggesting some kind of paternalism. What Native Americans need is what all Americans need: equitable state assistance in developing the quality and effectiveness of their educational system and opportunities to develop investment in productive entrepreneurial economic enterprise. Casino gambling purports to do this while undermining Native American work ethic, individual initiative, and private ownership.

Tribal sovereignty issues are very complex. On the one hand, Native American tribes are considered sovereign, that is to say a nation. On the other hand, Native Americans are American citizens who vote, pay taxes, receive government services, and so on. So should the legal system give standing to a somewhat defined group, like a tribe, or should it focus on individuals?

Part of the problem associated with legalization and expansion of commercial gambling is that some Native American tribes, via their legal standing with respect to the 1988 congressional act, have exercised favored nation status in instituting and operating commercial gambling establishments. They have sometimes done this to the consternation of state and local authorities who are less than enamored by casino gambling or who simply want some ability to influence economic development within their political jurisdiction.

Some of this may be mitigated by a 1996 U.S. Supreme Court ruling.

The Court invalidated the 1988 act's provision permitting tribes to sue in federal court if tribes believe states are failing to negotiate gambling agreements in good faith.[33]

The Supreme Court held that Congress does not have the power to override the eleventh amendment of the U.S. Constitution, which protects states from suits being filed against them in federal court. The Supreme Court preserved an option for tribes to go to the federal interior secretary when governors refuse to negotiate. So a modest step toward clarification has been made, but much of the legal labyrinth of a century remains yet to be sorted.

At a minimum, so-called "off-reservation" Native American casinos should be banned. Purchasing a parcel of land within a city boundary and labeling it a "reservation" is a sham, and it is unfair competition for other area businesses.[34]

*4. Reduce charity gambling by nonprofit organizations for fund-raising.* States could be more restrictive in granting gambling licenses. This can be done fairly and in a manner that furthers the public interest. However, the primary responsibility for reducing the use of gambling for fund-raising lies with nonprofit organizations, including churches.

A nonprofit organization's most precious resource is its reputation, for it is the public's appreciation for results and a well-accomplished mission that creates support for a cause. Gambling operations undercut a nonprofit organization's humanitarian reputation, and therefore, in the long run, lower the funds a nonprofit organization can expect to raise. Jettisoning gambling fund-raisers is an investment in a nonprofit organization's future.

*5. Ban publication of "point spreads" in national media, and create a federal task force to propose laws on sports betting.* Point spreads are more about betting than athletics; they always were. So banning their publication is a matter of public health, not free speech. Wagering on athletic events is one of the most accessible means of introduction to gambling by adolescents and is one of the primary engines of Internet gambling. Sports betting threatens the very integrity of competition based on talent and effort. Without significant cooperation of government, professional and collegiate sports, and existing gambling interests, to stop the continued growth of sports betting, sports betting scandals will increase. Strict sports betting policies should be developed by schools and universities, the NCAA and NAIA, and other sports agencies, similar to those already in place for alcohol and drug use. Laws should be developed that enact appropriate disincentives for sports betting, again similar to those shielding sports from alcohol and drug use, in order to protect the game and advance the quality of sporting competition.

6. *Ban advertising for gambling operations.* This policy is similar to the one operating in Great Britain. Word-of-mouth is still available to gambling operations, but at least the United States government could make it clear that gambling is not a "nice vice" that can be promoted.

7. *Pass legislation to regulate Internet gambling within U.S. borders.* The World Wide Web is the future of gambling, so legislation must be written and adopted to keep pace with the Internet's rapid development. Banning credit card companies and other financial institutions from using financial instruments to pay Internet-generated gambling debt is a beginning. Without such limitations and other similar efforts, money will continue to flow only one way—outside the U.S. with no attendant benefits to the American economy.

Somebody once said that "the devil is in the details." This was never more true than with gambling. On the surface, it looks good, but when you get into the details, you find ventures of chance that destroy values necessary for social vitality.

State legislators and governors will do well by their public trust if they begin to work toward the containment or curtailment of legalized commercial gambling, particularly where states are directly involved. If they do, their political and economic success will be more than illusory.

# 11

# INTERNET GAMBLING
## *The World's a Casino*

Dear Ann Landers:

I first gambled online a year ago and won several hundred dollars. That was unfortunate, because then I was hooked. Within a few short weeks, I was totally obsessed. No matter how much I won or lost, I kept gambling. I never actually saw any money change hands, and it all seemed like a series of fast-paced exciting games. The end result is that I am now $13,000 in debt.

I am overwhelmed with shame and humiliation because of this addiction. How could I have been so foolish? If my husband were to discover what I have done, he would probably leave me. Ann, I always thought that I could control my urge to gamble. It never occurred to me that my life would become hell because of it. I have miraculously stopped gambling, but there is still a long road ahead of me. I worry about making the next month's credit-card payment or having enough money to buy a birthday gift for my son. It will take years before I am out of debt. . . . I always prided myself on being a responsible adult, but now, I see how easy it is to lose your way. It could happen to me, it could happen to anyone.—Anonymous in the Midwest.[1]

Ann Landers told this anxious mother to connect with a local chapter of Gamblers Anonymous. "Anonymous in the Midwest" is one of thousands now gambling to excess and to possible financial destruction right in the convenience of their own homes. She demonstrates that you don't have to be a sports legend or a famous politician or corporate tycoon or a down-and-out person on his last dollar to gamble. You don't have to hit the boardwalk in Atlantic City or walk the Strip in Las Vegas. You just need access to an online computer—anywhere, anytime, all the time.

## Gambling with a Mouse

Since the world's first virtual online casino, Internet Casino, Inc., opened August 18, 1995, with an initial investment of $1.5 million, Internet gambling has become the fastest-growing segment of the gambling market in the country, if not the world.[2] Now you can gamble in your office, den, family room, bedroom, kitchen, hotel room, airport, internet café, school, anywhere you can gain access, online or wireless, to the World Wide Web. It's so easy. Players can "click their mouse and bet the house," says Ann Greer, chairman of the National Coalition Against Gambling Expansion.[3]

The Internet was first developed in the 1960s but became a popular phenomenon in the 1990s as an international network of interconnected computers. In the past decade the Internet has become a dominant force in business, communications, government, education, entertainment, and virtually every profession. "The Internet is the most rapidly spreading medium in history. It took radio 38 years to reach 50 million users. Television spread more quickly, attaining the 50 million mark in 13 years. The Internet reached its 50 millionth user just 5 years after it became readily available."[4]

The Internet can be and is used for many legitimate and productive purposes. But sin finds its way into all human endeavors, and cyberspace is no different. In a short time, gambling and pornography quickly surpassed computer software and hardware as the number one usage of the Internet. Estimates vary on just how many Americans are gambling on the Internet. The American Gaming Association estimates that nearly 4.5 million Americans gambled on the Internet in 2003.[5] In 2004, the Gaming Board of Great Britain projected 12 million online gamblers worldwide, 5.3 million of which were American; 4 million were Asian. By 2006, the number of Asians is expected to grow to 7.4 million.[6] In 2005, according to gambling analysts at River City Group in St. Louis, the number of Americans participating in Internet gambling will reach 7.4 million. CasinoFortune.com, one of the oldest online casinos, reports that its highest concentration of players, more than 420,000 annually, reside in the Midwest states of Michigan, Wisconsin, Minnesota, Indiana, Iowa, Missouri, and Ohio.[7]

CasinoFortune.com regularly calls high rollers at their homes to ask what the site can do for them to make their gambling experience more pleasant and to assure their repeat business. Most online gambling sites offer the same variety of games as land-based casinos. River City Group reports that some 68 percent of online gamblers are women.[8]

A 2001 Ontario, Canada, study found that women, divorced or widowed people, and senior citizens are more likely than others to dabble in Internet wagering. The rate of gambling online was nearly ten times higher than the year before.[9]

In 2003, River City Group reported that Internet gamblers represented all age and all income categories. River City Group found that 42.6 percent of online gamblers are over forty-five years of age, with 19.1 percent over fifty-five years of age. Some 30 percent of online gamblers report annual incomes between $25,000 and $49,999, 30 percent report incomes of $50,000 to $74,999, 15.6 percent have incomes of $75,000 to $99,999, and 14.5 percent earn more than $100,000 per year.[10]

So like other forms of gambling, Internet gambling seems to attract all types of people. Online casinos know this, for it is their bread and butter, and they are developing more sophisticated, exciting, and varied virtual gambling opportunities to entice an ever-growing market. One of the greatest economic advantages currently available to Internet gambling enterprises is that Internet usage is nowhere near a saturation point worldwide.

## Virtual Casinos

Internet gambling is growing rapidly because more Americans are becoming "wired," the Internet is easily accessible, technological advances make it faster and easier to download necessary software from gambling Web sites, and the speed of games is increasing, making it easier to place more bets.[11] Online virtual casinos simulate the real thing, and "online gambling is easier than onsite."[12]

From the first online casino in 1995, Internet gambling sites expanded to more than 500 in 1999.[13] By 2000, some 250 to 300 companies around the world were operating 1800 Internet gambling sites.[14]

"Since the mid-1990s, Internet gambling operators have established approximately 1,800 e-gaming Web sites in locations outside the U.S., and the global revenues from Internet gaming in 2003 are projected to be $5.0 billion." About 80 percent of Internet gambling sites offer casino gambling, 49.4 percent offer sports books, 22.8 percent provide access to horse/dog racing, and 6.8 percent connect gamblers with lotteries.[15] If all languages are taken into account, in 2002 gambling-related Internet sites, not all of which accepted wagers, numbered 32,991 worldwide and 44,076 in 2003, an increase of 34 percent in one year.[16] Some fifty governments and countries endorse Internet gambling within their borders, led by Antigua with more than one hundred gambling sites operating in or near the capital of St. John's.[17] The Caribbean and Central America account for about 79 percent of gambling Web sites.[18]

Internet gambling sites are increasing so rapidly that numerous online directories have been developed to guide players to new and more exotic gambling opportunities. Two of the larger and well-known gateway sites are www.internet-gambling-places-4U.com and www.internetgambling .reciprocalinks.com/, which provide players with listings and links to gambling sites.

## "Net" Gambling Revenues

Internet gambling is a money-making machine. "Because players make more bets per hour than they would at Caesar's Palace, they literally lose money to the house twice as fast," said Peter Kjaer, who runs an Internet gambling site. "Of the two industries on the Internet that make money, this is the one I can tell my mother about."[19]

Annual Internet gambling revenues have increased by more than 1600 percent between 1976 and 1997.[20] Internet gambling revenues doubled from $300 million in 1997 to $651 million in 1998, then redoubled again to $1.2 billion in 1999.[21] By 2001, some 2.5 million Americans gambled online, putting an estimated $5.5 billion into online, off-shore casinos.[22] Another report by the Government Accounting Office placed online gambling at over $4 billion in 2003, nearly two-thirds of it from Americans, and the amount of profit estimated at three times the profits from pornography on the Internet.[23] Other sources suggest that total Internet gambling revenues in 2003 were closer to $5.691 billion, with the same sources projecting revenues will triple by 2009 to $16.929 billion.[24]

By 2010, Online Gambling Research and Markets Group projects gross revenue from worldwide online wagers will be $18.4 billion, while Merrill Lynch estimates $42 billion by the same year. For 2015 the two companies both project enormous increases but again with differing tallies: Online Gambling predicts $125 billion in worldwide online wagers, while Merrill Lynch predicts $177 billion in worldwide online wagers, some $100 billion of which will be from online sports betting alone.[25]

Typical land-based casinos' profit ranges from 8 percent to 16 percent on each dollar, while virtual casinos' cut is closer to 24 percent.[26]

Since Internet gambling debts are not enforceable in the United States, online players take cash advances on their credit cards. "Online casinos generally require that a player set up an account. To do this, the player must first register by furnishing a variety of personal information. The player is asked to provide a user or account name and a password for security purposes. In some cases the casino provides them. Most casinos accept four methods of depositing funds: a direct mail check or money order; a direct withdrawal from a bank; a bank or Western Union wire transfer; or a direct debit to a credit card account, which is known as 'electronic cash' (or 'e-cash' for short) and is the fastest method. . . . Account numbers are encrypted with coding software that employs complex algorithms to render confidential information indecipherable to a hacker."[27]

At the world's largest online book maker, Sportsbook.com, players can deposit funds in an EFS account off-shore, then this money is transferred into V-chips to be used while gambling online. Players click "I agree" that they are familiar with gambling laws in their jurisdictions. Other options include bank wires, Western Union, or credit cards. Sportsbook .com processes more than $100 million in wagers from around the world. Other online sites use Net Cash or Digicash for their operations. Given the electronic ease with which players can "charge" their gambling, it is not too surprising to discover that player bankruptcies are a growing social and financial fallout.[28]

Off-shore Web sites pay no taxes to state governments. Nor do they generate the jobs or capital investments that land-based casinos and racetracks may produce. Governments only receive taxes from gamblers who voluntarily declare their winnings.[29]

## Online Sports Betting
Sports betting, what one former active gambler called "seasonal losing," is a perfect application for Internet gambling.[30] Online sports bets collect more money from the Super Bowl than from all the sports books in Las Vegas combined.[31]

Gross online sports wagering in 2003 was $63.5 billion.[32] Perhaps of more interest is the fact that in 2001, sports wagering accounted for the largest average one-day losses per gambler by online gambling activity at

$284. This was followed by racing at $271, casinos at $164, bingo at $104, and lotteries registering $95.[33]

Senator Jon Kyl (R-AZ) says,

> There are those who say we should just regulate Internet gambling. I don't believe it can be regulated, so we have to prohibit it. We have to keep sports clean in order to keep people believing in them. We can't let gambling intrude, and Internet gambling is the foot in the door. That's why the NFL, the NCAA, and the NHL are so behind what we're doing. They're worried. They fear the influence of gambling, and the Internet could allow it to happen with so much ease.

Jeff Pash, executive vice president of the NFL, said this in testimony before Congress: "Sports gambling breeds corruption and undermines the values our games represent. We do not want our games or our players used as gambling bait."[34]

"College students . . . have for a decade been the fastest growing segment of the gambling population even without the help of the Internet."[35] Sports gambling is still a key entry point to more gambling by adolescents and college students. Given the younger generation's facility with computers, and given that they are growing up in a time when gambling is so available and all-but-endorsed by adults, it is not illogical to assume that greater gambling-related social and economic problems will characterize our future.

## Online Problem Gambling

As Internet gambling increases so does problem gambling—at the speed of a computer. Internet gambling, like its land-based forebears, contributes to increased gambling disorders, especially among youth; crime; and burdens on government.[36] Kevin Whyte, executive director of the National Council on Problem Gambling, said, "Internet gambling provides the holy trinity of risk factors—immediate access, anonymity, and with the use of a credit card, the ability to gamble with money you don't really have."[37]

Internet gamblers may be more likely to have or to develop serious gambling problems than other gamblers, because the Web is so easily accessible and because it attracts those trying to hide their addiction. The risk of increased problem gambling includes the availability of the

Web twenty-four hours per day in one's own home, greater exposure and access of children (all they need is an adult's credit card), absorption on the computer, leading people to lose track of time while gambling, and a decrease of the perception of the value of cash; that is, players forget they are spending money.[38]

A survey of gambling behavior by Dr. George Ladd and Dr. Nancy Petry of the University of Connecticut Health Center "warns that the explosive growth of the Internet will lead to more online betting opportunities—and thus the risk of more people suffering from the health and emotional difficulties associated with compulsive gambling. These include substance abuse, circulatory disease, depression, and risky sexual behaviors." Although Internet gambling was the least common form of gambling reported by study participants, the study found that a majority of those with Internet gambling experiences had the most serious problems with addiction. "Only 22 percent of the participants without any Internet gambling experience had problems compared with 74 percent of those who used the web." In this study, Internet gamblers were more likely unmarried and younger people with lower education and income levels. The researchers estimated that people under twenty-five years of age are three times more likely to become problem gamblers.[39]

Dr. Jeffrey Derevensky, codirector of the International Center for Youth Gambling Problems at McGill University in Montreal, worries about Internet gambling sites that incorporate video-game technology and their likely lure for adolescents. "They give you an illusion of control, a sense that the more you play, the better you get," he said. "It's training a whole new generation of kids. Once they get their credit cards, they're off and running."[40]

Online poker tournaments sponsored by such groups as www .collegepokerchampionships.com target students and do not publish help lines or warn about addictions. "It's actively soliciting kids to gamble, and in some states that may be illegal," said Kevin Whyte of the National Council on Problem Gambling. "You wouldn't have a college drinking championship, or a college smoking championship.com."[41]

The primary reason to anticipate an increase in compulsive gambling from 5 to 7 million up to 20 million people is that Internet gambling is more addictive.[42] One Internet gambling site operator cynically (but unfortunately realistically) tapped into cybergambling's potential, "Internet sex sites can only simulate the real thing, but online casinos *are* the real thing."[43]

## Cyberslacking

Internet gambling, along with other misuses of the Internet on company time, is now a growing problem for businesses worldwide, contributing to a gradual shift of personnel Internet use policies from Information Technology to Human Resources departments.[44] Websense, Inc., the worldwide leader of employee Internet management solutions, warns that as online gambling sites continue to increase dramatically, "cyberslacking" will increasingly threaten a company's bottom line. In Hong Kong, for example, a Websense survey found that 76 percent of employers considered online gambling their number one problem, while 69 percent identified online pornography. The challenge is for employers to detect and manage productivity, as well as resource and bandwidth draining activity.[45]

Chief technology officer for Websense, Harold Kester, says, "We track the online gambling category very carefully for our customers. Many of our clients, including nearly half of the Fortune 500, are becoming increasingly aware of the productivity and legal issues surrounding online gambling at work."[46]

Internet gamblers can literally go for days with no job creation, no state revenues produced, no increases in tourism generated, and no taxes contributed to the local economy.[47] "Gambling is a habit-forming, addictive means of pleasure for many adults," said Dr. David Greenfield, director of The Center for Internet Studies in West Hartford, Connecticut, "Couple that with the already addictive nature of the Internet and corporations could be in big trouble for creating an environment where these types of abuses can take place."[48] Internet gambling is an escape, a leap into cyberspace creating a seemingly unlimited horizon of opportunities. Like all gambling, Internet gambling is "often a way of adding intensity to an experience after we've lost the ability to experience that intensity on its own."[49]

## Governing Internet Gambling?

"Internet gambling is essentially a borderless activity that poses regulation and enforcement challenges."[50] The United States Wire Act of 1961 prohibits the use of a wire transmission facility to foster any gambling pursuit.[51] The law was passed as a direct response to sports gambling over the telephone.

Also relevant to Internet gambling regulation is "the Professional and Amateur Sports Protection Act of 1992, which prohibited sports wagering in all states except those with pre-existing operations (Nevada, Oregon, and Delaware). The Justice Department in both the Clinton and Bush administrations has expressed the view that the U.S. Wire Act of 1961 applies to all forms of Internet gambling, and therefore it is illegal under existing law." However, some U.S. courts have variously ruled on cases applying to both sports betting and online casinos. Consequently, periodic concerns about Internet gambling are raised in the United States Congress, ranging from attempts to ban all Internet gambling to efforts to stop use of credit cards and other financial instruments for the purpose of Internet gambling, to recommendations for study commissions to explore licensing, regulations, and taxation of Internet gambling sites.[52] Internet payment systems like PayPal have responded to federal lawmakers by blocking charges from online casinos, as have several credit card companies, including Citibank, Discover Card, MBNA, and American Express.[53]

Several federal attempts to regulate Internet gambling have so far failed, for example the Internet Gambling Prohibition Act of 2000 that failed to pass both houses of Congress. U.S. Representative Jim Leach (R-IA) and Senator Jon Kyl (R-AZ) have tried unsuccessfully for the past few years to get Congress to enact Internet gambling legislation (the Unlawful Internet Gambling Funding Prohibition Act). "There is no easier way to launder money than through gambling, and no easier methodology than Internet gambling," Leach says.[54]

"Follow the money" has been a workable maxim for centuries for both crime-doers and crime-stoppers, and Internet gambling kicks both the principle and its potential into warp speed. Online betting is itself now a target for cyberextortion when hackers demand money by attacking and shutting down online casinos, which are particularly vulnerable since they have little legal recourse given the illegal status of Internet gambling in the United States. BetWTTS.com in Antigua was forced to pay $30,000 when hackers attacked its site, preventing thousands of bets totaling $5 million from being placed. While some might consider this poetic justice, law enforcement officials worry about the transferability of hackers' skills to online banking and other financial institutions.[55]

A few states have attempted to regulate Internet gambling, passing laws making it illegal. Florida reached an agreement with Western Union stopping the transfer of money from that state to off-shore sports books. "But the states themselves recognize the limits of their enforceable authority."[56] Notwithstanding, Illinois, Louisiana, Michigan, Oregon, and

South Dakota have all passed legislation banning Internet gambling within their borders, and attorneys general in Minnesota, Missouri, New Jersey, New York, and Wisconsin have declared they would use existing law to fight Internet gambling in their states.[57]

In November 2004, a World Trade Organization panel said Washington, D.C. should drop its prohibition on Americans placing bets via online casinos, saying the ban represented an unfair trade barrier.[58] Whether the United States yields to this international pressure or maintains its stance toward illegal Internet gambling remains to be seen. One sure bet is that the challenge will not go away.

## Cybergambling Tomorrow

"Gambling is the future of the Internet," says Simon Noble, executive director of the online gambling division of Intertops. "You can only look at so many dirty pictures."[59] Indeed, online betting is one of the most profitable forms of making money in history.

It's possible that Internet gambling is just the tip of the technological iceberg. Interactive TV betting and use of various handheld computer devices, including mobile phones, for playing games and making wagers could be the next commercial development.[60] "The gambling games possible for the future are only limited by the imagination of software designers."[61] Future Web technology will likely allow interaction between land-based and online casinos, allowing the latter to coordinate offerings, in real time, with conventions and major events taking place in Las Vegas and other gambling meccas.[62] Cockfights, dogfights, crab races, frog jumping, country-club Calcuttas, floating craps games, election betting, two-bit Mah-jongg games, happy hour gambling, sports pools, and more, there is no end of Internet gambling possibilities.[63]

Gambling on the Internet may seem new and exciting, but it's still gambling. People are still being bilked of their wages, money in massive amounts is still being redistributed in a manner that leaves one party of the transaction impoverished and the other enriched, people are still developing compulsive gambling problems, and no one really benefits except those who own the Internet gambling operation. So like Solomon said centuries ago, "There's nothing new under the sun." Internet gambling takes a centuries-old vice and puts it online, making sin more available, accessible, and seemingly less accountable.

# 12

# CULTURAL ALCHEMY
## *The Irrationality of Gambling*

In George Orwell's *1984*, gambling becomes the principal form of entertainment in the English-speaking world state, Oceania. In their boredom, pessimism, and ignorance, the working classes turn to inane and interminable discussions focusing on the daily lottery.

Religion in a biblical or even traditional sense is virtually nonexistent in totalitarian Oceania. The elite give obeisance to the ruling party, while the working classes worship shallow pleasures of the moment. There is no past, and there is no future—only the present. Life has no rhyme or reason. The senselessness of gambling makes sense.[1]

### A Celebration of Irrationality
Gambling demands that the gambler abandon reason. It's a venue of superstition, a religion-free religion. Gambling is a celebration of irrationality and as such is the perfect postmodern game. In a time when valuelessness is valued, gambling fits. The 9/11 calamity did not even get our attention for very long. "The worst terror attack to date in the nation's history caused barely a stutter in overall casino attendance."[2]

Gambling has entered mainstream culture today because of a collapse of taboos. The question is, Who pushed over the taboos? Gambling is not a national craze because unscrupulous gambling tycoons got into bed with money-grubbing legislators. Gambling is not mainstream entertainment because of a mob conspiracy. Perhaps these things happened along the way, but the real source of gambling fever lies with the American people.

Vicki Abt, James Smith, and Eugene Martin Christiansen believe that our culture has shifted away from certain bedrock beliefs. First, we've lost faith in the idea that individuals can influence their destiny by their own efforts. Second, we no longer believe that a person is rewarded with what he or she deserves or has earned. Contemporary Americans are less confident in their ability to control their own destiny. We're a more fatalistic and superstitious people. They issue a warning: "A civilization cannot survive for very long . . . on wishful thinking and illusions."[3]

*Gambling . . . flourishes in cultures where people no longer*
*believe they can influence their present, much less their future.*

Ironically, gambling is built on a losing not a winning mentality. Gambling is correlated with social pessimism. It flourishes in cultures where people no longer believe they can influence their present, much less their future. Gambling blossoms from a mood of despair, powerlessness, and hopelessness. That's why gambling became dominant in Orwell's Oceania. Life is luck, uncertainty, chance, a crap shoot.

## Dame Fortune

American culture has lost confidence in hard work, ingenuity, and a better tomorrow. We're casting about looking for good fortune to shine on us, hoping somehow we'll get lucky. That's why winning the lottery is the number one American fantasy.

Yet why do Americans think we're immune to the hazards of gambling when every civilization in the past five hundred years has sought to curtail gambling or its effects?[4] It is because we've embraced moral relativism—the postmodern belief in *mobile truths*. Something may be true for you or true for me, but nothing is objectively and absolutely true. We no longer believe in absolute truth, in right and wrong.

Despite our great religiosity, we Americans have become practical agnostics. If God exists, we don't believe he has anything to say to us. We reject him, we reject his Word, and we reject his morality. The only thing left is uncertainty—and luck.

In a culture that believes the universe began by chance, that our existence and our morality are nothing more than the luck of the draw, gambling is oddly logical. Gambling is a metaphor for the current cultural zeitgeist. It grows out of our cultural philosophy. We believe in a world of undefined chaos.

Gambling has become a surrogate religion—a pathological hope—a concession to life based on luck—an admission that there is nothing to life but determinism, fatalism, nihilism. Gambling is rabbit's foot religion. It's our postmodern paganism. It's idolatry.

We believe only in Dame Fortune. But Dame Fortune is no more real than Mother Nature, Santa Claus, or the tooth fairy. We know this, yet we grasp at it anyway. We're victims of Orwell's doublethink. We hold two contradictory beliefs simultaneously, and we seem to accept them both.

In the postmodern American culture, any philosophy will do, except biblical Christianity.[5] No new belief is too odd, too arcane, too absurd. We live our lives by the helter-skelter of the latest religious fad even while we chase back to Christian or at least traditional religion for weddings, births, and funerals. American culture is in a spiritual morass.

American politics is not going to provide the way out. Neither political party is addressing the deeper moral crisis of this age. Leadership is difficult to find. We have only positioned and positioning politicians—motivated more by power than principle.

The mainline institutional church is not going to provide the way out of our spiritual morass. Theological liberalism has robbed it of its prophetic voice. The mainline church is lost within itself. It's like an aging lion with no teeth. It periodically roars, but no one pays any attention.

Academia is not going to point the way out of the spiritual morass. American academia looks strong, and in some ways is strong, but it's spiritually weak. Academia, especially at higher educational levels, is like a great Samson seduced by the Delilah of moral pluralism.

## Higher Values

Is it possible that theologically conservative churches are going to provide the way out? American culture's greatest need is ultimately not political or economic, it is moral and therefore spiritual. What America needs is a spiritual revival, beginning with the individual and spreading to the community. When that happens, gambling will fall by the wayside.

*What America needs is a spiritual revival, beginning with the individual and spreading to the community.*

The Bible depicts the reality of sin and Satan, but for all the darkness of sin in the world, biblical Christianity is forever an optimistic faith. God—not luck—is in control. Jesus Christ has paid the penalty of sin and offers salvation to all who accept him.

Human and divine choices influence life. Various sterile determinisms are just that: sterile, impotent. Biblical values provide not bondage but liberty for mind, body, and soul.

Christian values are radically different from the values of the gambling industry. Yet Christian silence on gambling is deafening.

Gambling is fundamentally contradictory not only to biblical teachings of individual stewardship and divine sovereignty but also to the socially borrowed Christian values that made this country strong—the Protestant work ethic, individual value and responsibility, and rationality. Why aren't Christians pointing people away from superstition and toward the supernatural?

Where are the pastors preaching accountability before God for our money and our time? Jeremiads against Las Vegas or the Mafia will not be helpful. We need sound biblical exposition applied to this daily practical problem. Pastors need to make sure that there is not a person in their pews who can't explain the scriptural principles and doctrines pertaining to gambling.

Contemporary Christian understanding of a biblical theology of work and leisure is at best anemic and would be considered shameful by earlier generations of believers. Christians must rediscover God's principles of creation and recreation relating not just to gambling but to all of life.

### Shaping Our Moral Destiny

Gambling drains the economic order and undermines philanthropy. When will responsible civic, business, and academic leaders make their voices heard in state capitals more often, more vigorously, and more effectively, other than just when a casino campaign comes to their back yard?

Gambling threatens the moral foundations of the culture. It's a package loaded with hidden economic costs. Gambling is bad for business. It's a made-to-order conservative issue.

Gambling threatens people sometimes listed among the weaker or more vulnerable in the population: the poor, the elderly, and children. Gambling is a regressive tax. It's a made-to-order liberal issue.

When will conservatives and liberals alike realize that the gambling issue is win-win for them and a rare political issue providing a clear opportunity for a conservative/liberal governing coalition? Conservatives should be reacting to the moral principles discarded by a casino culture. Liberals should be reacting to gambling's demolition of the working class.

The same is true for Democrats and Republicans. But to date, neither party has assumed an anti- or a pro-gambling position. Too many politicians among conservatives and liberals and in both parties have been seduced by the lure of wealth without work, increased revenues without taxes.

The social pressure must be enormous, but the question still must be asked: Where are the responsible Native American leaders who see the moral bust on the other side of the economic boom? Some have spoken, sometimes at their peril, but no one has yet galvanized a Native American anti-gambling movement.

Native Americans are not a monolithic ethnic group any more than any other ethnic group. As a people, Native Americans deserve better than to be cast by the media, casino kings, or Native American pro-gambling interests as one great voice in favor of selling their souls to gambling.

We also need more senior citizens setting a moral and financially responsible example. They're out there, but they're not being heard. A "Grandparents Against Gambling" (GAG) movement would be helpful. Mothers Against Drunk Driving (MADD) and Students Against Drunk Driving (SADD) have orchestrated much-needed and nationally successful campaigns. Perhaps GAG could emulate their success but be preemptive. Stop gambling before gambling stops teenagers. The country needs seniors to step forward and lead.

When will the American people recognize that gambling is both a stimulant and a tranquilizer? It's just the latest opiate of the people. Whether all Americans accept the argument that gambling is intrinsically wrong is beside the point. Certainly Americans should recognize that gambling is extrinsically dangerous, deleterious, and destructive.

What will it take to get Americans, their state legislatures, and their federal Congress to realize that gambling is not a free lunch? We want cradle to grave government services, but we do not want to pay for them. What's a body to do? Answer: gambling.

If we persist in this kind of foolish illogic, our greed will be our gateway to destiny. In our desire for more, we will create a future with less.

Gambling is a bottomless pit. Gambling asks us to play the odds, and gambling always wins in the long run.

Gambling is bad business, bad recreation, bad fund-raising, bad religion, bad politics, bad economics, and bad morality.

Gamblers know the truth. "You can win a race, but you can't beat the races."

# Appendix

# WHERE TO FIND HELP
# AND INFORMATION

**Master Web Site**

"Compulsive Gambling Links," a thorough listing of state (36) and national (U.S. and Canada) problem gambling counseling agencies and help sites.
www.azccg.org/links/links.html

**Problem Gambling Counseling Agencies in the United States**

Gamblers Anonymous
P.O. Box 17173
Los Angeles, CA 90017
Gamblers Anonymous Helpline: 213-386-8779
Phone:      213-386-8790
Fax:        213-386-0030
Web site:   http://gamblersanonymous.org
E-mail:     isomain@gamblersanonymous.org

Gam-Anon (for spouses and family members of compulsive gamblers)
P.O. Box 157
Whitestone, NY 11357
Phone:      718-352-1671
Fax:        718-746-2571
Web site:   www.gam-anon.org

The Gambling Treatment and Research Center
at the University of Connecticut Health Center

263 Farmington Ave, Suite LG006
Farmington, CT 06030-3949
Phone:          877-400-0570
Fax:            860-679-1312
Web site:       www.gamblingtreatment.net/

The National Council on Problem Gambling, Inc.
216 G Street NE
Washington, DC 20002
Keith Whyte, Executive Director
Nationwide helpline: 800-522-4700
Phone:          202-547-9204
Fax:            202-547-9206
Web site:       www.ncpgambling.org
E-mail:         ncpg@ncpgambling.org

**National Gambling Opposition Agency**
National Coalition Against Legalized Gambling
100 Maryland Ave. NE, Room 311
Washington, DC 20002
Rev. Tom Grey, Executive Director
Phone:          800-664-2680
Fax:            307-587-8082
Web site:       www.ncalg.org
E-mail:         ncalg@vcn.com

**Selected State Problem Gambling Counseling Agencies**
California Council on Compulsive Gambling, Inc.
121 S. Palm Canyon Dr., Suite 225
Palm Springs, CA 92262
Bebe Smith, Acting Executive Director
Helplines:      800-FACTS-4-U (322-8748) (CA only)
                800-GAMBLER© (AK/AZ/CA/IL/KY/MS/NJ/
                NM/NV/NY/PA/TN/TX/WV)
Phone:          760-320-0234
Fax:            760-416-1349
Web site:       www.calproblemgambling.org
E-mail:         info@calproblemgambling.org

Michigan Council on Problem and Compulsive Gambling
18530 Mack Ave., #552
Detroit, MI 48236
Warren Biller, Executive Director
Statewide helpline: 800-270-7117
Phone:        313-396-0402
Fax:          313-396-0407
E-mail:       mi@ncpgambling.org

Nevada Council on Problem Gambling, Inc.
4340 S. Valley View, Suite 220
Las Vegas, NV 89103
Carol O'Hare, Executive Director
Phone:        702-369-9740
Fax:          702-369-9765
Helplines:    800-522-4700
              800-GAMBLER©
Web site:     www.nevadacouncil.org
E-mail:       NevCouncil@aol.com

Compulsive Gambling Center
924 E. Baltimore Street
Baltimore, MD 21202
Valerie Lorenz, Executive Director
Toll free:    800-LOST-BET (800-567-8238)
Phone:        410-332-1111
Fax:          410-685-2307

Council on Compulsive Gambling of New Jersey, Inc.
3635 Quakerbridge Road, Suite 7
Hamilton, NJ 08619
Ed Looney, Executive Director
Helpline:     1-800-GAMBLER© (426-2537; for the
              following states: AK, AZ, CA, IL, KY, MS, NJ,
              NM, NV, NY, PA, TN, TX, WV)
Phone:        609-588-5515 ext. 17
Fax:          609-588-5665
Web site:     www.800gambler.org
E-mail:       ccgnj@800gambler.org

**Problem Gambling Counseling Agencies in Canada**
Canadian Foundation on Compulsive Gambling (Ontario)
Helpline:        888-391-1111 (Nationwide)
Phone:           416-499-8260
                 416-499-9800
Fax:             416-499-8260
Web site:        www.cfcg.on.ca/

Canadian Foundation on Compulsive Gambling (Saskatchewan)
Suite 2332 11th Avenue
Regina, Saskatchewan S4P OK1
Doug Moran, Executive Director
Helpline:        800-306-6789 (Provincial)
Phone:           306-352-9988
Fax:             306-352-2266
E-mail:          dougm.cfcg@dlcwest.com

International Centre for Youth Gambling Problems and High
Risk Behaviors
3724 McTavish St.
Montreal, Quebec, Canada H3A 1Y2
Phone:           514-398-1391
Fax:             514-398-3401
Web site:        www.youthgambling.org/

Responsible Gambling Council (Ontario)
505 Consumers Road, Suite 801
Toronto, Ontario M2J 4V8
Morrie Behrmann, Director of Information Services
Phone:           416-499-9800 ext. 226
Toll free:       888-391-1111
Fax:             1-416-499-8260 Fax
Web site:        www.responsiblegambling.org/
E-mail:          infosource@rgco.org

2109 Ottawa St., Suite 401 (Windsor Office)
Windsor, Ontario N8Y 1R8
Phone:           519-2542112
Fax:             519-254-0093

Web site:    www.responsiblegambling.org/
E-mail:    infosource@cfcg.org

## Selected Online Gambling Help Sites

www.gamblock.com
Software that blocks access to all online gambling sites.

www.femalegamblers.org/
Women Helping Women.

www.childnet-int.org
www.cyberpatrol.com
www.netnanny.com
Protecting children from accessing gambling on the Internet.

# NOTES

## Chapter 1: Taking a Chance

1. Except for the names, this story is true and comes from a community in Michigan.
2. Vicki Abt, James F. Smith, and Eugene Martin Christiansen, *The Business of Risk: Commercial Gambling in Mainstream America* (Lawrence, Kans.: University Press of Kansas, 1985), 35.
3. William N. Thompson, *Legalized Gambling: A Reference Handbook* (Santa Barbara, Calif.: ABC-CLIO, 1994), 2.
4. Samuel Johnson, as quoted in Mark Clapson, *A Bit of a Flutter: Popular Gambling and English Society, 1823–1961* (Manchester, England: Manchester University Press, 1992), 1.
5. Abt, Smith, and Christiansen, *Business of Risk,* 74.
6. For a discussion of types of gambling, see ibid., 118–37.
7. Francis Emmett Williams, *Lotteries, Laws, and Morals* (New York: Vantage Press, 1958), 81; see also Ross Coggins, ed., *The Gambling Menace* (Nashville: Broadman Press, 1966), 55–56.
8. Michael B. Walker, *The Psychology of Gambling* (New York: Pergamon Press, 1992), 151.
9. Thompson, *Legalized Gambling,* 3.
10. Carroll Bogert, "Fool's Gold in Black Hawk?" *Newsweek* (28 March 1994): 22–24; Gene and Adele Malott, "Mississippi Beach Booms as Little Vegas," *The Grand Rapids Press,* 25 December 1994, K4; James Sterngold, "Are Casinos a Gamble Worth Taking?" *The Grand Rapids Press,* 3 December 1995, A3.
11. Henry R. Lesieur, "Compulsive Gambling," *Society* (May–June 1992): 43.
12. Each fall, the gambling industry's flagship publication,

*International Gaming and Wagering Business Magazine,* details current annual as well as comparative gambling industry statistics over several years. Of particular value was gambling experts Eugene Martin Christiansen and Will E. Cummings's article, "Double-Edged Growth," *International Gaming and Wagering Business Magazine* (1 August 1995): 31–32.

13. Pam Schmid, "Gambling Habit Proves Addicting to Growing Number of Teenagers," *The Grand Rapids Press,* 9 January 1994, A5; William B. Falk, "Workless Wealth," *The Grand Rapids Press,* 15 December 1995, A2; Frank Rich, "America on Big Bender with Gaming," *Las Vegas Sun,* 10 May 1996, 15B.

14. Christiansen and Cummings, "Double-Edged Growth," 31; Joseph P. Shapiro, "America's Gambling Fever," *U.S. News and World Report* (15 January 1996): 53.

15. Rachel A. Volberg, *When the Chips Are Down: Problem Gambling in America* (New York: The Century Foundation Press, 2001), 24; Eugene M. Christiansen, "The Gross Annual Wager in the U.S.," www.cca-i.com/insight/issue_guide.htm, accessed 15 October 2004.

16. "Casino Markets by Annual Revenue," www.americangaming.org/industry/factsheets/statistics_detail.cfv?id=4, accessed 15 October 2004.

17. "Gaming Revenue: 10-Yr Trends," www.americangaming.org/industry/factsheets/statistics_detail.cfv?id=8, accessed 15 October 2004.

18. "Gaming Revenue: Current Year Data," August 2004, www.americangaming.org/industry/factsheets/statistics_detail.cfv?id=7, accessed 15 October 2004.

19. Shapiro, "Gambling Fever," 59.

20. Christiansen and Cummings, "Double-Edged Growth," 31–32.

21. Robert Goodman, *The Luck Business: The Devastating Consequences and Broken Promises of America's Gambling Explosion* (New York: The Free Press, 1995); James Popkin with Katia Hetter, "America's Gambling Craze," *U.S. News and World Report,* 14 March 1994, 42.

22. As cited in John Fetto, "Off the Map: The Legal Gambling Industry Grows in Popularity," *American Demographics,* www.findarticles.com/p/articles/mi_m4021/is_2002_Sept_1/ai_90957513, accessed 15 October 2004.

23. Christiansen and Cummings, "Double-Edged Growth," 31–32.
24. Eugene M. Christiansen and Sebastian Sinclair, "The Gross Annual Wager of the United States, 2000," www.cca-i.com/insight/issue_guide.htm, accessed 15 October 2004.
25. Christiansen and Cummings, "Double-Edged Growth," 31–32.
26. Chris Welles, "America's Gambling Fever," *Business Week* (24 April 1989): 112–13.
27. Christiansen and Cummings, "Double-Edged Growth," 31–32.
28. Edward W. Packel, *The Mathematics of Games and Gambling* (Washington, D.C.: The Mathematical Association of America, 1981), 4.
29. *Report of the Governor's Blue Ribbon Commission on Michigan Gaming*, Robert J. Danhof, Chairman (Lansing, Mich.: Michigan Court of Appeals, April 1995), 15; Shapiro, "Gambling Fever," 55.
30. Thompson, *Legalized Gambling*, 13.
31. Cristopher Lasch, as quoted in Abt, Smith, and Christiansen, *Business of Risk*, 22.
32. Abt, Smith, and Christiansen, *Business of Risk*, 148.
33. David Weinstein and Lillian Deitch, *The Impact of Legalized Gambling: The Socioeconomic Consequences of Lotteries and Off-Course Betting* (New York: Praeger, 1974), 144.
34. Quoted in David Neff and Thomas Giles, "Feeding the Monster Called 'More,'" *Christianity Today* (25 November 1991): 19.
35. Commission on the Review of the National Policy Toward Gambling, Charles H. Morin, Chairman, *Gambling in America: Final Report of the Commission on the Review of the National Policy Toward Gambling* (Washington, D.C.: GPO, 1976), 229.
36. John Zipperer, "Against All Odds," *Christianity Today* (14 November 1994): 58–59.
37. Quoted in William Safire, "GOP Should Add Gaming to Moral Agenda," *The Grand Rapids Press*, 15 September 1995, A14.
38. Ralph Reed, as quoted in Margot Hornblower, "No Dice: The Backlash Against Gambling," *Time*, 1 April 1996, 30.
39. Gary L. Bauer, *Our Hopes Our Dreams: A Vision for America* (Colorado Springs: Focus on the Family Publications, 1996), 115–16.
40. James W. Brosnan, "Battle Lines Drawn over Federal Gaming Controls," *The Grand Rapids Press*, 12 May 1996, E1; Ralph Reed, *Active Faith: How Christians Are Changing the Soul of*

*American Politics* (New York: The Free Press, 1996), 223.

41. See the United Methodist Church publication "A $pecial Issue on Gambling," *Christian Social Action* 7, no. 7 (July–August 1994).

42. Brosnan, "Battle Lines"; Lee Ranck, "We're Selling Out to a Bunch of Looters?" *Christian Social Action* 7, no. 7 (July–August 1994): 12–16; Shapiro, "Gambling Fever," 53–54.

43. Hornblower, "No Dice," 29.

44. Durand Jacobs, as quoted in Richard Chavira, "The Rise of Teenage Gambling," *Time* (25 February 1991): 78.

## Chapter 2: Seven Come Eleven

1. P. T. Barnum, as quoted in David Johnston, *Temples of Chance: How America Incorporated Bought Out Murder Incorporated to Win Control of the Casino Business* (New York: Doubleday, 1992), 25.

2. Ross Coggins, ed., *The Gambling Menace* (Nashville: Broadman Press, 1966), 17.

3. Several texts give details on the historical data referenced in this chapter. They include David D. Allen, *The Nature of Gambling* (New York: Coward-McCann, 1952); Larry Braidfoot, *Gambling: A Deadly Game* (Nashville: Broadman Press, 1985); Henry Chafetz, *Play the Devil: A History of Gambling in the United States from 1492 to 1955* (New York: Potter Publishers, 1960); John Samuel Ezell, *Fortune's Merry Wheel: The Lottery in America* (Cambridge: Harvard University Press, 1960); Commission on the Review of the National Policy Toward Gambling, Charles H. Morin, Chairman, *Gambling in America: Final Report of the Commission on the Review of the National Policy Toward Gambling* (Washington, D.C.: GPO, 1976); Rufus King, *Gambling and Organized Crime* (Washington, D.C.: Public Affairs Press, 1969).

4. William N. Thompson, *Legalized Gambling: A Reference Handbook* (Santa Barbara, Calif.: ABC-CLIO, 1994), 4–5.

5. Lord Beaconsfield, as quoted in James Hastings, ed., *Encyclopedia of Religion and Ethics* (Edinburgh: T and T Clark, 1913), 165.

6. Allen, *Nature of Gambling,* 44.

7. Commission on the Review of the National Policy Toward

Gambling, *Gambling in America*, 1.

8. Coggins, *Gambling Menace*, 13.
9. Allen, *Nature of Gambling*, 45.
10. Chafetz, *Play the Devil*, 31; and Allen, *Nature of Gambling*, 45.
11. Commission on the Review of the National Policy Toward Gambling, *Gambling in America*, 1–15.
12. Samuel Johnson, as quoted in E. Benson Perkins, *Gambling in English Life* (London: Epworth Press, 1950), 4.
13. Sandra Chereb, "Slot Machines Go High-Tech Thanks to Computer Advances," *The Grand Rapids Press*, 30 November 1995, B2.
14. Chris Welles, "America's Gambling Fever," *Business Week*, 24 April 1989, 114.
15. "Lemons in a Row," *The New York Times*, 13 July 2004, www .nytimes.com/2004/07/13/opinion/13tue1.html.
16. Eugene Martin Christiansen and Will E. Cummings, "Double-Edged Growth," *International Gaming and Wagering Business Magazine* (1 August 1996): 40.
17. Chereb, "Slot Machines," B2; "Gaming As Entertainment," *Las Vegas Style* (May 1996): 13; *Casino Gambling: The Myth and the Reality* (Lansing, Mich.: Michigan Interfaith Council on Alcohol Problems, 1988), 16.
18. See www.insiderv/v.com/didyoukno.html, accessed 19 October 2004.
19. J. Taylor Buckley, "The Quest for Gambling's 'Holy Grail': Industry Seeks Next-Generation Slot Machine," *USA Today*, 20 May 1996, 1A; Buckley, "For Many, the 'Whisper' Is Money," *USA Today*, 20 May 1996, 2A.
20. As quoted in Gary Rivlin, "The Tug of the Newfangled Slot Machines," The New York Times, 9 May 2004, http://www .nytimes.com/2004/05/09/magazine/09SLOTS .html?ex=111457 4400&en=1719e31141e72f24&ei=5070 (accessed November 19, 2004).
21. Benjamin Blake and Hannah Erickson, *Amazing Las Vegas Trivia* (Las Vegas: Las Vegas Trivia, 1994); Dan Nesmith, *The Casino Slot Machine: What You Need to Know* (Mobile: SMI, 1993).
22. *Casino Gambling*, 16.

23. "Schools Win in Lottery," *The Grand Rapids Press*, 11 May 1995, A18.

24. "Underbelly of Vegas," *The Grand Rapids Press*, 4 July 2004, C11.

25. Buckley, "Holy Grail," 1A.

26. Johnston, *Temples of Chance*, 19, 57.

27. Chereb, "Slot Machines," B2.

28. Dick Sadler, as quoted in Ibid.

29. "Casino Technology Can Track Slot Machine Players," *The Grand Rapids Press*, 26 December 1995, B7.

30. D. Kirk Davidson, *Selling Sin: the Marketing of Socially Unacceptable Products* (Westport, Conn.: Praeger, 2003), 70.

31. "CNN for Gamblers," *The Grand Rapids Press*, 26 December 1995, A3.

32. John Zipperer, "Against All Odds," *Christianity Today* (14 November 1994): 58; David Bennahum, "Pay-Per-Play," www .wired.com/wired/archive/2.06/eword.html?pg=6, accessed 26 February 2005; "New Gaming Network Bets On Success," www.cnn.com/2003/SHOWBIZ/TV/10/26/gambling.channel .ap/, accessed 26 February 2005.

33. Eugene Martin Christiansen, "Table Games Are Back," www.caa-i.com/insight/, accessed 15 October 2004.

34. David G. Schwartz, *Suburban Xanadu: The Casino Resort on the Las Vegas Strip and Beyond* (New York: Rutledge, 2003), 1; and Howard Stutz, "Poker Renaissance, The Game's Popularity Is Fueled by Telecasts and Corporate Sponsorships," *International Gaming and Wagering Business* 25, no. 1 (January 2004): 22.

35. Troy Reimink, "Poker's Wild: For Many, Card Play Craze Not Just a Passing Fad," *The Grand Rapids Press*, 22 November 2004, D1; and Lori Johnston, "College Deal: TV Poker Shows Spark Campus Card Craze," *The Grand Rapids Press*, 4 April 2004, A9.

36. Rex M. Rogers, "Think Youth Gambling Is Harmless Fun? Don't Bet on It," *The Grand Rapids Press*, 27 November 2004, A13.

37. Richard Grimes, "The Odds Are Against Phone Bets," *Charleston Daily Mail*, 6 June 1995, 6A.

38. Marc Cooper, *The Last Honest Place in America: Paradise and Perdition in the New Las Vegas* (New York: Nation Books, 2004), 15.

39. Ibid., 12–13; and Laura Holston, "The Lure of Sin City: Las

Vegas's Nicely Naughty Image Moves Upscale," *The Grand Rapids Press,* 24 October 2004, M5.

40. Dave Palermo, "Perception Is Reality: Many Casino Company CEOs Think the Time Has Come to Craft a New Image for the Gaming Industry," *International Gaming and Wagering Business* 23, no. 2 (February 2002): 23.

41. Glenn Puit, "2001 Coroner's Statistics: Suicides in County a Record," www.reviewjournal.com/lvrj_home/2002/Mar-26-Tue-2002/news/18387136.html, accessed 19 October 2004.

42. Cooper, *Last Honest Place in America,* 71–72.

43. Brendan Riley and Michelle DeArmond, "Criminals Most Likely to Get Away with Violent Crime in Las Vegas," *The Grand Rapids Press,* 12 February 1996, D7.

44. Roy Maynard, "Against the Odds," *World* (21 October 1995): 16.

45. Eugene H. Winkler, "Betting Our Future," *Christian Social Action* (July–August 1994): 29.

46. Mark Shaffer, "Business Booming in Las Vegas," *The Grand Rapids Press,* 14 January 1996, A5; Blake and Erickson, *Las Vegas Trivia.*

47. Thompson, *Legalized Gambling,* 9–10; Johnston, *Temples of Chance,* 54.

48. Thompson, *Legalized Gambling,* 21.

49. Jenny Deam, "Dice Still Rolling for Atlantic City Residents," *The Grand Rapids Press,* 13 October 1994, A6.

50. Thompson, *Legalized Gambling,* 48–49.

51. James Popkin with Katia Hetter, "America's Gambling Craze," *U.S. News and World Report,* 14 March 1994, 46; Robert Goodman, *The Luck Business: The Devastating Consequences and Broken Promises of America's Gambling Explosion* (New York: The Free Press, 1995), 20–26.

52. "Atlantic City Still Crumbles Despite Gambling Revenues," *The Grand Rapids Press,* 8 April 1993, D16.

53. *Casino Gambling,* 32.

54. Ibid.

55. Arnie Wexler, as quoted in Ibid.

56. I. Nelson Rose, as quoted in Popkin with Hetter, "Gambling Craze," 46.

## Chapter 3: Gambling Goes Mainstream

1. "Celebrity Oddsmaker Jimmy 'the Greek' Dies," *The Grand Rapids Press*, 22 April 1996, C2; Frank Deford, "A Long Shot Takes Leave," *Newsweek*, 6 May 1996, 74.
2. I. Nelson Rose, as quoted in James Popkin with Katia Hetter, "America's Gambling Craze," *U.S. News and World Report*, 14 March 1994, 46. Cited in William N. Thompson, *Legalized Gambling: A Reference Handbook* (Santa Barbara, Calif.: ABC-CLIO, 1994), 6.
3. This section and the following section owe much to the Commission on the Review of the National Policy Toward Gambling, Charles H. Morin, Chairman, *Gambling in America: Final Report of the Commission on the Review of the National Policy Toward Gambling* (Washington, D.C.: GPO, 1976), 18–107.
4. Rufus King, *Gambling and Organized Crime* (Washington, D.C.: Public Affairs Press, 1969), 74.
5. Commission on the Review of the National Policy Toward Gambling, *Gambling in America*, 59.
6. In 1969, Canada followed suit by changing its criminal code to allow lotteries and charitable gambling (Thompson, *Legalized Gambling*, 8). America's southern neighbor, Mexico, is also flirting with expanded legalized gambling. While a national lottery, horse racing, sports betting, and cockfighting have been available for years, the Mexican Congress outlawed casino gambling in the 1930s. Most Mexicans don't want expanded legalized casinos, however. A poll in the Mexico City *Reforma* indicated that 68 percent oppose and 30 percent favor casinos. See Hayes Ferguson, "Mexico Officials Debate Legalizing Casino Gambling to Aid Economy," *The Grand Rapids Press*, 12 November 1995, A20.
7. Eugene Martin Christiansen and Will E. Cummings, "Double-Edged Growth," *International Gaming and Wagering Business Magazine* (1 August 1995): 31–32. Thompson, *Legalized Gambling*, 3.
8. Thompson, *Legalized Gambling*, 3.
9. I. Nelson Rose, "Gambling and the Law: The New Millennium," in ed. Gerda Reith, *Gambling: Who Wins? Who Loses?* (Amherst, N.Y.: Prometheus Books, 2003), 114.

10. Owen Wood, "Gambling: Risky Business," www.cbc.ca/news/background/gambling/, accessed 17 July 2004.

11. www.family.org/cforum/fosi/gambling/gitus/, accessed 19 October 2004.

12. "Gambling Addiction Near Epidemic," *The Bottom Line on Alcohol in Society* 14, no. 1 (spring 1993): 7.

13. Matthew Brown, "Gaming Industry Has No Chance in Utah," *The Grand Rapids Press*, 5 May 1996, A15.

14. Ibid.

15. Charles T. Clotfelter and Philip J. Cook, *Selling Hope: State Lotteries in America* (Cambridge: Harvard University Press, 1989), 45; Commission on the Review of the National Policy Toward Gambling, *Gambling in America*, 91; Vicki Abt, James F. Smith, and Eugene Martin Christiansen, *The Business of Risk: Commercial Gambling in Mainstream America* (Lawrence, Kans.: University Press of Kansas, 1985), 5.

16. "Many Christians Say Gambling Is OK," www.Gambling Magazine.com/managearticle.asp?c=280&a=8799, accessed 18 July 2004.

17. www.barna.org/FlexPage.aspx?Page=BarnaUpdate&BarnaUpdateID=123, accessed 18 July 2004.

18. www.barna.org/FlexPage.aspx?Page=BarnaUpdate&BarnaUpdateID=155, accessed 18 July 2004.

19. Eugene Martin Christiansen, as quoted in David Johnston, *Temples of Chance: How America Incorporated Bought Out Murder Incorporated to Win Control of the Casino Business* (New York: Doubleday, 1992), 20.

20. This section owes much to Abt, Smith, and Christiansen, *Business of Risk*, 55–67; Clotfelter and Cook, *Selling Hope*; John Samuel Ezell, *Fortune's Merry Wheel: The Lottery in America* (Cambridge: Harvard University Press, 1960).

21. Neal Lawrence, "Gambling on a New Life," *Midwest Today* 3, no. 1 (1995): 16.

22. See www.naspl/.org/rankpercap.html, accessed 19 October 2004.

23. Tom Watson Jr., *Don't Bet on It* (Ventura, Calif.: Regal Books, 1987), 25; Norman L. Geisler and Thomas A. Howe, *Gambling a Bad Bet: You Can't Win for Losing in More Ways Than You Can Imagine* (Grand Rapids: Revell, 1990), 11.

24. "Kids Gambling and Losing," 14 July 2003, www.cbsnews

.com/stories/2003/07/14/health/main563015.shtml, accessed 19 October 2004.

25. D. Kirk Davidson, *Selling Sin: The Marketing of Socially Unacceptable Products* (Westport, Conn.: Praeger, 2003), 77.

26. See www.naspl.org/history.html, accessed 19 October 2004.

27. *California v. Cabazon Band of Mission Indians,* 480 US 202 (1987).

28. As quoted in Greg Gattuso, "What's Ahead for Charity Gambling?" *Fund Raising Management,* September 1993, 21.

29. Lawrence, "New Life," 16. The number of Native American tribes keeps going up, a function of the economic opportunity some Native Americans see in the operation of gambling establishments. See www.indiangaming.org/library/index.html, accessed 20 November 2004.

30. Alan Meister, "Economic Evolution of Indian Gaming," *International Gaming and Wagering Business* 24, no. 10 (October 2003): 14–15.

31. See the National Indian Gaming Association's Web site at www .indiangaming.org, accessed 20 November 2004.

32. Carroll Bogert, "Casino Clout for Native Americans," *Newsweek,* 28 March 1994, 24.

33. "Casino Plans to Up the Ante with Expansion," *The Grand Rapids Press,* 28 May 1995, A9.

34. Tina Lam, "Indian Casinos," *Detroit Free Press,* 21 March 1996, 13A; Ted Roelofs, "Tribal War: Identity Issue Splits Chippewa," *The Grand Rapids Press,* 23 June 1996, A1.

35. Joel J. Smith and Eric Morath, "Expansion Threatens Michigan Gaming Jackpot," *The Detroit News,* 15 August 2004, www .detnews.com/2004/casinonews/0409/23/A01-242640.htm, accessed 19 October 2004.

36. Lawrence, "New Life," 16.

37. Steve Wilson, "This Indian Casino Willing to Give State a Piece of the Pie," *The Arizona Republic,* 22 January 1995, A2; "Colorado's Gambling Guide," *A Pocket Guide to Limited Stakes Gambling in Colorado,* vol. 4, no. 4, 1994.

38. Jim Nesbitt, "Betting on the Future," *The Grand Rapids Press,* 17 October 1993, A1; "Gamblers Don't Care If It Cruises," *The Grand Rapids Press,* 6 April 1995, A10.

39. Popkin with Hetter, "Gambling Craze," 43.

40. Timothy M. Ito et al., "Racing's Rough Ride," *U.S. News and World Report* (12 June 1995): 41–42; Michael B. Walker, *The Psychology of Gambling* (New York: Pergamon Press, 1992), 17.

41. Smith and Morath, "Expansion Threatens Michigan Gaming Jackpot."

42. Charlotte Olmsted, *Heads I Win; Tails You Lose* (New York: Macmillan, 1962), 230.

43. See www.greyhoundracingsucks.com/grs_statistics.htm, accessed 20 November 2004.

44. Rick Haglund, "Casinos Are Hobbling Michigan Horse Racing," *The Grand Rapids Press,* 23 October 1994, A1.

45. *Report of the Governor's Blue Ribbon Commission on Michigan Gaming,* Robert J. Danhof, Chairman (Lansing, Mich.: Michigan Court of Appeals, April 1995), 3.

46. Ito et al., "Racing's Rough Ride," 41–42; Jim Bolus, "Has Racing Missed the Boat?" *Las Vegas Style,* May 1996, 22.

47. "MRC Betting Parlor Plan Delayed by Cancellation," *The Grand Rapids Press,* 25 January 1996, B2.

48. Robert Goodman, *The Luck Business: The Devastating Consequences and Broken Promises of America's Gambling Explosion* (New York: The Free Press, 1995), 91.

49. Ito et al., "Racing's Rough Ride," 42.

50. "Dollars Pile Up as Fans Bet on Game," *USA Today,* 29 January 1996, 6C; Richard O. Davis and Richard G. Abram, "Sports Betting: The American Pastime," in *Gambling: Examining Pop Culture,* ed. James Haley (San Diego: Greenhaven Press, 2004), 132.

51. Richard O. Davis and Richard G. Abram, "Sports Betting: The American Pastime," in *Gambling: Examining Pop Culture,* ed. James Haley (San Diego: Greenhaven Press, 2004), 132.

52. Benjamin Blake and Hannah Erickson, *Amazing Las Vegas Trivia* (Las Vegas: Las Vegas Trivia, 1994), 12.

53. John Lyman Mason and Michael Nelson, *Governing Gambling* (New York: Century Foundation Press, 2001), 87.

54. Neil David Isaacs, *You Bet Your Life: The Burdens of Gambling* (Lexington, Ky.: University Press of Kentucky, 2001), 3.

55. Walter Byers, as quoted in "Forum on Gambling Looks at Newspapers," *The Grand Rapids Press,* 1 April 1995, C6.

56. NCAA, "Rules and Bylaws," www2.ncaa.org/legislation_and_

governance/ rules_and_bylaws/ (accessed March 2, 2005).

57. "Task Force Named to Confront Gambling Threat," *The NCAA News,* 24 May 2004, www.ncaa.org/news/2004/20040524/active/ 4111n01.html, accessed 19 October 2004.

58. Myles Brand, as quoted in "NCAA Study Finds Sports Wagering a Problem Among Student-Athletes," 12 May 2004, www.ncaa .org/releases/research/2004/2004051201re.htm, accessed 19 October 2004.

59. "Initial Findings from the NCAA National Study on Collegiate Sports Wagering and Associated Behaviors," 12 May 2004, www .ncaa.org/gambling/2003NationalStudy/slideshow/, accessed 19 October 2004.

60. Myles Brand, as quoted in Malcolm Moran, "Gambling Survey Reveals 'Risk Is Real,' NCAA Leader Says," *USA Today,* 15 May 2004, 1C. Cited in John Lyman Mason and Michael Nelson, *Governing Gambling* (New York: Century Foundation Press, 2001), 88.

61. "Most College Game Officials Gamble," *The Grand Rapids Press,* 30 March 2000, D2.

62. "Gambling Industry, Colleges Point Fingers," *The Grand Rapids Press,* 30 March 2000, D2.

63. Erik Christianson, "NCAA Sports Wagering Task Force and AFCA Partner on 'Don't Bet On It' Campaign," 27 October 2004, http://www2.ncaa.org/media_and_events/press_ room/2004/october/20041027_dont_bet_on_it.html (accessed March 2, 2005); Gail Dent, "NCAA, NABC and WBCA Partner on National 'Don't Bet on It' Campaign," 23 February 2005, http://www2.ncaa.org/media_and_events/press_room/2005/ february/20050223_dontbetonitreleasebkb.html (accessed March 2, 2005).

64. Christiansen and Cummings, "Double-Edged Growth," 31–32; Glenn Puit, "2001 Coroner's Statistics: Suicides in County a Record," www.reviewjournal.com/lvrj_home/2002/mar-26-the -2002/news/18387136.html, accessed 19 October 2004.

65. Lark Ellen Gould, "Statistics Show First-Time Visitors Are Fair Game," *Las Vegas/Travel Agent,* 4 March 1996, 2.

66. Johnston, *Temples of Chance,* 12.

67. John L. Smith, *Running Scared: The Life and Treacherous Times*

*of Las Vegas Casino King Steve Wynn* (New York: Barricade Books, 1995).

68. Dennis Tanner, "St-I-I-I-LL Growing," *The Grand Rapids Press*, 4 February 1996, I1; Richard Corliss, "Just What VEGAS Needed," *Time*, 6 May 1996, 75.

69. Frank Rich, "America on Big Bender with Gaming," *Las Vegas Sun*, 10 May 1996, 15B.

70. Blake and Erickson, *Las Vegas Trivia*.

71. Ibid.

72. Tanner, "St-I-I-I-LL Growing," I2.

73. Ibid.

74. Ibid.

75. Christiansen and Cummings, "Double-Edged Growth," 38.

76. As cited in Mark Shaffer, "Business Booming in Las Vegas," *The Grand Rapids Press*, 14 January 1996, A5.

77. James Haley, ed., *Gambling: Examining Pop Culture* (San Diego: Greenhaven Press, 2004), 107–8; see also www.insidervlv.com/visitorstatistics1.html, accessed 19 October 2004; Marc Cooper, *The Last Honest Place in America: Paradise and Perdition in the New Las Vegas* (New York: Nation Books, 2004), 14.

78. See www.unlv.edu/research_centers/cber/tour.html/, accessed 19 October 2004.

79. See www.insidervlv.com/visitorstatistics1.html, accessed 19 October 2004.

80. Haley, *Gambling*, 108; Cooper, *Last Honest Place in America*, 73–74.

81. Chris Woodyard, "MGM Mirage Plans Hotel-Condo Complex That Would Be Las Vegas 'Hub,'" *USA Today*, 11 November 2004, 3B.

82. Abt, Smith, and Christiansen, *Business of Risk*, 99; Joseph P. Shapiro, "America's Gambling Fever," *U.S. News and World Report*, 15 January 1996, 61.

83. Frank Fahrenkopf, as quoted in Christiansen and Cummings, "Double-Edged Growth."

84. Johnston, *Temples of Chance*, 49.

85. Ibid., 9–10, 12–13.

86. Cooper, *Last Honest Place in America*, 43–44; D. Kirk Davidson, *Selling Sin: The Marketing of Socially Unacceptable Products* (Westport, Conn.: Praeger, 2003), 73.

87. As quoted in Ibid., 9.
88. Gary Rivlin, "The Tug of the Newfangled Slot Machines," The New York Times, 9 May 2004, http://www.nytimes .com/2004/05/09/magazine/09SLOTS .html?ex=1114574400 &en=1719e31141e72f24&ei=5070 (accessed November 19, 2004).
89. "Slot Machines Are Most Addictive Form of Gambling," www .pastors.com/article.asp?ArtID=7429, accessed 19 October 2004.
90. Thompson, *Legalized Gambling*, 11.
91. Shapiro, "Gambling Fever," 61.
92. Abt, Smith, and Christiansen, *Business of Risk.*

## Chapter 4: God, Games, and the Good Life

1. The quote is genuine and reflects the experience of a friend.
2. John Samuel Ezell, *Fortune's Merry Wheel: The Lottery in America* (Cambridge: Harvard University Press, 1960), 17–18; David Neff and Thomas Giles, "Feeding the Monster Called 'More,'" *Christianity Today* (25 November 1991): 18; Lycurgus M. Starkey Jr., *Money, Mania and Morals: The Churches and Gambling* (Nashville: Abingdon Press, 1964), 35–38.
3. Henry Chafetz, *Play the Devil: A History of Gambling in the United States from 1492 to 1955* (New York: Potter Publishers, 1960), 21; Commission on the Review of the National Policy Toward Gambling, Charles H. Morin, Chairman, *Gambling in America: Final Report of the Commission on the Review of the National Policy Toward Gambling* (Washington, D.C.: GPO, 1976), 1–40.
4. *New Catholic Encyclopedia*, s.v. "gambling"; and as quoted in William N. Thompson, *Legalized Gambling: A Reference Handbook* (Santa Barbara, Calif.: ABC-CLIO, 1994), 31.
5. *Catechism of the Catholic Church* (Washington, D.C.: United States Catholic Conference, Liberia Editrice Vaticana, 1994), 580; and as quoted in Michigan Catholic Conference, "Betting on the Future: Gambling Issue Raises Many Difficult Questions," *Focus* 23, no. 2 (June 1995): 1–2.
6. Thompson, *Legalized Gambling*, 32.
7. Michigan Catholic Conference, "Betting on the Future," 2 (italics in original).

8. As quoted in Tom Watson Jr., *Don't Bet on It* (Ventura, Calif.: Regal Books, 1987), 241.

9. This paragraph and the following section owe much to Raymond C. Bell, "Moral Views on Gambling Promulgated by Major American Religious Bodies," in *Gambling in America*, by Commission on the Review of the National Policy Toward Gambling, 161–240.

10. As quoted in Ibid., 169.

11. "Gambling and Christian Faith: A New Look at an Old Dilemma," www.2preslex.org/gambling.htm, accessed 18 July 2004; "A Seventh Day Adventist Statement on Gambling," www .Adventist.org/beliefs/statements/main_stat49.html, accessed 18 July 2004; "Assemblies of God Beliefs," www.ag.org/top/beliefs/ Christian_character/charctr_12_gambling.cfm, accessed 18 July 2004.

12. Lee Ranck, "A Menace to Society . . . Destructive of Good Government," *Christian Social Action* 7, no. 7 (July–August 1994): 2.

13. The paragraphs that follow draw on excellent research in *Gambling in America*, by Commission on the Review of the National Policy Toward Gambling.

14. Bell, "Moral Views," 186.

15. "Gambling—1985," resolution adopted by the National Association of Evangelicals, Carol Stream, Illinois, 6 March 1985; Bell, "Moral Views," 189.

16. James Hastings, ed., *Encyclopedia of Religion and Ethics* (Edinburgh: T and T Clark, 1913), 244.

17. Cotton Mather, as quoted in Chafetz, *Play the Devil*, 14.

18. R. H. Charles, *Gambling and Betting: A Study Dealing with Their Origins and Their Relation to Morality and Religion* (Edinburgh: T and T Clark, 1924), 61.

19. Ibid., 52–53.

20. Hastings, *Religion and Ethics*, 163.

21. Fyodor Dostoyevsky, *The Gambler*, trans. Victor Terras (Chicago: University of Chicago Press, 1972).

22. Stephen Katz, *Gambling Facts and Fiction: The Anti-Gambling Handbook to Get Yourself to Stop Gambling, Quit Gambling, or Never Start Gambling* (Bloomington, Ind.: AuthorHouse, 2004), 5.

23. Robert D. Herman, ed., *Gambling* (New York: Harper and Row,

1967), 227.

24. Larry Braidfoot, *Gambling: A Deadly Game* (Nashville: Broadman Press, 1985), 182.

25. Starkey, *Money, Mania and Morals,* 112.

26. Eugene Martin Christiansen and Will E. Cummings, "Double-Edged Growth," *International Gaming and Wagering Business Magazine,* 1 August 1995, 40.

27. Vicki Abt, James F. Smith, and Eugene Martin Christiansen, *The Business of Risk: Commercial Gambling in Mainstream America* (Lawrence, Kans.: University Press of Kansas, 1985), 216.

28. George Brushaber, "You Bet, We Lose," *Christianity Today* (7 February 1994): 17.

29. Ross Coggins, *The Gambling Menace* (Nashville: Broadman Press, 1966), 102.

30. Ibid., 95; Charles, *Gambling and Betting,* 51.

31. Coggins, *Gambling Menace,* 57–58.

32. D. James Kennedy, ed., *Gambling: America's Hidden Addiction* (Fort Lauderdale: Coral Ridge Ministries Media, 1995), 6, 14.

33. William Temple as quoted in Starkey, *Money, Mania and Morals,* 103–4.

34. Francis Emmett Williams, *Lotteries, Law, and Morals* (New York: Vantage Press, 1958), 76.

35. Watson, *Don't Bet on It,* 62.

36. Rex M. Rogers, *Christian Liberty: Living for God in a Changing Culture* (Grand Rapids: Baker, 2003).

37. Blaise Pascal, as quoted in Starkey, *Money, Mania and Morals,* 27.

38. Tertullian, as quoted in Hastings, *Religion and Ethics,* 164; E. Benson Perkins, *Gambling in English Life* (London: Epworth Press, 1950), 8.

39. Rex M. Rogers, "Everyone Loses at Gambling," *The West Michigan Christian,* May 2002, 6.

40. Stanley Hauerwas, as quoted in Neff and Giles, "Feeding the Monster," 20.

## Chapter 5: Government's Wheels of Fortune

1. Mark Twain, as quoted in Norman L. Geisler and Thomas A. Howe, *Gambling a Bad Bet: You Can't Win for Losing in More Ways Than You Can Imagine* (Grand Rapids: Revell, 1990), 73.

2. Quoted in "A $pecial Issue on Gambling," *Christian Social Action,* July–August 1994, 6.

3. Eugene Martin Christiansen and Will E. Cummings, "Double-Edged Growth," *International Gaming and Wagering Business Magazine,* 1 August 1995, 31–32.

4. "Tax Payments," www.americangaming.org/industry/factsheets/general_info_detail.cfv?id=10, accessed 20 November 2004.

5. "FY02 & FY03 Sales and Profit," www.naspl.org/sales&profits.html, accessed 19 October 2004.

6. Joel J. Smith and Eric Morath, "Expansion Threatens Michigan Gaming Jackpot," *The Detroit News,* 15 August 2004, www.detnews.com/2004/casinonews/0409/23/a01-242640.htm, accessed 19 October 2004.

7. Adam Tanner, "California Governor Fights Indian Casino Expansion," http://wireservice.wired.com/wired/story.asp?section=Breaking&storyID+936677&tw=wn_wire_story, accessed 19 October 2004.

8. James M. Wall, "Unbinding the Devil in Georgia," *Christian Century,* 21–28 November 1990, 1083; Chris Welles, "America's Gambling Fever," *Business Week,* 24 April 1989, 114.

9. Robert Goodman, *The Luck Business: The Devastating Consequences and Broken Promises of America's Gambling Explosion* (New York: The Free Press, 1995), x.

10. Ibid., 59.

11. Ibid., 144.

12. Commission on the Review of the National Policy Toward Gambling, Charles H. Morin, Chairman, *Gambling in America: Final Report of the Commission on the Review of the National Policy Toward Gambling* (Washington, D.C.: GPO, 1976), 74.

13. Benjamin Blake and Hannah Erickson, *Amazing Las Vegas Trivia* (Las Vegas: Las Vegas Trivia, 1994).

14. Goodman, *Luck Business,* 88–90.

15. Ibid., xii.

16. William Safire, "Gambling Offers No Payoff to Society," *The Grand Rapids Press,* 11 April 1995, A15.

17. I. Nelson Rose, "Gambling and the Law: Endless Fields of Dreams," *Christian Social Action,* July–August 1994, 6.

18. David Johnston, *Temples of Chance: How America Incorporated Bought Out Murder Incorporated to Win Control of the Casino*

*Business* (New York: Doubleday, 1992), 18–19; Goodman, *Luck Business*, 20.

19. Quoted in Margot Hornblower, "No Dice: The Backlash Against Gambling," *Time*, 1 April 1996, 32. See also Earl Grinols, "Four Economic Fundamentals of Gambling," *Christian Social Action*, July–August 1994, 11.

20. Goodman, *Luck Business*, 26–32.

21. Rex M. Rogers, "Gambling Driven by Bankrupt Principles," *The Grand Rapids Press*, 10 February 2001, A11.

22. Ron French, "Gambling Bankruptcies Soar," *The Detroit News*, 3 December 1995, 1A.

23. *Report of the Governor's Blue Ribbon Commission on Michigan Gaming*, Robert J. Danhof, Chairman (Lansing, Mich.: Michigan Court of Appeals, April 1995), 16.

24. William N. Thompson, *Legalized Gambling: A Reference Handbook* (Santa Barbara, Calif.: ABC-CLIO, 1994), 42–43.

25. For a discussion of the revenue potential of state lotteries, see David Weinstein and Lillian Deitch, *The Impact of Legalized Gambling: The Socioeconomic Consequences of Lotteries and Off-Course Betting* (New York: Praeger, 1974), 3.

26. Thompson, *Legalized Gambling*, 43.

27. Charles T. Clotfelter and Philip J. Cook, *Selling Hope: State Lotteries in America* (Cambridge: Harvard University Press, 1989), 167–68.

28. Thompson, *Legalized Gambling*, 44.

29. William Thompson, as quoted in James Sterngold, "Are Casinos a Gamble Worth Taking?" *The Grand Rapids Press*, 3 December 1995, A3.

30. Thompson, *Legalized Gambling*, 43.

31. Ibid., 45.

32. Safire, "No Payoff," A15.

33. John Warren Kindt, as cited in Sterngold, "Gamble Worth Taking?" A3. Cited in Joseph P. Shapiro, "America's Gambling Fever," *U.S. News and World Report*, 15 January 1996, 55.

34. Christiansen and Cummings, "Double-Edged Growth," 31–32.

35. Thompson, *Legalized Gambling*, 46.

36. Shapiro, "Gambling Fever," 56.

37. Commission on the Review of the National Policy Toward Gambling, *Gambling in America*, 51–63.

38. Robert F. Kennedy, "The Baleful Influence of Gambling," in *Gambling*, ed. Robert D. Herman (New York: Harper and Row, 1967), 169.

39. Commission on the Review of the National Policy Toward Gambling, *Gambling in America*, 63.

40. Vicki Abt, James F. Smith, and Eugene Martin Christiansen, *The Business of Risk: Commercial Gambling in Mainstream America* (Lawrence, Kans.: University Press of Kansas, 1985), 28; Commission on the Review of the National Policy Toward Gambling, *Gambling in America*.

41. Richard Thompson, as quoted in "Christian Coalition Antes with Anti-Casino Petitions," *The Grand Rapids Press*, 27 June 1995, A9.

42. Parris N. Glendenning, as quoted in Greg Gattuso, "What's Ahead for Charity Gambling?" *Fund Raising Management*, September 1993, 6, 24.

43. David Johnston, "The Dark Side of Charity Gambling," *Money*, October 1993, 133.

44. Ibid., 134–35.

45. Clotfelter and Cook, *Selling Hope*, 132.

46. Thompson, *Legalized Gambling*, 52.

47. Neal Lawrence, "Gambling on a New Life," *Midwest Today* 3, no. 1 (1995): 16.

48. Ibid.; Levi A. Rickert, "Indian Gaming Poses No Great Threat," *The Grand Rapids Press*, 8 December 1996, A19.

49. Lawrence, "New Life," 16.

50. "Indian Gaming Facts," www.indiangaming.org/library/index .html, accessed 20 November 2004.

51. Sandra Ann Harris, "Indians Bet Casinos' Future on Gambling School," *The Grand Rapids Press*, 24 September 1995, A6.

52. Donald L. Barlett and James B. Steele, "Wheel of Misfortune," *Time*, 16 December 2002, 47.

53. Ibid., 48.

54. Donald L. Barlett and James B. Steele, "Who Gets the Money?" *Time*, 16 December 2002, 49.

55. Harris, "Indians Bet Casinos' Future on Gambling School," A6.

56. Ted Roelofs, "Tribal War: Identity Issue Splits Chippewa," *The Grand Rapids Press*, 23 June 1996, A1; "Tribe Cuts Off Shares

in Casino Action to 484 Members," *The Grand Rapids Press*, 13 June 1996, B4.

57. D. Kirk Davidson, *Selling Sin: The Marketing of Socially Unacceptable Products* (Westport, Conn.: Praeger, 2003), 74.

58. As quoted in Brett Duval Fromson, *Hitting the Jackpot: The Inside Story of the Richest Indian Tribe in History* (New York: Atlantic Monthly Press, 2003), 221, 223.

59. Ibid., 161–67, 211–16.

60. "Casinos Will Mean Jobs, Gambling Panel Is Told," *The Grand Rapids Press*, 23 February 1995, C5; Richard Grimes, "The Odds Are Against Phone Bets," *Charleston Daily Mail*, 6 June 1995, 6A.

61. Gattuso, "Charity Gambling," 21–22.

62. Roy Romer, as quoted in Ibid., 22.

63. See, for example, David Yeagley, "Liberals Gamble Away Indians' Future," 17 May 2004, www.frontpagemag.com/articles/readarticle.asp?id=13399, accessed 19 October 2004.

64. Ibid., 24. Leon Shenandoah, leader of the Onondaga Indians and the spiritual steward of the Six Nations of the Iroquois Confederacy, who died in July 1996, spoke out against his people's involvement in gambling ventures, "N.Y. Indian Tribe Leader," *The Grand Rapids Press*, 23 July 1996, C10.

65. Linda Kanamine, "Tribal Windfall Fulfills Dream, Creates Strife," *USA Today*, 13–15 May 1994, 1A.

66. Sandra Sanchez, "Clash Over Casinos Could Close Highways," *USA Today*, 5 January 1996, 3A.

67. "Casinos Will Mean Jobs, Gambling Panel Is Told," C5; "Right Bet for Future," *The Grand Rapids Press*, 22 March 1996, A12.

68. I. Nelson Rose, as cited in James Popkin with Katia Hetter, "America's Gambling Craze," *U.S. News and World Report*, 14 March 1994, 46.

69. Goodman, *Luck Business*, 81; Dave DeWitte, "Gaming Industry Hits Few Jackpots as Casino Openings Stumble in '94," *The Grand Rapids Press*, 10 July 1994, D5; William Petroski, "Foes Aim to Sink Casino Boat," *The Des Moines Register*, 10 February 1995, 1A; Hornblower, "No Dice," 33; William Safire, "Voters Bet on Morality over Gambling," *The Grand Rapids Press*, 25 November 1996, A9.

70. John Warren Kindt, "The Negative Impacts of Legalized

Gambling on Businesses," *Business Law Journal* 4, no. 2 (spring
1994): 93–124.

71.  "The Right Call on Gambling," *The Grand Rapids Press*, 29 June
1995, A20.

## Chapter 6: To Gamble or Not to Gamble

1.  This story is true and comes from a Michigan community.
2.  James Popkin with Katia Hetter, "America's Gambling Craze,"
*U.S. News and World Report*, 14 March 1994, 42.
3.  Commission on the Review of the National Policy Toward
Gambling, Charles H. Morin, Chairman, *Gambling in America:
Final Report of the Commission on the Review of the National
Policy Toward Gambling* (Washington, D.C.: GPO, 1976), 69–70.
4.  Vicki Abt, James F. Smith, and Eugene Martin Christiansen, *The
Business of Risk: Commercial Gambling in Mainstream America*
(Lawrence, Kans.: University Press of Kansas, 1985), 158–59.
5.  Charles T. Clotfelter and Philip J. Cook, *Selling Hope: State
Lotteries in America* (Cambridge: Harvard University Press,
1989), 121–22; Evan Moore, "Lotto Win Is Bad News for Two
'Good Friends,'" *The Grand Rapids Press*, 5 May 1996, A7.
6.  Clotfelter and Cook, *Selling Hope*, 70.
7.  Quoted in David D. Allen, *The Nature of Gambling* (New York:
Coward-McCann, 1952), 13.
8.  David Weinstein and Lillian Deitch, *The Impact of Legalized
Gambling: The Socioeconomic Consequences of Lotteries and Off-
Course Betting* (New York: Praeger, 1974), 7.
9.  Abt, Smith, and Christiansen, *Business of Risk*, 66.
10.  Linda Chavez, "There's No Future in Lady Luck," *USA Today*,
13 September 1995, 11A; George Will, "Life's a Gamble, Rise in
'Gaming' Is Sad," *The Grand Rapids Press*, 4 January 1996, A11.
11.  Robert Goodman, *The Luck Business: The Devastating
Consequences and Broken Promises of America's Gambling
Explosion* (New York: The Free Press, 1995), 135.
12.  Valerie Lorenz, as quoted in Ricardo Chavira, "The Rise of
Teenage Gambling," *Time*, 25 February 1991, 78; Rufus King,
*Gambling and Organized Crime* (Washington, D.C.: Public
Affairs Press, 1969), 11, 74; Chris Welles, "America's Gambling
Fever," *Business Week*, 24 April 1989, 113.
13.  Weinstein and Deitch, *Legalized Gambling*, 3; "Compulsive

Gambling: Addiction of Choice for the 90's?" *The Bottom Line on Alcohol in Society* 2, no. 4 (1991): 8.

14. Quoted in Mark Clapson, *A Bit of a Flutter: Popular Gambling and English Society, 1823–1961* (Manchester, England: Manchester University Press, 1992), viii.

15. "Gambling Addiction Near Epidemic," *The Bottom Line on Alcohol in Society* 14, no. 1 (spring 1993): 27.

16. *Casino Gambling: The Myth and the Reality* (Lansing, Mich.: Michigan Interfaith Council on Alcohol Problems, 1988), 9; Abt, Smith, and Christiansen, *Business of Risk*, 76–77.

17. Phil Satre, as quoted in "Gambling Addiction Near Epidemic," 11.

18. Charlotte Olmsted, *Heads I Win; Tails You Lose* (New York: Macmillan, 1962), 3.

19. Lycurgus M. Starkey Jr., *Money, Mania and Morals: The Churches and Gambling* (Nashville: Abingdon Press, 1964), 105.

20. Norman L. Geisler and Thomas A. Howe, *Gambling a Bad Bet: You Can't Win for Losing in More Ways Than You Can Imagine* (Grand Rapids: Revell, 1990), 65–66.

21. *Casino Gambling.*

22. Virgil W. Peterson, "Legalization Solves Nothing," quoted in *Gambling in America,* by Commission on the Review of the National Policy Toward Gambling, 55.

23. James Hastings, ed., *Encyclopedia of Religion and Ethics* (Edinburgh: T and T Clark, 1913), 166.

24. Clotfelter and Cook, *Selling Hope,* 133; Abt, Smith, and Christiansen, *Business of Risk,* 198–99.

25. Abt, Smith, and Christiansen, *Business of Risk,* 22.

26. As quoted in Goodman, *Luck Business,* 145.

27. Clotfelter and Cook, *Selling Hope,* 244.

28. Olmsted, *Heads I Win,* 252.

## Chapter 7: Charity Gambling Strikes It Rich

1. This story is fictitious, but it is based on countless stories similar to the ones found in William C. Lhotka, "B-4 the Fall: Casinos Drive Church Bingo from Paradise," *The Grand Rapids Press,* 20 May 1996, A2.

2. David Johnston, "The Dark Side of Charity Gambling," *Money,* October 1993, 130.

3. Eugene Martin Christiansen and Will E. Cummings, "Double-

Edged Growth," *International Gaming and Wagering Business Magazine*, 1 August 1995, 31–32.

4. Sarah Schweitzer, "The Decline of Charity Bingo," in *Gambling: Examining Pop Culture*, ed. James Haley (San Diego: Greenhaven Press, 2004), 147–48.

5. "2003 Gross Annual Wager of the United States" from Christiansen Capital Advisors LLC, www.cca-i.com/ primary%20navigation/online%20data%20store/ free%20research/2003%20revenue%20by%20industry.pdf, accessed 20 November 2004.

6. Robyn Taylor Parets, "Refreshing a Classic," *International Gaming and Wagering Business* 22, no. 8 (20 August 2001): 25.

7. Johnston, "Dark Side"; Greg Gattuso, "What's Ahead for Charity Gambling?" *Fund Raising Management*, September 1993, 20.

8. Gattuso, "Charity Gambling," 20; "Gambling in Maryland a Private Matter Between Player and Charity," *The Grand Rapids Press*, 24 December 1994, D6.

9. Gattuso, "Charity Gambling," 20; *Report of the Governor's Blue Ribbon Commission on Michigan Gaming*, Robert J. Danhof, Chairman (Lansing, Mich.: Michigan Court of Appeals, April 1995), 44.

10. Johnston, "Dark Side," 130.

11. "Donations to Charities Up More Than 10%," *The Grand Rapids Press*, 22 May 1996, A14.

12. "2002 Annual Report on Charitable Gaming in North America," www.naftm.org/, accessed 20 November 2004.

13. "Out of Control Bingo Needs Tough Cop," *The Virginia-Pilot*, 9 August 2004, www.home.hamptonroads.com/stories/story .cfm?story=74047&ran=41505, accessed 19 October 2004.

14. Christiansen and Cummings, "Double-Edged Growth," 31–32.

15. George Will, "Life's a Gamble, Rise in 'Gaming' Is Sad," *The Grand Rapids Press*, 4 January 1996, A11.

16. Charles T. Clotfelter and Philip J. Cook, *Selling Hope: State Lotteries in America* (Cambridge: Harvard University Press, 1989), 40–41; Gattuso, "Charity Gambling," 20.

17. John L. Smith, *Running Scared: The Life and Treacherous Times of Las Vegas Casino King Steve Wynn* (New York: Barricade Books, 1995), 32.

18. Arnie Wexler, as quoted in James Popkin with Katia Hetter,

"America's Gambling Craze," *U.S. News and World Report,* 14 March 1994, 46.

19. David Briggs, "Church Activists Want Legalized Gambling to Fold," *The Grand Rapids Press,* 6 August 1994, B4.

20. Ross Coggins, ed., *The Gambling Menace* (Nashville: Broadman Press, 1966), 101.

21. David L. McKenna, "Gambling: Parasite on Public Morals," *Christianity Today,* 8 June 1973, 4.

22. Robert D. Herman, ed., *Gambling* (New York: Harper and Row, 1967), 229.

23. McKenna, "Gambling," 6.

24. Larry Burkett, "A Principle under Scrutiny: Gambling," *How to Manage Your Money* (Gainesville, Ga.: Christian Financial Concepts, n.d.), 2. See also Larry Burkett's booklet, *The Truth About . . . Gambling and Lotteries* (Gainesville, Ga.: Christian Financial Concepts, 1996), 18.

25. Stephen Katz, *Gambling Facts and Fictions: The Anti-Gambling Handbook to Get Yourself to Stop Gambling, Quit Gambling, or Never Start Gambling* (Bloomington, Ind.: AuthorHouse, 2004), 71–72.

26. "England," *National and International Religion Report* 10, no. 8 (1 April 1996): 7.

27. *Blue Ribbon Commission,* 13; Michigan Catholic Conference, "Betting on the Future: Gambling Issue Raises Many Difficult Questions," *Focus* 23, no. 2 (June 1995): 3.

28. *California v. Cabazon Band of Mission Indians,* 480 US 202 (1987); Gattuso, "Charity Gambling," 23.

29. Gattuso, "Charity Gambling," 6.

**Chapter 8: Tarnished Glitter**

1. "Rose Takes Chance with Confession," USA Today, 7 January 2004, 9C; "Fear of Gambling Goes Way Back in Baseball," USA Today, 7 January 2004, 9C; D. Kirk Davidson, Selling Sin: The Marketing of Socially Unacceptable Products, (Westport, Conn.: Praeger, 2003) 79-80; David Weinstein and Lillian Deitch, The Impact of Legalized Gambling: The Socioeconomic Consequences of Lotteries and Off-Course Betting (New York: Praeger, 1974), 88; Mark Starr, "The Gambling Man," Newsweek, 14 June 1993, 72; "Liquor, Gambling Clip Ex-Eagles Owner's

Wings," The Arizona Republic, 16 March 1996, A6.

2. Durand Jacobs, as quoted in Pam Schmid, "Gambling Habit Proves Addicting to Growing Number of Teen-Agers," *The Grand Rapids Press*, 9 January 1994, A5.

3. Harold Voorhees, as quoted in Ed Golder, "Bill Aims to Chill Lotto Fever," *The Grand Rapids Press*, 31 March 1996, A1.

4. Charlotte Olmsted, *Heads I Win; Tails You Lose* (New York: Macmillan, 1962), 70.

5. See also "Types of Gamblers" and "The Three Phases of Problem Gambling," www.ca\problemgambling.org/, accessed 19 October 2004.

6. Lyn Barrow, as quoted in Commission on the Review of the National Policy Toward Gambling, Charles H. Morin, Chairman, *Gambling in America: Final Report of the Commission on the Review of the National Policy Toward Gambling* (Washington, D.C.: GPO, 1976), 95–96.

7. Ibid.

8. Norman L. Geisler and Thomas A. Howe, *Gambling a Bad Bet: You Can't Win for Losing in More Ways Than You Can Imagine* (Grand Rapids: Revell, 1990), 81–84.

9. *Report of the Governor's Blue Ribbon Commission on Michigan Gaming*, Robert J. Danhof, Chairman (Lansing, Mich.: Michigan Court of Appeals, April 1995), 16.

10. John M. Barron, Michael E. Staten, and Stephanie M. Wilhusen, "The Impact of Casino Gambling on Personal Bankruptcy Filing Rates" 18 August 2000, www.msb.edu/prog/crc/pdf/wp63.pdf, accessed 15 October 2004.

11. Stuart Winston and Harriet Harris, *Nation of Gamblers: America's Billion Dollar a Day Habit* (Englewood Cliffs, N.J.: Prentice-Hall, 1984), 5; "Compulsive Gambling: Disease or Moral Weakness?" *The Bottom Line on Alcohol in Society* 14, no. 1 (spring 1993): 19; "Half the Story on Gambling," *The Grand Rapids Press*, 3 March 1995, A12.

12. As quoted in Joseph P. Shapiro, "America's Gambling Fever," *U.S. News and World Report*, 15 January 1996, 59.

13. Geisler and Howe, *Bad Bet*, 37.

14. Robert Goodman, *The Luck Business: The Devastating Consequences and Broken Promises of America's Gambling Explosion* (New York: The Free Press, 1995), 50–51.

15. "Twenty Questions," www.gamblersanonymous.org/20questions
    .html, accessed 19 October 2004.

16. Stephen Katz, *Gambling Facts and Fictions: The Anti-Gambling
    Handbook to Get Yourself to Stop Gambling, Quit Gambling,
    or Never Start Gambling* (Bloomington, Ind.: AuthorHouse,
    2004), 23.

17. Margot Hornblower, "East St. Louis Places Its Bet," *Time,* 1 April
    1996, 33.

18. Geisler and Howe, *Bad Bet,* 37.

19. As cited in Shapiro, "Gambling Fever," 59.

20. "Gamblers' Families Lament Losing Side," *The Grand Rapids
    Press,* 23 March 1995, A14; Olmsted, *Heads I Win,* 185–93;
    Geisler and Howe, *Bad Bet,* 35.

21. Charles T. Clotfelter and Philip J. Cook, *Selling Hope: State
    Lotteries in America* (Cambridge: Harvard University Press,
    1989), 87.

22. Henry R. Lesieur, *The Chase: Career of the Compulsive Gambler*
    (Cambridge, Mass.: Schenkman, 1984).

23. Ibid., 23, 194.

24. Paul R. Ashe, as quoted in Patty Ryan, "Beaten by the Odds,"
    *Tampa Tribune,* 31 January 1993, 1.

25. Vicki Abt, James F. Smith, and Eugene Martin Christiansen, *The
    Business of Risk: Gambling in Mainstream America* (Lawrence,
    Kans.: University Press of Kansas, 1985), 85–86.

26. I. Nelson Rose, as quoted in J. Taylor Buckley, "Nation Raising
    Generation of Gamblers," *USA Today,* 5 April 1995, 4D; Ryan,
    "Beaten by the Odds," 15.

27. "Wider Legalized Gambling Can Be Another Lousy Bet," *USA
    Today,* 2 April 1992, 8A; "Teen Gambling: Hidden Habit, Public
    Problem," *USA Today,* 5 April 1995, 8A.

28. George Will, "Country Gambling with Its Future," *The Grand
    Rapids Press,* 8 February 1993, A15.

29. Jeffrey J. Derevensky and Rina Gupta, eds., *Gambling Problems
    in Youth: Theoretical and Applied Perspectives* (New York: Kluwer
    Academic Publishers, 2004), 232–33.

30. Earl L. Grinols, *Gambling in America: Costs and Benefits*
    (Cambridge, U.K.: Cambridge University Press, 2004), 139.

31. Stephen Katz, *Gambling Facts and Fictions: The Anti-Gambling
    Handbook to Get Yourself to Stop Gambling, Quit Gambling, or*

*Never Start Gambling* (Bloomington, Ind.: AuthorHouse, 2004), 3, 16, 26.

32. *Blue Ribbon Commission,* 67; Henry R. Lesieur, "Compulsive Gambling," *Society* 29 (May–June 1992): 43.
33. Lesieur, *The Chase,* 239; idem, "Compulsive Gambling," 46.
34. Joanna Franklin, as quoted in Lesieur, "Compulsive Gambling," 47.
35. *Blue Ribbon Commission,* 2.
36. Michael J. Stoil, "Gambling Addiction: The Nation's Dirty Little Secret," *Behavioral Health Management* (July–August 1994): 36; Neal Lawrence, "Gambling on a New Life," *Midwest Today* 3, no. 1 (1995): 18–19.
37. William N. Thompson, *Legalized Gambling: A Reference Handbook* (Santa Barbara, Calif.: ABC-CLIO, 1994), 58.
38. Fyodor Dostoyevsky, *The Gambler,* trans. Victor Terras (Chicago: University of Chicago Press, 1972).
39. Lesieur, *The Chase,* 242; Gerda Reith, ed., *Gambling: Who Wins? Who Loses?* (Amherst, N.Y.: Prometheus Books, 2003), 20.
40. Ibid., 242–43.
41. Ibid., 246–47.
42. Quoted in Barbara Deane, "Women and Gambling: Risking It All," *Woman's Day,* 1 February 1996, 44.
43. "Gambling Addiction Near Epidemic," *The Bottom Line on Alcohol in Society* 14, no. 1 (spring 1994): 19; Joseph Ciarrocchi, "Pathological Gambling and Pastoral Counseling," in *Clinical Handbook of Pastoral Counseling,* ed. Robert J. Wicks and Richard D. Parsons (New York: Integration Books, Paulist Press, 1993), 2:594; Lesieur, *The Chase,* 44.
44. "Gambling Addiction Near Epidemic," 43.
45. As cited in Ciarrocchi, "Pathological Gambling," 595–99.
46. As cited in Tom Watson Jr., *Don't Bet on It* (Ventura, Calif.: Regal Books, 1987), 228.
47. The last two paragraphs are from Thompson, *Legalized Gambling,* 55.
48. Valerie Lorenz, as quoted in Stoil, "Gambling Addiction," 37.
49. Eugene Martin Christiansen and Will E. Cummings, "Double-Edged Growth," *International Gaming and Wagering Business Magazine* (1 August 1995): 31–32.
50. Ciarrocchi, "Pathological Gambling," 604–9.

51. Deane, "Women and Gambling," 45.
52. "Gambling Addiction Near Epidemic," 41–46.
53. One city press is beginning to recognize the problem. The "Casino Guide Home Page" of the *Detroit News* offered these tips for what it called "money management advice":
    1. Set a limit—and don't spend more. This is the cardinal rule of gambling for entertainment. When you lose your set amount, stop. Leave if you can't bear to watch others gamble.
    2. Quit while you're ahead. This is tough, but it's what the pros do. Pick a sum, such as the amount of money you're willing to wager, and stop when you've won that amount.
    3. Don't increase bets to try and win back losses. This is dangerous and foolish.
    4. Set time limits. Go with a group and pick a time monitor, the equivalent of a designated driver. This person herds fellow gamblers out the door when the pre-set time is up.
    5. Don't take checkbooks, ATM cards, or credit cards to a casino.
    6. Never go in debt to gamble.
    7. Keep records of winnings and losses. Winnings of more than $1,200.00 must be reported to the IRS. The same amount can be claimed as losses if you can document it with a gambler's diary that lists places, amounts, machines, and fellow gamblers.
    8. Don't get drunk.
    9. Beware of compulsive gambling. Signs of this serious addiction include betting more than you can afford to lose, going in debt to gamble, and selling assets to gamble.
54. Goodman, *Luck Business*, 46.
55. Valerie Lorenz, quoted in "Compulsive Gambling: Addiction of Choice for the 90s?" *The Bottom Line on Alcohol in Society* 2, no. 4 (1991): 5; Lesieur, *The Chase*, 257.

## Chapter 9: Casino Culture

1. Frank Rich, "America on Big Bender with Gaming," *Las Vegas Sun*, 10 May 1996, 15B.
2. Barbara Deane, "Women and Gambling: Risking It All,"

*Woman's Day,* 1 February 1996, 43. While gambling is illegal in Japan, the same trend is taking place there. As long as cash is not dispensed inside the parlors, authorities look the other way. Upright pinball machine parlors called *pachinko* collected $305 billion in 1994, almost double the amount of five years ago. The increase is attributable largely to greater patronization by women and youth. The parlors are well lighted and clean, offer quality prizes, and provide a safe environment in which women can gamble. Joseph Coleman, "Japanese Gambling 'Halls' Becoming 'Parlors,'" *The Grand Rapids Press,* 11 February 1996, A22.

3. See www.insidervlv.com/visitorstatistics1.html, accessed 19 October 2004.

4. Quoted in Deane, "Women and Gambling," 44–45.

5. The information included in this section comes from The Council on Compulsive Gambling of New Jersey, "Is Gambling Running Over the Rest of Your Life?" (1993), 2–3.

6. Deane, "Women and Gambling."

7. Laura Klepacki, "Having a Gray Old Time," *International Gaming and Wagering Business Magazine,* October 1995, 135–37; The Council on Compulsive Gambling of New Jersey, "Gambling Away the Golden Years: Compulsive Gambling and New Jersey's Senior Citizens" (1993).

8. "Women, Seniors, and Teens," www.calproblemgambling.org/womenseniorsteen.html, accessed 19 October 2004.

9. Gary Rivlin, "The Tug of the Newfangled Slot Machines," *The New York Times,* http://lair.exent.com/pipermail/fork/Week-of-Mon-20040510/030192.html, accessed 19 November 2004.

10. Noted in William N. Thompson, *Legalized Gambling: A Reference Handbook* (Santa Barbara, Calif.: ABC-CLIO, 1994), 24–25.

11. See www.insidervlv.com/visitorstatistics1.html, accessed 19 October 2004.

12. As quoted in "Kids Wait and Wait as Parents Gamble," *The Bottom Line on Alcohol in Society* 14, no. 1 (spring 1993): 26–28.

13. As cited in "Kids Gambling—and Losing," www.cbsnews.com/stories/2003/07/14/health/main563015.shtml, accessed 19 October 2004.

14. Lark Ellen Gould, "Las Vegas Is Targeting the Young at Heart,

Not the Young," *Las Vegas/Travel Agent,* 4 March 1996, 8–9.

15. Robert Goodman, *The Luck Business: The Devastating Consequences and Broken Promises of America's Gambling Explosion* (New York: The Free Press, 1995), 44.

16. Matt Connor, "The Kids Are Alright," *International Gaming and Wagering Business Magazine,* October 1995, 74.

17. See www.insidervlv.com/visitorstatistics1.html, accessed 19 October 2004.

18. Marc Cooper, *The Last Honest Place in America: Paradise and Perdition in the New Las Vegas* (New York: Nation Books, 2004), 74.

19. Ibid., 75.

20. Rachel A. Volberg, "The Prevalence and Demographics of Pathological Gamblers: Implications for Public Health," *American Journal of Public Health* 84, no. 2 (February 1994): 240.

21. See www.healthteacher.com/lessonguides/gambling/index.asp, accessed 19 October 2004.

22. Durand F. Jacobs, "Juvenile Gambling in North America: Considering Past Trends and Future Prospects," in *Futures at Stake: Youth, Gambling, and Society,* ed. Howard J. Schaffer (Reno, Nev.: University of Nevada Press, 2003), 265.

23. See www.healthteacher.com/lessonguides/gambling/whoandwhy.asp, accessed 19 October 2004.

24. Delaware Council on Gambling Problems Newsletter 16, no. 5 (March-April 2001), as cited in "Is All Gambling the Same?" www.healthteacher.com/lessonguides/gambling/isallgamblingthesame.asp, accessed 19 October 2004.

25. The Council of Compulsive Gambling of New Jersey, "Adolescent Compulsive Gambling: The Hidden Epidemic," n.d. This section owes much to J. Taylor Buckley, "Nation Raising 'A Generation of Gamblers,'" *USA Today,* 5 April 1995, 1A.

26. Ricardo Chavira, "The Rise of Teenage Gambling," *Time,* 25 February 1991, 78; Buckley, "Generation of Gamblers," 1A; Durand Jacobs, as cited in "Is All Gambling the Same?"

27. *Report of the Governor's Blue Ribbon Commission on Michigan Gaming,* Robert J. Danhof, Chairman (Lansing, Mich.: Michigan Court of Appeals, April 1995), 15; Laurel Shaper Walter, "More Teens Play Games of Chance," *The Christian Science Monitor,* 25 April 1990, 16; Howard J. Schaffer, ed.,

*Future at Stake: Youth Gambling and Society* (Reno, Nev.: University of Nevada Press, 2003).

28. Chavira, "Teenage Gambling," 78; "Teen Gambling: Hidden Habit, Public Problem," *USA Today,* 5 April 1994, 8A.

29. Buckley, "Generation of Gamblers," 2A; Valerie Lorenz, as quoted in Ronald A. Reno, "The Diceman Cometh," *Policy Review,* March–April 1996, 42.

30. Art Levine, "Playing the Adolescent Odd," *U.S. News and World Report* (18 June 1990), quoted in *Blue Ribbon Commission,* 15; Chavira, "Teenage Gambling," 78; "Adolescent Compulsive Gambling," 1.

31. J. Taylor Buckley, "Parents Often Shrug Off an Addiction with Few Visible Signs," *USA Today,* 5 April 1995, 4D.

32. See www.addictionrecov.org/youthgam.htm, accessed 19 October 2004; Jeffrey J. Derevensky and Rina Gupta, ed., *Gambling Problems in Youth: Theoretical and Applied Perspectives* (New York: Kluwer Academic Publishers, 2004), 4.

33. See www.education.mcgill.ca/gambling/en/problemgambling .htm, accessed 19 October 2004.

34. Keith Whyte, as quoted in "Kids Gambling—and Losing."

35. Warren Richey, "Youth Gambling, Even at Elementary Level, Spreads Across US," www.csmonitor.com/cgi-bin/ durableRedirect.pl?/durable/1998/08/07/p3s2.htm, accessed 19 October 2004.

36. Durand Jacobs, as quoted in Ibid.

37. Jay Teitel, "Are Kids Addicted to Gambling? You Can Bet on It." www.todaysparent.com/behaviordevelopment/allages/article .jsp?content=20030905.html, accessed 19 October 2004.

38. Dervensy and Gupta, *Gambling Problems in Youth,* 248.

39. Michael Frank, as quoted in Tim Layden, "Bettor Education," *Sports Illustrated,* 3 April 1995, 74.

40. Buckley, "Parents Often Shrug Off," 4D.

41. *Blue Ribbon Commission,* 67.

42. Arnie Wexler, as quoted in Layden, "Bettor Education," 76.

43. Arnie Wexler, as quoted in Stuart Winston and Harriet Harris, *Nation of Gamblers: America's Billion Dollar a Day Habit* (Englewood Cliffs, N.J.: Prentice-Hall, 1984), 29–30.

44. As quoted in Delaware Council on Gambling Problems Newsletter 16, no. 5 (March–April 2001). Cited at www

.healthteacher.com/lessonguides/gambling/index.asp, accessed 19 October 2004.

45.   As quoted in Erica Meera, "Wanna Bet? Online Gambling Tempting Youth," 3 November 2003, www.thevarsity.ca/ news/2003/11/03/News/Wanna.Bet.Online.Gambling.Tempting. For.Youth-546670.shtml, accessed 19 October 2004.

46.   Mark Griffiths, *Gambling and Gaming Addictions in Adolescence* (Oxford, U.K.; Malden, Mass.: BPS/Blackwell, 2002), 6.

47.   Melissa Raimondi, "X Marks the Spot," *Casino Player*, July 1995, 33.

48.   Layden, "Bettor Education," 70–71.

49.   Arnie Wexler, as quoted in Ibid.

50.   As quoted in ibid., 83.

51.   Ibid., 71; Michael J. Stoil, "Gambling Addiction: The Nation's Dirty Little Secret," *Behavioral Health Management*, July–August 1994, 35.

52.   Arnie Wexler, as quoted in Layden, "Bettor Education," 71–72.

53.   Arnie Wexler, as quoted in Ibid., 74.

54.   Janice Karlovich, "Central Michigan Students Study Casino Management," *Michigan Monthly*, April 1996, 8.

55.   "Casino Can Be Dicey to CMU Crowd," *The Grand Rapids Press*, 15 January 1996, B3.

56.   Ibid.

## Chapter 10: Jackpot Junkies

1.   Fred Girard, "Gambling Shatters Ex-Tiger's Dream Life," *The Detroit News and Free Press*, 17 October 2004, 1A; "Ex-Tiger Fielder Loses All to Gambling," *The Grand Rapids Press*, 22 October 2004, E5.

2.   "Lisa and Gambling," www.christians-in-recovery.com/ testimony/lisa_gamble.html, accessed 18 July 2004.

3.   Jim Bolus, "Has Racing Missed the Boat?" *Las Vegas Style*, May 1996, 21.

4.   Suzanne Morton, *At Odds: Gambling and Canadians, 1919–1969* (Toronto; Buffalo: University of Toronto Press, 2003), 4.

5.   Vicki Abt, James F. Smith, and Eugene Martin Christiansen, *The Business of Risk: Gambling in Mainstream America* (Lawrence, Kans.: University Press of Kansas, 1985), 37, 174–75, 213–15.

6.   David D. Allen, *The Nature of Gambling* (New York: Coward-

McCann, 1952), 49, 55–56.

7. Stephen Katz, *Gambling Facts and Fictions: The Anti-Gambling Handbook to Get Yourself to Stop Gambling, Quit Gambling, or Never Start Gambling* (Bloomington, Ind.: AuthorHouse, 2004), 3.

8. Earl L. Grinols, *Gambling in America: Costs and Benefits* (Cambridge, U.K.; New York: Cambridge University Press, 2004), 139, 175–76, 182–83, 186–87.

9. Gerda Reith, ed., *Gambling: Who Wins? Who Loses?* (Amherst, N.Y.: Prometheus Books, 2003), 9, 12.

10. I. Nelson Rose, "Gambling and the Law: The New Millennium," in *Gambling: Who Wins? Who Loses?* ed. Reith, 125–26.

11. Jeffrey J. Derevensky and Rina Gupta, eds., *Gambling Problems in Youth: Theoretical and Applied Perspectives* (New York: Kluwer Academic Publishers, 2004), 232.

12. I. Nelson Rose, "Gambling and the Law," 125.

13. Peter Collins, *Gambling and the Public Interest* (Westport, Conn.: Praeger, 2003), 7, 10.

14. Ibid., 7.

15. See www.ohioroundtable.org/issues/gambling/index.cfm, accessed 19 October 2004.

16. Patrick Alan Pierce and Donald E. Miller, *Gambling Politics: State Governments and the Business of Betting* (Boulder, Colo.: Lynne Rienner Publishers, 2004), 197–98.

17. Robert Goodman, *The Luck Business: The Devastating Consequences and Broken Promises of America's Gambling Explosion* (New York: The Free Press, 1995), 46, 84.

18. Denise Von Herrmann, *The Big Gamble: The Politics of Lottery and Casino Expansion* (Westport, Conn.: Praeger, 2002), 2.

19. Pierce and Miller, *Gambling Politics*, 198–99.

20. "Historical Listing of Statewide Initiatives, 1904–2001," www.inandrinstitute.org/ballotwatch.htm#2003, accessed 20 October 2004.

21. Chad Hills, "Score Card: Gambling Expansion in 2003," 20 January 2004, www.family.org/cforum/fosi/gambling/facts/a0029827.cfm, accessed 19 October 2004.

22. Initiative and Referendum Institute, University of Southern California, www.iandrinstitute.org/bw%202004-10%20(election%20summary).pdf, accessed 21 November 2004.

23. Eugene Martin Christiansen, as quoted in Joel J. Smith and Eric Morath, "Expansion Threatens Michigan Gaming Jackpot," *The Detroit News*, 15 August 2004, www.detnews.com/2004/casinonews/0409/23/a01-242640.htm, accessed 19 October 2004.

24. "Gambling Expansion Big Loser in 2003," www.ncalg.org/library/pdf/ncalg%20scorecard/3.pdf, accessed 19 October 2004.

25. David Johnston, *Temples of Chance: How America Incorporated Bought Out Murder Incorporated to Win Control of the Casino Business* (New York: Doubleday, 1992), 301; William N. Thompson, *Legalized Gambling: A Reference Handbook* (Santa Barbara, Calif.: ABC-CLIO, 1994), 57.

26. Bill Clinton, as quoted in Goodman, *Luck Business*, 106.

27. Margot Hornblower, "No Dice: The Backlash Against Gambling," *Time*, 1 April 1996, 30.

28. Frank J. Fahrenkopf, as quoted in James Sterngold, "Are Casinos a Gamble Worth Taking?" *The Grand Rapids Press*, 3 December 1995, A3.

29. As quoted in Hornblower, "No Dice," 31.

30. "National Gambling Impact Study Commission," http://govinfo.library.unt.edu/ngisc/reports/fullrpt.html, accessed 15 October 2004; David G. Schwartz, *Suburban Xanadu: The Casino Resort on the Las Vegas Strip and Beyond* (New York: Rutledge, 2003), 209–10.

31. Rex M. Rogers, "Michigan Needs Gambling Moratorium," *The Detroit News*, 22 March, 2001, 11A.

32. Rex M. Rogers, "Gambling and Native Americans," *Business Update*, September 1997, 6.

33. "Casino Supporters, Opponents Dispute Impact of Court Ruling," *The Grand Rapids Press*, 28 March 1996, F4; Dennis Camire, "Gaming Ruling Unclear: High Court Confuses Indian Casino Issue," *Las Vegas Sun*, 10 May 1996, 16A.

34. "Roll of the Dice on Tribal Casinos," *The Grand Rapids Press*, 22 July 1996, A10.

## Chapter 11: Internet Gambling

1. "Online Gambling Leads to Great Shame," Dear Ann Landers, *The Grand Rapids Press*, 19 August 1999, D4.

2. Margie McEvoy, "The Political and Social Implications of

Internet Gambling," 6 March 2000, www.ncalg.org/library/pdf/ InternetGamblingPaper.pdf, accessed 15 October 2004.

3. Ann Greer, as quoted in Ryan D. Hammer, "Does Internet Gambling Strengthen the U.S. Economy? Don't Bet on It," www.law.indiana.edu/fdj/pubs/v54/no1/Hammer.pdf, accessed 24 November 2004.

4. John Lyman Mason and Michael Nelson, *Governing Gambling* (New York: The Century Foundation Press, 2001), 80.

5. "Internet Gambling," www.americangaming.org/industry/ factsheets/issues_detailscfv?id=17, accessed 20 November 2004.

6. See http://answers.google.com/answers/threadview?id=393352, accessed 15 October 2004.

7. "Internet Gambling Approaches Tenth Anniversary," *Casino News,* 17 November 2004, www.casinocitytimes.com/news/ article.cfm?contentid=146677, accessed 24 November 2004.

8. Ibid.

9. Tom Blackwell, "Internet Gambling Up Tenfold, Study Finds," 28 November 2001, www.nationalpost.com/news/story.html?f=/ stories/20011128/807893.html, accessed 28 November 2001.

10. "Virtual Vegas," *Newsweek,* 21 April 2003, E18.

11. Mason and Nelson, *Governing Gambling,* 82.

12. Robin Gareiss and John Soat, "Gambling on the Internet," in *Gambling: Examining Pop Culture,* ed. James Haley (San Diego: Greenhaven Press, 2004), 152.

13. Mason and Nelson, *Governing Gambling,* 81.

14. "Internet Gambling," www.americangaming.org/industry/ factsheets/issues_detailscfv??id=17, accessed 20 November 2004.

15. "Internet Gambling: An Overview of the Issues," A Report of the U.S. General Accounting Office to Congressional Requesters, December 2002. See document at http://www.gao.gov/new .items/d0389.pdf.

16. "Online Gambling Sites Show Steady Worldwide Growth, Warns Websense," 19 November 2003, www.shoutasia.com/websense/ clients_websense_gamble.htm, accessed 25 November 2004.

17. "Online Gambling Sites Are Going Global, Creating Big Headaches for Corporations, Warns Websense, Inc.," *San Diego Business Wire,* 20 June 2001, www.findarticles.com/p/ articles/mi_m0ein/is_2001_June_20/a1_75663509, accessed 27 November 2004.

18. "Virtual Vegas."

19. Peter Kjaer, as quoted in John Horn, "Point and Bet," *Newsweek*, 28 October 2002, 50.

20. Bryan Knowles, "Should the Federal Government Prohibit Internet Gambling?" 15 June 2000, http://speakout.com/ activism/issue_briefs/1324b-1.html.

21. Mason and Nelson, *Governing Gambling*, 81.

22. John Fetto, "Off the Map—The Legal Gambling Industry Grows in Popularity," *American Demographics*, www.findarticles.com/ p/articles/mi_m4021/is_2002_Sept_1/ai_90957513, accessed 15 October 2004.

23. "Internet Gambling Approaches Tenth Anniversary"; John W. Kennedy, "Addiction a Click Away," April 2003, www .christianitytoday.com/ct/2003/004/8.25.html, accessed 19 October 2004.

24. "Internet Gambling," www.americangaming.org/Industry/ factsheets/issues_detail.cfv?id=17, accessed 15 October 2004.

25. See http://answers.google.com/answers/threadview?id=393352, accessed 15 October 2004.

26. McEvoy, "The Political and Social Implications of Internet Gambling."

27. James Rutherford, "The Newest Casinos," *Casino Player*, December 1997, 41.

28. McEvoy, "The Political and Social Implications of Internet Gambling."

29. Mason and Nelson, *Governing Gambling*, 84.

30. Stephen Katz, *Gambling Facts and Fictions: The Anti-Gambling Handbook to Get Yourself to Stop Gambling, Quit Gambling, or Never Start Gambling* (Bloomington, Ind.: AuthorHouse, 2004), 153.

31. Hammer, "Does Internet Gambling Strengthen the U.S. Economy?"

32. See http://answers.google.com/answers/threadview?id=393352, accessed 15 October 2004.

33. "Virtual Vegas."

34. Jeff Posh, as quoted in Steven Crist, "All Bets Are Off," *Sports Illustrated*, 26 January 1998, 85–86.

35. Ibid., 91.

36. Mason and Nelson, *Governing Gambling*, 83.

37. Kevin Whyte, as quoted in "Kids Gambling—and Losing," 14 July 2003, www.cbsnews.com/stories/2003/07/14/health/main563015.shtml, accessed 19 October 2004.

38. See www.gamcare.org.uk/site.builder/onlinehelp.html, accessed 25 November 2004; Kevin O'Neill, "Internet Gambling: Year 2000," www.800gambler.org/ArticleDetails.aspx?ContentID=12, accessed 24 November 2004.

39. "Internet Gambling Breeds Addiction," 17 March 2002, http://news.bbc.co.uk/1/hi/health/1872731.stm, accessed 25 November 2004.

40. Jeffrey Derevensky, as quoted in "Kids Gambling—and Losing."

41. Kevin Whyte, as quoted in Lori Johnston, "College Deal, TV Poker Shows Spark Campus Card Craze," *The Grand Rapids Press*, 4 April 2004, A9.

42. Hammer, "Does Internet Gambling Strengthen the U.S. Economy?"

43. As quoted in Horn, "Point and Bet."

44. Mark Fox, Larry Phillips, and Ganesh Vaidyanathan, "Managing Internet Gambling in the Workplace," http://firstmonday.org/issues/isssue8_4/fox/index.html, accessed 24 November 2004.

45. "Online Gambling Sites Show Steady Worldwide Growth, Warns Websense," 19 November 2003, www.shoutasia.com/websense/clients_websense_gamble.htm, accessed 25 November 2004.

46. Harold Kester, as quoted in Ibid.

47. David G. Schwartz, *Suburban Xanadu: The Casino Resort on the Las Vegas Strip and Beyond* (New York: Rutledge, 2003), 214.

48. David Greenfield, as quoted in "Online Gambling Sites Show Steady Worldwide Growth, Warns Websense."

49. Jay Teitel, "Are Kids Addicted to Gambling? You Can Bet on It," www.todaysparent.com/behaviordevelopment/allages/article.jsp?content=20030905_150814_3936&page-1, accessed 19 October 2004.

50. "Internet Gambling: An Overview of the Issues, A Report of the U.S. Government Accounting Office," December 2002, www.GAO.gov/new.items/d0389.pdf, accessed 19 October 2004.

51. Michael E. Hammond, "Is It a Crime to Bet on the Net?" in *Gambling: Who Wins? Who Loses?* ed. Gerda Reith (Amherst, N.Y.: Prometheus Books, 2003), 134.

52. "Internet Gambling," www.americangaming.org/Industry/

factsheets/issues_detail.cfv?id-17, accessed 15 October 2004.

53. Horn, "Point and Bet."

54. Kennedy, "Addiction a Click Away"; Jim Leach, as quoted in Bill Cahir, "Bill to Ban Internet Gambling Faces Long Odds," *The Grand Rapids Press,* 5 May 2003, B3.

55. Jon Swartz, "Online Betting Sites Fight Cyberextortion," *USA Today,* 9 March 2004, 1B.

56. Mason and Nelson, *Governing Gambling,* 81.

57. "Internet Gambling," www.americangaming.org/Industry/factsheets/issues_detail.cfv?id=17, accessed 15 October 2004.

58. Jonathan Fowler, "WTO Says US Should Drop Ban on Off-Shore Internet Gambling," 10 November 2004, www.technologyreview.com/articles/04/11/asp/ap_11/004.asp, accessed 24 November 2004.

59. Simon Noble, as quoted in Crist, "All Bets Are Off," 85.

60. Gerda Reith, *Gambling,* 39; also http://www.gamcare.org.uk/site.builder/onlinehelp.html, accessed 25 November 2004.

61. Katz, *Gambling Facts and Fictions,* 233.

62. James H. Burnett III, "Everything Clicking for Internet Gambling," *Milwaukee Journal Sentinel,* 18 November 2004, www.kansascity.com/mld/kansascity/news/nation/10213594.htm?1c, accessed 24 November 2004.

63. Neil D. Isaacs, *You Bet Your Life: The Burdens of Gambling* (Lexington, Ky.: University Press of Kentucky, 2001), 2.

## Chapter 12: Cultural Alchemy

1. George Orwell, *1984* (New York: Harcourt Brace Jovanovich, 1949).

2. David G. Schwartz, *Suburban Xanadu: The Casino Resort on the Las Vegas Strip and Beyond* (New York: Rutledge, 2003), 211.

3. Vicki Abt, James F. Smith, and Eugene Martin Christiansen, *The Business of Risk: Gambling in Mainstream America* (Lawrence, Kans.: University Press of Kansas, 1985), 217.

4. R. H. Charles, *Gambling and Betting: A Study Dealing with Their Origin and Their Relation to Morality and Religion* (Edinburgh: T and T Clark, 1924), 10.

5. Stanley J. Grenz, *A Primer on Postmodernism* (Grand Rapids: Eerdmans, 1996).

# SELECTED BIBLIOGRAPHY

Abt, Vicki, James F. Smith, and Eugene Martin Christiansen. *The Business of Risk: Commercial Gambling in Mainstream America.* Lawrence, Kans.: University Press of Kansas, 1985.

Allen, David D. *The Nature of Gambling.* New York: Coward-McCann, 1952.

Anderson, Kerby. "What's Wrong with State Lotteries?" *Moody Monthly* 85, no. 5 (January 1985): 10.

Bell, Raymond C. "Moral Views on Gambling Promulgated by Major American Religious Bodies." In *Gambling in America: Final Report of the Commission on the Review of the National Policy Toward Gambling.* Charles H. Morin, Chairman. Washington, D.C.: GPO, 1976, 161–239.

Braidfoot, Larry. *Gambling: A Deadly Game.* Nashville: Broadman Press, 1985.

*Casino Gambling: The Myth and the Reality.* Lansing, Mich.: Michigan Interfaith Council on Alcohol Problems, 1988.

Chafetz, Henry. *Play the Devil: A History of Gambling in the United States from 1492 to 1955.* New York: Potter Publishers, 1960.

Charles, R. H. *Gambling and Betting: A Study Dealing with Their Origin and Their Relation to Morality and Religion.* Edinburgh: T and T Clark, 1924.

Ciarrocchi, Joseph. "Pathological Gambling and Pastoral Counseling." In *Clinical Handbook of Pastoral Counseling,* edited by Robert J. Wicks and Richard D. Parsons. Vol. 2. New York: Integration Books, Paulist Press, 1993.

Clapson, Mark. *A Bit of a Flutter: Popular Gambling and English Society, 1823–1961.* Manchester, England: Manchester University Press, 1992.

Clotfelter, Charles T., and Philip J. Cook. *Selling Hope: State Lotteries in America.* Cambridge: Harvard University Press, 1989.

Coggins, Ross, ed. *The Gambling Menace.* Nashville: Broadman Press, 1966.

Collins, Peter. *Gambling and the Public Interest.* Westport, Conn.: Praeger, 2003.

Colson, Charles. "The Myth of the Money Tree." *Christianity Today,* 10 July 1987, 64.

Commission on the Review of the National Policy Toward Gambling, Charles H. Morin, Chairman. *Gambling in America: Final Report of the Commission on the Review of the National Policy Toward Gambling.* Washington, D.C.: GPO, 1976.

Cooper, Marc. *The Last Honest Place in America: Paradise and Perdition in the New Las Vegas.* New York: Nation Books, 2004.

Davidson, D. Kirk. *Selling Sin: The Marketing of Socially Unacceptable Products.* Westport, Conn.: Praeger, 2003.

Denton, Sally and Roger Morris. *The Money and the Power: The Making of Las Vegas and Its Hold On America, 1947–2000.* New York: Vintage, 2001.

Derevensky, Jeffrey J., and Rina Gupta, eds. *Gambling Problems in Youth: Theoretical and Applied Perspectives.* New York: Kluwer Academic Publishers, 2004.

Dostoyevsky, Fyodor. *The Gambler.* Translated by Victor Terras. Chicago: University of Chicago Press, 1972.

Evans, Anthony T. *Tony Evans Speaks Out on Gambling and the Lottery.* Chicago: Moody Press, 1995.

Ezell, John Samuel. *Fortune's Merry Wheel: The Lottery in America.* Cambridge: Harvard University Press, 1960.

Froman, Brett Duval. *Hitting the Jackpot: The Inside Story of the Richest Indian Tribe in History.* New York: Atlantic Monthly Press, 2003.

"Gambling Addiction Near Epidemic." *The Bottom Line on Alcohol in Society* 14, no. 1 (spring 1993): 4–50.

Gaughn, Shasta, ed. *Teen Addiction.* San Diego: Greenhaven Press, 2002.

Geisler, Norman L., and Thomas A. Howe. *Gambling a Bad Bet: You Can't Win for Losing in More Ways Than You Can Imagine.* Grand Rapids: Revell, 1990.

Goodman, Robert. *The Luck Business: The Devastating Consequences and*

*Broken Promises of America's Gambling Explosion.* New York: The Free Press, 1995.

Grenz, Stanley J. *A Primer on Postmodernism.* Grand Rapids: Eerdmans, 1996.

Griffiths, Mark. *Gambling and Gaming Addictions in Adolescence.* Oxford, U.K.; Malden, Mass.: BPS/Blackwell, 2002.

Grinols, Earl L. *Gambling in America: Costs and Benefits.* Cambridge, U.K.; New York: Cambridge University Press, 2004.

Haley, James, ed. *Gambling: Examining Pop Culture.* San Diego: Greenhaven Press, 2004.

Hastings, James, ed. *Encyclopedia of Religion and Ethics.* Edinburgh: T and T Clark, 1913.

Herman, Robert D., ed. *Gambling.* New York: Harper and Row, 1967.

Isaacs, Neil David. *You Bet Your Life: The Burdens of Gambling.* Lexington, Ky.: The University Press of Kentucky, 2001.

Jensen, Marten. *Casino Gambling Secrets.* New York: Cardozo Publishers, 2004.

Johnston, David. *Temples of Chance: How America Incorporated Bought Out Murder Incorporated to Win Control of the Casino Business.* New York: Doubleday, 1992.

Katz, Stephen. *Gambling Facts and Fictions: The Anti-Gambling Handbook to Get Yourself to Stop Gambling, Quit Gambling, or Never Start Gambling.* Bloomington, Ind.: AuthorHouse, 2004.

Kennedy, D. James, ed. *Gambling: America's Hidden Addiction.* Fort Lauderdale: Coral Ridge Ministries Media, 1995.

King, Rufus. *Gambling and Organized Crime.* Washington, D.C.: Public Affairs Press, 1969.

Land, Barbara. *Las Vegas with Kids.* Rocklin, Calif.: Prima Publishing, 1995.

Lesieur, Henry R. *The Chase: Career of the Compulsive Gambler.* Cambridge, Mass.: Schenkman, 1984.

Lorence, Jordan. "State Lotteries: A Bad Bet." *Focus on the Family,* March 1989, 7–8.

Marotta, Jeffrey J., Judy A. Cornelius, and William R. Eadington, eds. *The Downside: Problem and Pathological Gambling.* Reno, Nev.: Institute for the Study of Gambling and Commercial Gaming, College of Business Administration, University of Nevada, Reno, 2002.

Martinez, Thomas M. *The Gambling Scene: Why People Gamble.* Springfield, Ill.: C. C. Thomas, 1983.

Mason, John Lyman and Michael Nelson. *Governing Gambling*. New York: The Century Foundation Press, 2001.

Mason, W. Dale. *Indian Gaming: Tribal Sovereignty and American Politics*. Norman, Okla.: University of Oklahoma Press, 2000.

Morton, Suzanne. *At Odds: Gambling and Canadians, 1919–1969*. Toronto; Buffalo: University of Toronto Press, 2003.

Nesmith, Dan. *The Casino Slot Machine: What You Need to Know*. Mobile: SMI, 1993.

Olmsted, Charlotte. *Heads I Win; Tails You Lose*. New York: Macmillan, 1962.

Orwell, George. *1984*. New York: Harcourt Brace Jovanovich, 1949.

Packel, Edward W. *The Mathematics of Games and Gambling*. Washington, D.C.: The Mathematical Association of America, 1981.

Pasquaretta, Paul. *Gambling and Survival in Native North America*. Tucson, Ariz.: University of Arizona Press, 2003.

Pavalko, Ronald M. *Risky Business: America's Fascination with Gambling*. Australia; Belmont, Calif.: Wadsworth, 2000.

Perkins, E. Benson. *Gambling in English Life*. London: Epworth Press, 1950.

Pierce, Alan Patrick and Donald E. Miller. *Gambling Politics: State Governments and the Business of Betting*. Boulder, Colo.: Lynne Rienner Publishers, 2004.

Quinn, John Philip. *Gambling and Gambling Devices*. Montclair, N.J.: Patterson Smith, 1969.

Reith, Gerda, ed. *Gambling: Who Wins? Who Loses?* Amherst, N.Y.: Prometheus Books, 2003.

*Report of the Governor's Blue Ribbon Commission on Michigan Gaming*. Robert J. Danhof, Chairman. Lansing, Mich.: Michigan Court of Appeals, April 1995.

Rogers, Rex M. *Christian Liberty: Living for God in a Changing Culture*. Grand Rapids: Baker, 2003.

Sasuly, Richard. *Bookies and Bettors: Two Hundred Years of Gambling*. New York: Holt, Rinehart and Winston, 1982.

Schaffer, Howard J., ed. *Futures at Stake: Youth, Gambling, and Society*. Reno, Nev.: University of Nevada Press, 2003.

Schumacher, Geoff. *Sun, Sin, and Suburbia: An Essential History of Modern Las Vegas*. Las Vegas: Stephens Press, 2004.

Schwartz, David G. *Suburban Xanadu: The Casino Resort on the Las Vegas Strip and Beyond*. New York: Rutledge, 2003.

Smith, John L. *Running Scared: The Life and Treacherous Times of Las Vegas Casino King Steve Wynn*. New York: Four Walls Eight Windows, 2001.

"A $pecial Issue on Gambling." *Christian Social Action* 7, no. 7 (July–August 1994).

Starkey, Lycurgus M., Jr. *Money, Mania and Morals: The Churches and Gambling*. Nashville: Abingdon Press, 1964.

Stoil, Michael J. "Gambling Addiction: The Nation's Dirty Little Secret." *Behavioral Health Management* (July–August 1994): 35–37.

Thompson, William N. *Gambling in America: An Encyclopedia of History, Issues, and Society*. Santa Barbara, Calif.: ABC-CLIO, 2001.

_____. *Legalized Gambling: A Reference Handbook*. Santa Barbara, Calif.: ABC-CLIO, 1994.

Time-Life Editors. *The Gamblers*. Alexandria, Va.: Time-Life Books, 1978.

Torr, James D. *Gambling: Opposing Viewpoints*. San Diego: Greenhaven Press, 2002.

Volberg, Rachel A. *When the Chips Are Down: Problem Gambling in America*. New York: The Century Foundation Press, 2001.

Von Hermann, Denise. *The Big Gamble: The Politics of Lottery and Casino Expansion*. Westport, Conn.: Praeger, 2002.

Walker, Michael B. *The Psychology of Gambling*. New York: Pergamon Press, 1992.

Watson, Tom, Jr. *Don't Bet on It*. Ventura, Calif.: Regal Books, 1987.

Weinstein, David, and Lillian Deitch. *The Impact of Legalized Gambling: The Socioeconomic Consequences of Lotteries and Off-Course Betting*. New York: Praeger, 1974.

"Will It Really Rain Pennies from Heaven? An Evaluation of the Prospects for Casino Gambling in Detroit." *A Report of the Michigan Family Forum*. Lansing, Mich., n.d.

Williams, Francis Emmett. *Lotteries, Law, and Morals*. New York: Vantage Press, 1958.

Winston, Stuart, and Harriet Harris, *Nation of Gamblers: America's Billion Dollar a Day Habit*. Englewood Cliffs, N.J.: Prentice-Hall, 1984.

# ABOUT THE AUTHOR

**Rex M. Rogers** (Ph.D. in political science, University of Cincinnati) is president of Cornerstone University, Grand Rapids, Michigan. He has participated in more than 150 media interviews on gambling, including *Janet Parshall's America*, Moody Radio's *Open Line*, Larry Burkett's *Money Matters* and *How to Manage Your Money*, Dr. James Dobson's *Focus on the Family*, and Rev. H. B. London's *Pastor to Pastor: Difficult Issues*. Dr. Rogers has also testified about gambling on several occasions before the Michigan state legislature. He is the author and voice of the daily radio program *Making a Difference*, which is also syndicated in a column to 89 newspapers in 31 states. *Making a Difference* applies biblical principles to a wide range of contemporary issues and concerns, such as family and church challenges, biomedical ethics questions, business and economics, philosophy and culture, music and the arts, and education, and offers brief, practical, and straightforward Christian commentary for immediate everyday use. Rogers also writes and speaks on Christian higher education, leadership, and socio-cultural trends. In 2003, he published *Christian Liberty: Living for God in a Changing World* (Baker).

Cornerstone University is a Christian institution of higher learning comprised of the undergraduate college; the graduate program, including Grand Rapids Theological Seminary and Asia Baptist Theological Seminary based in Singapore; and Cornerstone University Radio, a Christian radio division that includes three radio stations, an internationally syndicated program called *Mission Network News*, and a nationally distributed children's radio ministry called "His Kids Radio." More can be learned about the university at www.cornerstone.edu.